MANAGING EMPLOYEE RETENTION:
A Strategic Accountability Approach

Series Editor: Jack J. Phillips, Ph.D.

Accountability in Human Resource Management
Jack J. Phillips

Achieving the Perfect Fit
Nick Boulter, Murray Dalziel, Ph.D., and Jackie Hill, Editors

Bottom-Line Training
Donald J. Ford

Corporate Performance Management
David Wade and Ronald Recardo

Developing Supervisors and Team Leaders
Donald L. Kirkpatrick
The Global Advantage
Michael J. Marquardt

Handbook of Training Evaluation and Measurement Methods, 3ʳᵈ Edition
Jack J. Phillips

Human Performance Consulting
James S. Pepitone

Human Performance Improvement
William J. Rothwell, Carolyn K. Hohne, and Stephen B. King

The Human Resources Scorecard
Jack J. Phillips, Patricia Pulliam Phillips, and Ron D. Stone

HR to the Rescue
Edward M. Mone and Manuel London

HRD Survival Skills
Jessica Levant

HRD Trends Worldwide
Jack J. Phillips

Learning in Chaos
James Hite, Jr.

Linking Learning and Performance
Toni K. Hodges

Managing Change Effectively
Donald L. Kirkpatrick

The Power of 360° Feedback
David A. Waldman and Leanne E. Atwater

The Project Management Scorecard
Jack J. Phillips, G. Lynne Snead, and Timothy W. Bothell

Return on Investment in Training and Performance Improvement Programs, Second Edition
Jack J. Phillips

Bottom-Line Organization Development
Merrill Anderson

FORTHCOMING TITLES

Building a World-Class First-Level Management Team
Jack J. Phillips and Ron D. Stone

The Diversity Scorecard
Edward E. Hubbard

Bottom-Line Call Center Management
David L. Butler

The ROI Fieldbook
Patricia Pulliam Phillips and Holly Burkett

MANAGING EMPLOYEE RETENTION:

A Strategic Accountability Approach

JACK J. PHILLIPS, Ph.D.
ADELE O. CONNELL, Ph.D.

ELSEVIER
BUTTERWORTH
HEINEMANN

An Imprint of Elsevier

SOCIETY FOR
HUMAN
RESOURCE
MANAGEMENT

Amsterdam   Boston   Heidelberg   London   New York   Oxford   Paris   San Diego
San Francisco   Singapore   Sydney   Tokyo

ELSEVIER
BUTTERWORTH
HEINEMANN

SOCIETY FOR
HUMAN
RESOURCE
MANAGEMENT

Butterworth-Heinemann

An Imprint of Elsevier

Copyright © 2003 by Franklin Covey. All rights reserved.

Permissions may be sought directly from Elsevier's Science and Technology Rights Department in Oxford, UK. Phone: (44) 1865 843830, Fax: (44) 1865 853333, e-mail: permissions@elsevier.co.uk. You may also complete your request on-line via the Elsevier homepage: http://www.elsevier.com by selecting "Customer Support" and then "Obtaining Permissions".

Library of Congress Cataloging-in-Publication Data

Phillips, Jack J., 1945–
    Managing employee retention : a strategic accountability approach / Jack J. Phillips, Adedle O. Connell.
        p.   cm.—(Improving human performance series)
    Includes bibliographical references and index.
    ISBN 0-7506-7484-9 (alk. paper)
    1. Employee retention.   2. Labor turnover.   I. Connell, Adele O.   II. Title.
III. Series.
HF5549.5.R58P45 2003
658.3′14—dc21
                                                                2003048168

British Library Cataloguing-in-Publication Data
A catalogue record for this book is available from the British Library.

The publisher offers special discounts on bulk orders of this book.
For information, please contact:

Manager of Special Sales
Elsevier
200 Wheeler Road
Burlington, MA 01803
Tel: 781-313-4700
Fax: 781-313-4882

For information on all Butterworth-Heinemann publications available, contact our World Wide Web home page at: http://www.bh.com

10 9 8 7 6 5 4 3 2

Printed in the United States of America

Contents

14 Case Study Application: Southeast Corridor Bank, 326

Preface

The Need

During the last decade, employee retention has become a serious and perplexing problem for all types of organization. Managing retention and keeping the turnover rate below target and industry norms is one of the most challenging issues facing businesses. From all indications, the issue will compound in the future, even as economic conditions change. Employee retention will continue to be an important issue for most job groups in the first decade of the 21st century.

Employee turnover continues to be one of the most unappreciated and undervalued issues facing business leaders. This stems from several important assumptions and conclusions about turnover:

1. All stakeholders involved in the issue, including Human Resource managers, underestimate the true cost of employee turnover.
2. The causes of turnover are not adequately identified in most organizations.
3. The solutions to reduce turnover are sometimes mismatched with the cause of turnover and do not generate the desired results.
4. Many of the preventive measures for turnover are either overkill or they often miss the mark altogether.
5. A process to measure the success of retention solutions and place a monetary value on managing retention does not exist in most organizations.

These assumptions and conclusions create the need for a book to address these issues.

FEATURES OF THIS BOOK

Based on proven strategies, this is a practical book to provide direction to managers and specialists who are concerned about retention. First, it shows how to accurately cost turnover, providing examples and actual data from hundred of organizations. Second, it presents effective ways to identify the causes of turnover so the problems can be quickly identified and rectified. Third, it shows how to lower an excessive turnover rate by implementing carefully designed and selected solutions to match the cause of turnover. Fourth, it reveals how to keep the turnover in an acceptable range by implementing a variety of preventive measures, tracking leading indicators, and placing alerts along the way to signal when action is needed. Finally, it demonstrates how to actually place monetary value on the implementation of solutions to improve or maintain retention. In summary, this is a practical, indispensable tool to show how the retention issue can be carefully managed and monitored so that appropriate levels of turnover can be controlled and appropriate solutions can be implemented.

TARGET AUDIENCE

Several audiences will find this new publication appropriate. First and foremost are the Human Resources managers and executives who must address retention issues on a routine basis. This book provides practical and useful information to address the issue and manage it in a realistic, practical way.

Second, the various specialists involved in different types of HR practices such as recruiting and selection, learning and development, career management, job design, communications, compensation, reward systems, and employee relations will find this book helpful. These specialists, who design solutions to help prevent or reduce turnover, will discover extremely valuable information as they confront this critical issue in their organization.

Third, managers at all levels, who must live with the consequences of turnover, will find this book useful in helping them fully understand the key issues and problems and, more important, the cost of the turnover. It will show them, in bottom-line terms, what turnover is actually costing them and what they must do to improve it in the future.

Finally, the fourth target audience group is professors who teach Human Resource courses and consultants who assist HR managers with this issue. This book will offer proven strategies to deal with what is perhaps the number one issue facing the human capital management field.

How This Book Is Different

Several books are available to address employee retention. Most books on this issue focus on retention solutions without showing how to match solutions to need. Some of them attempt to show the impact of turnover although they sometimes fall short of addressing the fully-loaded costs. Other books show how to retain employees by focusing on human relations programs and practices to increase job satisfaction. Still others focus on how to recruit the best employees in an effort to minimize future turnover. While these are all important issues, there is no book that focuses on the turnover issue from all vantage points beginning with the impact, working toward solutions, and showing the actual value of those solutions as they are implemented. For the first time in a major book—in one volume—an indispensable tool is developed to deal with this nightmare issue.

Structure and Flow

The book presents a logical process of managing retention. Chapter 1, *Why Retention is a Serious Problem . . . Still*, explains why retention continues to be a serious problem, even in times of economic ups and downs. It explores the negative impact of retention on both organizations and on individuals, including what's driving the persistent retention issue. This chapter also dispels some of the myths of turnover and explains why this should be tackled immediately as a strategic issue in organizations.

Chapter 2, *A Strategic Accountability Approach to Managing Retention*, presents the overall approach for the book. In eight distinct steps, this chapter summarizes the recommended approach to retention, beginning with measuring and monitoring turnover and cycling through all the issues of determining causes, matching needs to solutions, forecasting solutions, measuring the success, and continuing to make adjustments. This process is offered as a more systematic, methodical approach to the retention issue.

Chapter 3, *Measure and Monitor Turnover and Retention Data*, is the first step of the strategic accountability approach. It outlines what types of retention and turnover data should be collected, when data should be collected, and how data should be reported to the senior team. Additional data beyond the overall turnover rates are described.

Chapter 4, *Develop Fully Loaded Costs of Turnover*, discusses how to calculate the total impact of turnover, including both direct and indirect costs. In most cases, the indirect costs exceed the direct costs and the techniques for efficiently capturing these are described. This chapter provides the appropriate data to show the executive team if turnover is having a dramatic and sometimes devastating impact on the organization.

Chapter 5, *Diagnose Causes of Turnover*, is one of the critical chapters that explore how to pinpoint the causes of turnover in the organization. It shows how to use questionnaires, surveys, interviews, focus groups, exit interview data, as well as other techniques to identify the actual causes of turnover. This is an often-overlooked step as organizations sometimes review general research data about employee needs and attempt to develop solutions without uncovering the specific causes within the organization.

Chapters 6, 7, 8, and 9 are a major part of this book. They show a variety of typical solutions that are implemented. Each chapter begins with a discussion around a cluster of typical needs uncovered in organizations and outlines specific solutions that have been implemented to meet those needs.

Chapter 6, *Solution Set: Recruiting New Employees*, focuses on the initial processes that bring employees to an organization. Focusing on needs and solutions, the chapter examines what attracts employees to an organization and weaves through the recruitment, selection, orientation, indoctrination, and job assignment issues to ensure that the employee fits into the organization and the job.

Chapter 7, *Solution Set: Establishing an Appropriate Work Environment*, presents the essentials necessary for an acceptable work environment in today's climate. It explores such issues as job satisfaction, culture, climate, diversity, work life balance, and many other critical issues that employers take for granted. These are the basics and a variety of solutions are presented to provide them.

Chapter 8, *Solution Set: Creating Equitable Pay and Performance Processes*, deals with the economic and reward issues. This critical chapter identifies what employees seek in terms of pay and benefits and their need for adequate rewards and recognition on the job. It explores a variety of solutions economically matched to these needs. The need for non-economic rewards is also covered in this chapter.

Chapter 9, *Solution Set: Building Motivation and Commitment*, is perhaps the most important set of solutions. In addition to exploring the issues that cause employees to remain with the organization, this chapter explores solutions aimed at building commitment and growth. Organizational commitment, motivation systems, building trust, ethics, job growth, career advancement, and other key issues employees are demanding in the organization today are described.

Chapter 10, *Match Solutions to Needs*, shows how the solutions should be selected to focus directly on the specific needs of the employee within the organization. Given that there are many possible solutions, this chapter outlines practical ways to ensure that appropriate matches are made between the need and solution with care taken to ensure that mismatches and multiple solutions are avoided and that the solutions can be developed quickly.

Chapter 11, *Forecast the Value of Retention Solutions*, is probably the most innovative approach to managing retention. In this unique chapter, special techniques are offered to show how the value of a potential solution can be forecasted to determine the potential ROI before it is actually implemented. This approach provides executives with a profile of potential payoffs from several solutions, thus helping to ensure that the funds are not misallocated or wasted on low payoff opportunities or mismatched solutions.

Chapter 12, *Calculate the Return on Investment of Retention Solutions*, shows how the payoff of retention solutions can be developed. Using the ROI methodology, this chapter shows how six types of data can be collected from any type of retention solution (reaction, learning, application, impact, ROI, and intangible data). The ROI methodology provides the management team with the information necessary to determine the overall success of the solution.

Chapter 13, *Make Adjustments and Continue*, focuses on the heart of the retention process by showing how data from successful retention solutions can be utilized to ensure that the processes are working properly. It shows how results are communicated and actions are taken to continue to bring turnover down or keep turnover at an acceptable rate. This is the last step of the strategic accountability approach, and the cycle continues in a routine process from measuring turnover to making adjustments.

Finally, Chapter 14 presents a case study illustrating the processes described in the book. Taken from an actual setting, the study shows how a banking organization tackled an excessive turnover problem, using the step-by-step approaches in the book. More specifically, the case study shows how the causes of turnover were clearly pinpointed and how the impact of the solution was developed, including measuring ROI.

Jack J. Phillips
Adele O. Connell

Acknowledgments

FROM JACK PHILLIPS

No book is the work of the authors alone; many other individuals provided input and support to make this effort a reality. I am particularly grateful for the clients I have had the opportunity to work with in my years of consulting. I have learned from every assignment involving a retention issue and have translated that knowledge into this book. To all of my clients, I owe much appreciation for their willingness to engage our services and experiment with our approach.

I appreciate the efforts of Franklin Covey to support this publication. Franklin Covey is a leading global solutions firm with a variety of solutions that directly tackle the retention issue. I particularly appreciate the support of Val Christensen and Stephen M.R. Covey for this publishing effort.

Several other individuals were very helpful in developing this manuscript. Many thanks go to Francine Hawkins for typing, proofreading, and editing much of this manuscript. She assumed this task on top of a very busy schedule and performed admirably with this huge challenge. I would also like to thank Joyce Alff for her meticulous review, editing, and coordination. Joyce is a superb organizer, manager, and editor and was extremely valuable in making this book a reality.

I would like to acknowledge the continued support and assistance from my spouse and partner, Patti Phillips, who always inspires me to do my best and supports me in all my work.

FROM ADELE CONNELL

Who we are and what we accomplish are not just the result of our own efforts, but also a result of the efforts of the people who impact our lives. Without others, personal achievement is not possible because of our need for encouragement, support, kindness, generosity, and faith. With this in mind, I wish to thank the people who have made a difference in my life. First and foremost, I want to thank Stephen M. R. Covey and Dr. Jack Phillips for their faith in me. Without their faith and support, this work would never have been possible. I would also like to acknowledge the support and kindness of Alan Bentley, Ike Nicoll, and Mike Willis, PhD, who have encouraged my professional development and study of retention.

Within my military capacity, I have been fortunate to work with three individuals from the 96th Regional Readiness Command who have modeled superior leadership: Major General James P. Collins (Commanding General), Brigadier General Peter S. Cooke (Deputy Commanding General), and Command Sergeant Major Roger S. Fadel. Thank you, Sirs, for your mentorship and outstanding examples.

Next, I acknowledge the association and leadership of my DBM colleagues, Ana Hanna, Barbara Opoka, Greg Simpson, David Hightower, and Kathy Flora. Special thanks also goes to Alan Rex Mitchell for his suggestions, input, and help in editing.

On a more personal note, the friendship and kindness of good friends has been a real strength and joy. Thank you, Shawna Farmer, Nancy Sullivan, Mary Shumway, Haley Mackay, Jolene Reddish, and Rosie O'Connell. I have also been blessed with my own family version of the "Ya-Ya Sisterhood," aunts, Roxie Dobson, Joann Fleenor, (the late) Barbara Andersen, and (the late) Luana Williams. My "Ya-Ya Sisterhood" are models of strength, courage, faith, grace under pressure and beauty.

To my siblings, Jed, Mark, Paulette, Blake, and Charlene, I thank you. In particular, my sisters, Paulette Connell Baucom and Charlene Connell Dalto, have been my best friends. Your support is the very definition of love, kindness, support, and understanding. Next, I acknowledge the great support and love of my parents, Edward J. (Bud) and Faye J. Connell, who have always encouraged me and given me the confidence and desire to achieve my goals.

Most importantly, I must thank my four children for patiently waiting for mom to finish just one more sentence, one more paragraph, one more chapter, and one more re-write. My children will always be my greatest joy and greatest asset. You have each made completion of this whole effort possible: Melanie Faye Hall, Rachel Michelle Hall, Adam Joseph Herman, and Emily Mae Herman. Thanks, kids! It is my blessing to be your mother.

Above all, I thank and acknowledge my God for his blessings in helping me write and complete this work.

SOCIETY FOR
HUMAN
RESOURCE
MANAGEMENT

Selected Titles from the
Society for Human Resource Management
(SHRM®)

Diverse Teams at Work; By Lee Gardenswartz and Anita Rowe

Finding Diversity; By Luby Ismail and Alex Kronemer

HIPAA Privacy Source Book: A Collection of Practical Samples
By William S. Hubbartt

*Human Resource Essentials: Your Guide to Starting and Running
the HR Function* By Lin Grensing-Pophal, SPHR

*Performance Appraisal Source Book: A Collection of Practical
Samples*; By Mike Deblieux

*Practical HR Series: Legal, Effective References: How to Give and
Get Them;* By Wendy Bliss, J.D., SPHR

*Practical HR Series: Investigating Workplace Harassment: How to
Be Fair, Thorough, and Legal*
By Amy Oppenheimer, J.D., and Craig Pratt, MSW, SPHR

*Responsible Restructuring: Creative and Profitable Alternatives to
Layoffs;* By Wayne F. Cascio

Retaining Your Best Employees (In Action Case Studies)
Series Editor Jack J. Phillips

——————— TO ORDER SHRM BOOKS ———————

SHRM offers a member discount on all books that it publishes or sells. To order
this or any other book published by the Society, contact the SHRMStore.®

ONLINE: www.shrm.org/shrmstore
BY PHONE: 800-444-5006 (option #1); or 770-442-8633 (ext. 362);
or TDD 703-548-6999
BY FAX: 770-442-9742
BY MAIL: SHRM Distribution Center
P.O. Box 930132
Atlanta, GA 31193-0132   USA

CHAPTER 1

Why Retention Is a Serious Problem . . . Still*

"Employee turnover (leaving an organization) is a major organizational phenomenon. Employee turnover is important to organizations, individuals, and society. From the organizational perspective, employee turnover can represent a significant cost in terms of recruiting, training, socialization, and disruption, as well as a variety of indirect costs. Given the significance of turnover, it is important for the manager and prospective manager to be able to analyze, understand, and effectively manage employee turnover" (Mobley, 1982). The significance of this comment is that Mobley made it in 1982 in his classic book on employee turnover.

Employee turnover is not a new issue. It is relevant today and its importance will be even greater in the future. Many analysts believe that there may be 20 million jobs unfilled by the end of 2008. This is approximately twice the number of unfilled positions today. Some analysts are projecting a shortfall of up to 30 million employees (Galbreath, 2001). Those individuals who believe that this issue may fade with slight economic downturns might consider the following scenario. A blue-chip manufacturer announces 53,000 layoffs worldwide, a leading financial institution plans to shed 8,000 jobs, and a Big-Three automobile maker cuts 1,200 positions in a single plant. Given this situation, it appears that turnover might not be a problem. Digging a little deeper underscores the issue; the manufacturer in question was Boeing, the bank was CitiGroup, and the automobile

---

*Much of this first chapter is taken from a companion book of case studies, *Retaining Your Best Employees*. Patricia P. Phillips, ed. Alexandria, Va.: American Society for Training and Development, 2002.

maker was General Motors. These headlines are not from yesterday's paper—they are from the end of 1998, when the economy was at the height of a boom and employee turnover commanded everyone's attention (Bernasek, 2001).

Managing retention is a constant challenge for any organization. The awareness of the issue has heightened in the last decade, and, from all indications, the problem will be more serious in future decades. Even in slow economic times, most human resources (HR) executives find attracting and retaining talent to be a big problem. In a study during the 2001–2003 recession, 90 percent of the 109 executives surveyed said that they were finding it difficult to attract and retain the best people in the organization (Dell and Hickey, 2002). This chapter explores the seriousness of the issue and examines some of the major reasons for turnover and its consequences. It also dispels some of the myths about turnover and sets the stage for the remainder of the book.

Definitions

An understanding of the basic distinctions between retention, turnover, and other related topics is important. These distinctions among these definitions will help clarify the concepts in this book and establish the appropriate framework.

Retention is the percentage of employees remaining in the organization. High levels of retention are desired in most job groups.

Turnover, the opposite of retention, refers to the percentage of employees leaving the organization for whatever reason(s). "Avoidable" turnover is distinguished from "unavoidable" so that the proper emphasis can be placed on the avoidable portion.

Turnover rate refers to the rate of individuals leaving. Several formulas are discussed in this chapter and in Chapter 3.

Tenure is the length of time an individual is employed by the organization and is usually related to the concept of employee loyalty. A loyal employee usually remains with an organization for a long period. In many organizations it is desirable to have long-tenured employees, although this situation taken to extreme can also *create* problems.

Experience levels are often defined as the months or years of experience in a particular job or functional area of the organization. Average levels of experience are critical issues in some job categories and knowledge industries.

Retention as a Critical Issue

Recent publicity underscores the critical issues surrounding retention. The topic has reached widespread visibility through countless articles and books bringing the issue to the attention of managers and specialists. Retention articles are regularly included and sometimes on the cover of magazines such as *Fortune*, *Forbes*, and *Business Week*. Books describing the competition for talent and suggested solutions are readily available. Workshops and seminars are regularly conducted on the issue of retention and turnover. It has become a mainstream topic in business and professional literature.

The concept of employer-of-choice has intensified in the last decade. Employees want to work for the best employers. Organizations strive to be the "best company to work for" because that statement translates directly into lower rates of turnover. Fueled in part by the book *The 100 Best Companies to Work for in America* (Levering and Moskowitz, 1993), many companies attempt to build the type of organization that can be included in, or at least meet the standards for inclusion into, these impressive lists. The organizations listed in *Fortune* magazine's "100 Best Companies to Work for in America" and *Business Week*'s "Employers of Choice" are striving to be the preferred employer. Organizations included on these lists often use this recognition in print ads, recruiting literature, and other communications.

Becoming an employer-of-choice often involves the issue of acquiring the best talent for the organization, motivating employees to improve performance, keeping them satisfied and loyal, developing employees so they can grow and contribute skills, and ultimately retaining those employees (Fitz-enz, 2000).

Perhaps the most impressive development is the elevation of retention to the strategic levels of the organization. Consider the case of MicroStrategy, an information systems company whose software enables businesses to fine-tune their decision-making and add very healthy profits. With a market capitalization of $25 billion, MicroStrategy was known for recruiting the best and the brightest for its workforce of more than 2,000 and for sparing no expense to lure top talent. For example, it spent $5 million each year to conduct team-building exercises on a cruise ship in the Caribbean. Retention was an important part of strategy (Kiger, 2000).

Unfortunately for MicroStrategy, the retention strategy suffered because of financial difficulties. The company had to disclose that, because of accounting problems, it would have to restate earnings for several previous years. In a single day, the company's stock lost 60 percent of its market value, and over several months, plunged from more than $300 a share to below $30 a share. For the first time, the company was forced to rescind job offers and lay off 10 percent of its workforce while, at the same time, attempting to keep its key employees. In essence, its retention strategy shifted from attracting fresh new talent to retaining valued employees in the face of a financial blow. In both situations, retention was a key strategy driven by top executives. Most organizations now view the issue of retention and becoming an employer-of-choice as a strategic advantage.

Although employee retention is always important, the issue becomes even more important when the economy faces a temporary decline. *Fortune* magazine recently provided 13 strategies to deal with a downturn in business, along with three rules not to forget. One of the rules was "when times get tough, many organizations ease up on recruiting, figuring a slow economy will drive more applicants their way. They spend less on training as a way to raise profits quickly without doing immediate damage to the business." According to *Fortune*, "that approach is just dumb" (Charan and Colvin, 2001). This is one of the few major business publication that has taken a stand on the importance of recruiting quality people during a downturn while continuing to invest in their training and development.

These brief scenarios indicate how retention is constantly in the limelight. It has captured the attention of the business, financial, and executive community. It is a critical, strategic issue that now commands the attention it deserves. In many organizations, executives are creating integrated retention policies using internal and external data to shape focused retention solutions (Steel, Griffeth, and Hom, 2002).

NEGATIVE IMPACT OF TURNOVER ON THE ORGANIZATION

Although every manager and team member is aware of problems associated with turnover, a review of its major consequences puts retention in the proper perspective. Eleven categories frame the major negative consequences. Chapter 4 provides more detail on the financial impact of turnover.

High financial cost. Turnover has a huge economic impact on the organization, both in direct and indirect costs. Translating turnover into numbers that executives understand is essential because they need to appreciate the true costs (Dell and Hickey, 2002). Sometimes the cost impact alone causes it to become a critical strategic issue. The performance of companies has been inhibited by high turnover rates.

Survival is an issue. In a tight labor market where the success of the company depends on employees with critical skills, recruiting and retaining the appropriate talent can determine the success or failure of the organization.

Exit problems and issues. With increased litigation at the workplace, many organizations spend significant time and resources addressing the issues of disgruntled, and departing employees. Some individuals find the need to involve the legal system, leaving the organization with the challenge of facing an even bigger problem. Even employees who leave voluntarily can cost the company time and money.

Productivity losses and workflow interruptions. In most turnover situations, a person who exits abruptly leaves a productivity gap. This void not only causes problems for the specific job performed by the departing employee, but also for others on the same team and within the flow of work.

Service quality. With so much emphasis on providing excellent service to external and internal customers, high turnover has a tremendous negative impact on the quality of customer service. Turnover of front-line employees is often regarded as the most serious threat to providing excellent external customer service (Phillips, 2002).

Loss of expertise. Particularly in knowledge industries, a departing employee may have the critical skills needed for working with specific software, completing a step in an important process, or carrying out a task for a project. Sometimes an entire product line may suffer because of a departure. A lost employee may be impossible to replace—at least in the short term.

Loss of business opportunities. Turnover may result in a shortage of staff for a project or leave the remaining staff unprepared to take advantage of a new business opportunity. Existing projects or contracts may be lost or late because a key player is no longer available.

Administrative problems. In most organizations, turnover creates a burdensome amount of administrative effort, not only in additional paper work, but also in time spent confronting and addressing turnover-related issues. This takes precious time away from more important, productive responsibilities.

Disruption of social and communication networks. Every organization has an informal network. Turnover disrupts the communication and socialization patterns critical to the maintenance of teamwork and a productive work environment.

Job satisfaction of remaining employees. The disruptive nature of turnover is amplified when other employees are forced to assume the workload of departing colleagues or address problems associated with the departure. Remaining team members can be distracted by their concern and curiosity about why employees are leaving.

Image of the organization. High turnover creates the negative image of a company with a revolving door. Once this image has been established in the job marketplace, it is difficult to change, especially in the recruiting channels.

These are very significant, negative consequences. With such impact and pain, excessive turnover should command the attention of everyone in the organization.

NEGATIVE IMPACT OF TURNOVER ON INDIVIDUALS

This book primarily focuses on what organizations are (and should be) doing about managing retention because of the negative impact of turnover on the organization. At the same time, it is important to remember that turnover can have a negative impact on the individual, particularly if a person is leaving because of problems that could have been prevented. If the departure is involuntary, there are the usual issues about performance that could have been avoided. In addition, even a voluntary turnover, because of issues that could have been avoided, creates a variety of negative consequences.

Loss of employee benefits or job seniority. Some employee benefits are tied to tenure. Starting a new job almost always resets the clock, with the employee losing the vested interest in benefits at the previous organization.

Stress associated with the transition and change. In every job change, anxiety and stress associated with the transition will intensify, even if it is a desired transition. Job changes represent one of life's important stressors.

Financial difficulties. If a person leaves a job without having immediate employment, the transition can create a financial setback. Even in voluntary turnover, a short break in employment may occur.

Loss of social network. For many employees, the workplace is their primary social network; for some, their *only* social life. Relinquishing that connection and moving to another organization often destroys that network, along with the emotional support from the network.

Relocation costs. Although many organizations pay relocation costs, some do not. In almost every relocation situation, unreimbursed personal expenses are involved, as well as a tremendous amount of time and effort.

Wasted efforts and uncompleted projects. Particularly in knowledge industries, where employees work on developing and completing projects, a departure may mean wasted effort. This often leaves the employee feeling as if the entire time on the project was wasted.

Career problems. A situation in which the departure is a result of a performance issue can be devastating for the individual's career and can take a tremendous toll on self-esteem. Frequent job changes also can be difficult to explain to potential future employers.

With the significant negative impact of turnover—on organizations and individuals—turnover is clearly a critical issue.

External Drivers of the Retention Crisis

What has caused the retention crisis? Major changes have occurred in organizations—both internally and externally—making this issue more critical today than in previous years. Unfortunately, these changes will only worsen the crisis in the future.

Economic growth. Almost all industrialized nations, and many emerging countries, have experienced long economic expansions. As economies grow, job growth will continue. In almost all segments of the economy, economic expansions translate directly into new jobs, which in turn creates new opportunities for employees to leave current employment.

Slower growth of job seekers. Despite economic growth, the number of job seekers is not increasing as quickly as job growth. In the

United States, the job seeker growth rate is growing at a slower rate each year. Consequently, many organizations have the compounding problem of fewer job seekers and more jobs created (Bolch, 2001).

Unemployment rate at low levels. Low unemployment rates lead to increased turnover because more jobs are available. As shown in Figure 1-1, the unemployment rate in the United States continues to hover around a very low rate, from its high of 7.5 percent in 1992 to the 4 to 5 percent range in this millennium. Many economists agree that whenever the actual unemployment rate falls in the 5 percent range or lower, it creates serious problems for employers seeking to fill job vacancies.

Shortage of special skills. Compounding the situation is the short supply of workers with special skills, particularly in high-tech occupations, health care, and other critical areas. The news is often flooded with situations in which the number of candidates for jobs falls far short of the demand. This involves every spectrum from high-tech specialists, engineers, and scientists, where employment opportunities have outpaced the supply, to entry-level positions, such as those in the fast-food industry, where jobs go begging. This represents tremendous challenges for the future (Bernstein, 2002).

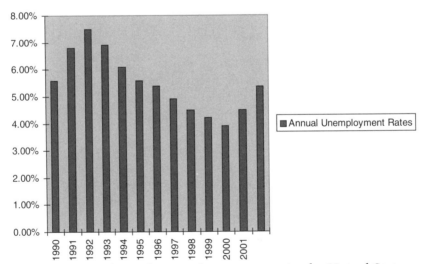

Figure 1-1. Annual unemployment rates in the United States.

Entrepreneurship. In recent years, growth in small businesses has been tremendous, particularly in those businesses created by individuals leaving large organizations and taking their expertise with them. In the United States, baby-boomers are taking early retirement to start their own businesses, sometimes in direct competition with the company they left. A global entrepreneur boom has developed, with the United States ranked No. 2 (behind South Korea and slightly ahead of Brazil) in the share of workers in new organizations (*The Economist*, 2001).

Job changes for more favorable climates. In recent decades, a significant number of jobs shifted to areas where the weather is considered more favorable. In the United States, this is particularly noticeable in the western states, the coastal areas, the southern states, and other areas where year-round climates are milder. Turnover is created as people migrate. This change has little to do with a specific organization, just the location of the jobs themselves.

From all indications, the problems outlined above are largely out of the employer's control and will only get worse. Figure 1-2 shows that the difference in the job growth rate and the workforce growth rate will cause the United States to have a shortfall in the future as birth rates are lower and baby-boomers are retiring early (Bernstein, 2002).

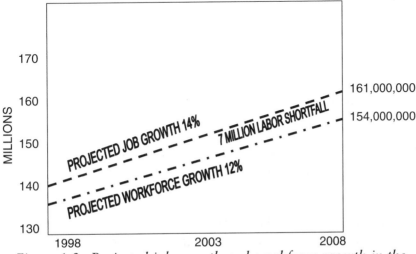

Figure 1-2. Projected job growth and workforce growth in the United States. Adapted from Branham (2001).

Internal Drivers

Internal changes in organizations operate in concert with the external influences to drive excessive turnover. Internal issues include structural changes within the organization and changes in employees' attitudes about work and their employers. The following internal drivers have a tremendous impact on turnover.

Lack of company loyalty. Perhaps one of the most frustrating issues is the growing lack of company loyalty. Many organizations show that much-needed loyalty has deteriorated in recent years. Some contend that allegiance is virtually nonexistent in most American companies (Capelli, 1999). Years ago employees appreciated their jobs and would strive to stay with an organization for a long time. There was a sense of pride in working for the same company for 40 years.

Studies continue to indicate that loyalty is not only low, but continues to remain low, perhaps even declining in recent times. Ironically, the research shows that employees want to remain with an organization for longer periods, creating an opportunity for the organizations to tackle this issue (Cole, 2000).

Desire for challenging and useful work. Employees want creative, challenging, and useful work, a desire that has been evolving for many years. For many employees, their jobs are their "identities"—who they are. They have a need to use their minds and make a significant contribution. If they cannot achieve this within the framework of the current job, they will find one where they can.

Need for autonomy, flexibility, and independence. Employees are becoming more accustomed to having the autonomy and flexibility to organize and control their work and work environment. Telecommuting is making it easier to work at home. This need is attracting many employees to organizations offering a flexible structure.

Need for performance-based rewards. More employees are seeking appropriate reward systems that reflect individual contribution and individual performance. If rewards are not in direct proportion to achievement, employees often will find jobs at organizations where they will be rewarded accordingly.

Need for recognition for participation, accomplishments, and contributions. In addition to monetary rewards, employees want credit for what they do and what they have accomplished. Periodic feedback and recognition has been an important part of motivational research for years. Employees seek workplaces where they can be acknowledged in a more systematic, routine fashion.

Desire for all types of benefits. Unfortunately, employees expect compensation in all forms. Some employees go to extremes to seek an organization with a particular benefit that is critical to their needs. Companies have had to adjust their programs and offer all types of perks, sometimes bordering on the absurd.

Need to learn new skills. Perhaps a more recent development is employees' desire to acquire new skills and skill sets. Employees want to learn new technology, processes, and projects and develop all types of skills, particularly in the technical area. Employees view skills acquisition—not seniority—as providing them with job security. Consequently, they seek organizations willing to invest in them. The availability of generous tuition payment, ample job-related training, and continuous development opportunities can be strong attractions.

Career growth in all directions. In addition to obtaining new skills, employees want the opportunity to advance within an organization as they grow and develop these skills. Some advancement is upward and other movement is lateral, such as growth of specialized skills, but if employees cannot advance inside the company, they will move to another one.

Desire to be on the leading edge. Employees are interested in organizations with a strong reputation, considered to be on the leading edge of technology or product development, or the best at what they do. These high-profile organizations—admired by many others and often the best in their field—are natural attractions for individuals who want to be associated with the best. If their current situation does not provide it, they may move to one that does.

Desire for competitive compensation. Increased salary schedules have probably been the most visible and discussed internal change in organizations. Compensation levels have grown significantly, sometimes outstripping other economic indicators. Employees want more money, with more disposable income. They also view their income level as an indication of their worth to the organization and their field.

Need for a caring, supportive environment. Some employees place a high level of importance on working in a caring, supportive environment. Gone are the days of willingness to tolerate harsh attitudes, continuous conflict, and unappreciative bosses. If they do not have the nurturing environment they want, they will move to another organization where they can find it.

Need for work/life balance. Many employees seek a job where they can establish a balance between their work and personal lives. Fewer employees are willing to work an excessive number of hours, cope with unusual working conditions, or tolerate highly stressful and demanding situations. They want time for more involvement in family activities and social networks—as well as time for religious commitments. They seek organizations that will provide the appropriate work/life balance (Brady, 2002).

In some cases, internal issues are affecting turnover rates more than external drivers, but collectively, the internal issues and external shifts provide a tremendous challenge for organizations to manage employee retention.

TURNOVER MYTHS

This introductory chapter would not be complete without discussing some of the myths about turnover. At one time or another, these myths surface in an organization and often inhibit efforts to manage retention in a proactive way.

Turnover costs are not too high. Turnover costs—both direct and indirect—are very high if turnover is excessive. This problem is often misunderstood; more precisely, the senior management team does not have a full appreciation for the high cost of excessive turnover. It is expensive and will be more costly in the future.

Turnover is just a cost of doing business. Some managers accept turnover, even in excessive numbers, as an acceptable cost—just a cost of doing business in the organization. Accepting this philosophy is analogous to accepting high accident rates in the construction industry as a cost of doing business. The best construction firms have low accident rates and low accident costs. This myth must be dispelled. If excessive turnover can be avoided, prevented, or controlled, the cost of doing business can be much lower.

Turnover is good; at least it has many positive consequences. Although *some* turnover can be a good thing, *excessive* turnover is not. (On the extreme, zero turnover is not desirable.) When the benefits of turnover outweigh the negative consequences, the scale tips quickly to the need for preventive measures. The key issue is to define excessive turnover and avoid it.

Turnover is an industry problem. Executives in some industries with unusually high turnover rates accept it as an industry problem. For example, the retail sales industry has an average turnover rate of 130 percent, and fast food an even higher one. Within this context, some organizations are able to achieve very low rates with proper attention to retention. It is a serious mistake to accept a high turnover, believing nothing can be done about it (Goldwasser, 2000).

Turnover is an HR problem. Pointing fingers at the HR executive or staff is unproductive in today's environment. Turnover is an organizational issue that must be addressed with leadership from the senior executive team. The HR function can have a tremendous impact on retention, but for the most part, HR staff provide the administrative support for measuring, monitoring, analyzing, and reducing excessive turnover rates.

The manager's role is minimal. Individual managers, particularly the first-level managers, actually have the critical role in turnover reduction. Most causes of turnover and subsequent retention solution strategies involve managers in some way. The adage "employees join organizations and leave managers" underscores the importance of the managers' role. Their influence is crucial, and they often underestimate their role and influence in the process.

Turnover is out of our control. Executives sometimes accept an unusually high turnover rate, assuming that it is all externally driven and therefore out of their control, which is not true. Most effective retention solutions are internally driven. In some organizations in geographical areas or industries where attracting employees is very difficult, turnover is still low. A high turnover rate need not be accepted as the norm.

Throwing money at the problem will solve it. Although retention strategies cost money, continuing to throw money at the problem can cause two other problems. First, the expense sometimes outweighs the cost of turnover, resulting in a negative return on investment. Second, excessive spending can render the entire process ineffective because there are too many solutions, with too many activities in place at the same time. Combating this situation requires a strategic accountability approach, where only those solutions that can produce the most results are tackled.

Turnover is a tactical issue only. The implementation of retention solutions requires a series of tactical steps. However, turnover is not only a tactical issue, it is also a strategic issue. Retention requires a commitment from the entire senior management team and must be addressed as a part of strategy. Only then will the tactical issues become a routine and supported step in the process. Technology and tools are now available to address getting and keeping talent, but if HR is not actively engaged in the planning process and does not receive corporate commitment from the top, the supply of talented employees will almost certainly be limited to ad hoc clusters of programs and boom and bust cycles of hiring and reductions that waste talent and inevitably cost more (Dell and Hickey, 2002).

TURNOVER RATES

When discussing turnover, it is important to define turnover rate early in the book. Chapter 3 provides more detail on definitions, measures, and reporting options. Turnover can be defined in many ways. The employer-of-choice definition for turnover follows three criteria:

1. **A standard rate—avoidable and unavoidable**—defined as the number of employees leaving during the month divided by the number of employees at mid-month. This rate includes all reasons for leaving the organization as the standard value. By itself, this measure has very little value.
2. **A standard rate—avoidable**—defined as the avoidable employee departures divided by the number of employees at mid-month. Although this is a more workable definition, there is still vagueness as to what is considered avoidable.
3. **New hire turnover rate** (early employee turnover rate)—defined as the number of employees leaving in the first 60 days of employment divided by the number of new employees hired in the same period.

These three measures should be appropriate for most monitoring situations. To some degree, they're consistent with the statistics available from many of the reporting agencies and benchmarking reports.

PAYOFFS OF RETENTION SOLUTIONS

Although it may appear obvious, it is helpful to recap the payoff of managing retention. Specific strategies aimed at overcoming the causes of turnover and implementing solutions to reduce turnover have important payoffs for organizations. Some studies have shown that the payoff for reducing turnover by 10 percent is greater than that of increasing productivity by 10 percent or reducing the actual inventories by 10 percent. Other studies have indicated that just reducing the turnover from industry average to the top 10 percent can increase profits by as much as 50 percent (Fitz-enz, 2000).

Turnover can have a devastating impact on the organization. Consider the comparison of CVS and Walgreens pharmacies. CVS experienced serious problems with a shortage of pharmacists, 650 to 750 a day. A Merrill Lynch analyst blamed the company's less than expected financial performance on the shortage and a failure to manage retention. CVS shareholders filed a class-action suit alleging that it failed to tell shareholders that it was unable to successfully manage the retention issue. Walgreens has not experienced the same serious problems and have met their financial targets (Raphael, 2001).

Because of the tremendous cost of turnover (both direct and indirect), any efforts to lower turnover have a tremendous payoff, particularly when the value of the turnover reduction is compared with the cost of the solution. In turnover reduction studies, the actual return on investment can be as high as 1,000 percent (Phillips, 1994, 1997, and 2001). This is achieved when comparing the actual monetary benefits from turnover reduction solutions to the actual cost of the solution.

One of the most visible payoffs of employee retention occurs in the operations areas and with the front line staff. Lower turnover translates into fewer operational problems, fewer delays, increased customer service, smoother flow of work, and improved quality of transactions. Organizations routinely report operational improvements as the most important payoff of managing retention (Phillips, 2002).

Because of the negative consequences of turnover to the organization as well as the individual, there are many intangible benefits associated with turnover reduction solutions. Intangible measures are defined as measures not converted to monetary values. Typical payoffs include improved job satisfaction, organizational commitment, customer satisfaction, and teamwork, as well as reduced conflicts, stress, and bottlenecks. In some situations, these measures are more important than the monetary benefits.

Final Thoughts

This chapter sets the stage for this book by exploring the serious nature of retention in organizations. In recent years, managing retention has become a critically important topic that commands the attention of top executives and has become a part of the organization's strategy. The consequences of excessive turnover are significant and costly—both from the perspective of the organization and employee. External and internal drivers of the increased turnover are examined in this chapter, and the myths of turnover are presented in an attempt to dispel them. Finally, specific definitions and acceptable rates are defined and the payoff of the process is briefly discussed. The remainder of this book will examine, in detail, the recommended approach for managing retention for the organizations.

References

Bernasek, A. "Help Wanted, Really." *Fortune* March 5, 2001:118.

Bernstein, A. "Too Many Workers? Not for Long." *Business Week* May 20, 2002:126–130.

Bolch, M. "The Coming Crunch." *Training Magazine* April 2001.

Brady, D. "Rethinking the Rat Race." *Business Week* August 26, 2002:142.

Branham, L. *Keeping the People Who Keep You in Business*. New York: Amacon Publishing, 2001.

Capelli, P. *The New Deal at Work: Managing the Market-Driven Workplace*. Boston: Harvard Business School Press, 1999.

Charan, R., and Colvin, G. "Managing for the Slowdown: 13 Moves to Make Before Your Competitors Do Plus 3 Rules Not to Forget." *Fortune* Feb. 5, 2001:80.

Cole, C.L. "Building Loyalty." *Workforce Magazine* August 2000:46.

Dell, D., and Hickey, J. *Attracting and Keeping Top Employees*. New York: The Conference Board, 2002.

"Entrepreneurial Fresh Air." *The Economist* January 13, 2001:60.

Fitz-enz, J. *The ROI of Human Capital*. New York: Amacom Publishing, 2000.

Galbreath, R. *The Good and Bad News about the Labor Market through 2008*. SHRM White Paper, Alexandria, Va.: The Society for Human Resource Management, 2001.

Goldwasser, D. "Retention Café." *Training Magazine* December 2000:44.

Kiger, P.J. "Retention on the Brink." *Workforce Magazine* November 2000:59–60.

Levering, R., and Moskowitz, M. *The 100 Best Companies to Work for in America.* New York: Bantam Doubleday Dell Publishing Group, Inc., 1993.

Mobley, W.H. *Employee Turnover: Causes, Consequences, and Control.* Reading, MA: Addison-Wesley Publishing Company, 1982.

Phillips, J. (Ed.). *Measuring Return on Investment, Volume 1.* Alexandria, Va.: American Society for Training and Development, 1994.

Phillips, J. (Ed.). *Measuring Return on Investment, Volume 2.* Alexandria, Va.: American Society for Training and Development, 1997.

Phillips, P. (Ed.) and Phillips, J. (Series Ed.). *Measuring Return on Investment, Volume 3*, Alexandria, VA: American Society for Training and Development, 2001.

Phillips, P. (Ed.). *Retaining Your Best Employees.* Alexandria, Va.: American Society for Training and Development, 2002.

Raphael, L. "HR and an Rx for the Bottom Line." *Workforce.* October, 2001:104.

Steel, R.P., Griffeth, R.W., and Hom, D.W. "Practical Retention Policy for the Practical Manager." Academy of Management Executive, 2002; 16(2):149–162.

FURTHER READING

Ahlrichs, N.S. Competing for Talent: Key Recruitment and Retention Strategies for Becoming an Employer of Choice. Palo Alto, Cal.: Davies-Black Publishing, 2000.

Ashby, F., and Pell, A.R. *Embracing Excellence: Become an Employer of Choice to Attract and Keep the Best Talent.* Paramus, N.J.: Prentice Hall Press, 2001.

Coffman, C., and Gonzalez-Molina, G. *Follow This Path: How the World's Greatest Organizations Drive Growth by Unleashing Human Potential.* New York: Warner Books, 2002.

Cohen, D.S. *The Talent Edge: A Behavioral Approach to Hiring, Developing, and Keeping Top Performers.* New York: John Wiley & Sons, 2001.

Gonthier, G., and Morrissey, K. *Rude Awakenings: Overcoming the Civility Crisis in the Workplace.* Chicago: Dearborn Trade Publishing, 2002.

Grantham, C. *The Future of Work: The Promise of the New Digital Work Society.* New York: McGraw-Hill, 2000.

Griffeth, R.W., and Hom, P.W. *Retaining Valued Employees.* Thousand Oaks, Calif.: Sage Publications, 2001.

Harris, J. *Getting Employees to Fall in Love with Your Company.* New York: Amacom Publishing, 1996.

Jensen, B. *Work 2.0. Rewriting the Contract.* Cambridge, Mass.: Perseus Publishing, 2002.

Johnson, M. *Talent Magnet: Getting Talented People to Work for You.* London: Prentice Hall, 2002.

Reichheld, F.F. *Loyalty Rules! How Today's Leaders Build Lasting Relationships.* Boston: Harvard Business School Press, 2001.

Sears, D. *Successful Talent Strategies: Achieving Superior Business Results through Market-Focused Staffing.* New York: Amacon Publishing, 2003.

CHAPTER 2

A Strategic Accountability Approach to Managing Retention

Some organizations do a superb job of managing retention, whereas others fail miserably. The issues are not always externally driven but often lie within the organization—sometimes in the approach to the problem. Finding a new approach requires shifting paradigms, changing perceptions, and throwing out old habits. A more rigorous, analytical, and strategic approach to addressing internal issues is often needed (Steel, Griffeth, and Hom, 2002).

The previous chapter underscores the seriousness of employee turnover. This chapter describes the recommended approach to address employee retention and is the basis for this book. Several issues pertaining to managing retention as a strategic initiative are explored. Eight distinct steps provide the basis for the strategic approach and bring the appropriate focus on accountability to the retention issue. This chapter briefly explains the rationale for the approach and the steps involved. More detail around certain steps is contained in later chapters.

PROBLEMS WITH EXISTING APPROACHES

Old and outdated approaches to managing retention have created six distinct problems. How many of these sound familiar?

Proactive versus Reactive (What Problem?)

Many organizations react to the retention issue—waiting until a problem surfaces, often developing enormous incentive packages to entice key employees to "stay with the ship." In these situations, the turnover issue results in severe stresses and financial impact in the organization before steps are taken to resolve it. The pressure is on—a solution must be implemented, now!

A proactive approach is needed to prevent the issue from ever surfacing. This is often easier said than done. Almost every manager will agree that employee turnover should be prevented before it becomes a problem. Unfortunately, many external environmental factors exacerbate the turnover issue. The human resources (HR) staff and management team is not fully prepared for these issues and the results are sometimes disastrous. A continuous improvement process cycle is needed so that the focus is always on improving the current situation. This will help manage the employee retention issue.

Developing Too Many Preventive Programs (If We Try This, and This, and This, We Can Prevent the Problem in the Future)

Just as the reactive approach can be a problem, implementing too many preventive programs can also be a problem. In an effort to be proactive, many organizations implement preventive programs with a "try it and see" mentality without understanding the real impact of turnover on the organization. The philosophy is this: If enough programs are implemented, eventually one of them will help maintain staffing at the appropriate level, eliminating unnecessary turnover. Without the appropriate accountability applied to the program, the results of the program's implementation may never be known. Meanwhile, far too much money is spent. The organization's landscape is littered with overspending in an attempt to prevent the turnover problem from occurring. Although prevention is important, some method to forecast the value of preventive programs must be in place. Forecasting value provides some assurance that the program will generate enough monetary benefit to offset the costs.

Searching for Solutions (Hey, They Have a Great Program over at the Hard Rock Café!)

Many HR managers and staff members are constantly searching for a solution, trying to find a program that has worked for another location. When workshops and conferences are offered about retention strategies, HR staff flock to sessions, taking copious notes, and feverishly attempting to apply newly discovered techniques or programs to their organization. Many times this approach results in failure. Searching for a solution without the proper analysis of the problem is a very serious issue and leaves the management team wondering if there *is* a solution in their situation. An up-front evaluation is needed to identify the specific causes of turnover.

Too Many Solutions (I Never Met a Solution I Didn't Like!)

Even when employee retention is identified as a problem, too many organizations, even some of the successful ones, base their approach to the issue on an excessive number of strategies. Turnover is a complex issue with many influences. Perhaps 500 specific solutions could be implemented. The published literature on retention does not help—often offering countless solutions. One publication offers 154 solutions to "keep good people"(Herman, 1999). Implementing, or at least attempting to implement, too many solutions can create disastrous results. The organization is burdened with an excessive number of new programs, projects, initiatives, plans, policies, and techniques. This can result in costly efforts with minimal, if any, results to show for them, while at the same time, leaving staff members confused and managers perplexed. The objective is to tackle only the most critical turnover solutions, using precious organizational resources wisely to develop the most effective approach.

Mismatches between Need and Solution (We Blew It on This One!)

Too often, a solution that does not actually address the need or problem is implemented. Maybe there is insufficient information to provide a clear understanding of the solution required. Maybe the wrong solution is selected or improperly implemented, resulting in a lack of added value. Maybe the solution did not address the need as anticipated. Maybe it was the wrong solution. Whatever the case, these mistakes can be avoided by clearly matching the solutions to the needs.

Lack of Payoff (What Results?)

When an expensive solution is implemented, taking precious time and resources, a familiar scenario often surfaces. The management team wonders if it made a difference. Did it add enough value to offset the costs of its implementation? Could a different, less expensive solution have similar results? Is the turnover rate still unacceptable? The solution might have successfully prevented further turnover deterioration or it could have left turnover unchanged, poised for further deterioration. The problem lies in not knowing. A process is needed to measure the results of a solution from a balanced perspective, collecting different types of data (tangible and intangible) so that management can clearly see the impact of major retention strategies (Dell and Hickey, 2002).

The problems with these six approaches, and the rationale for preventing them, form the basis for the approach presented in this chapter.

NEEDED: A STRATEGIC ACCOUNTABILITY APPROACH

The strategic accountability approach, outlined in Figure 2-1, is the basic model for this book. The process brings accountability to the retention issue in eight steps (Phillips and Phillips, 2002).

The strategic accountability approach has five very important advantages, as follows. *It considers the retention issue to be an important part of strategy.* The executive team is very involved in the retention issue. With many firms, retention has become a strategic issue because it makes the difference between financial mediocrity and excellence. It is a critical issue that deserves proper attention and management throughout the process.

The retention issues are measured with bottom-line results. Accountability is incorporated throughout the process so those involved can fully understand the cost of the problem, cost of the solutions, potential impact of the solutions, and the actual impact of the solutions—all in monetary terms. This level of accountability is often missing in other approaches to retention analysis.

The approach moves logically from one issue to another. A series of steps, not necessary to manage the process, are followed with this

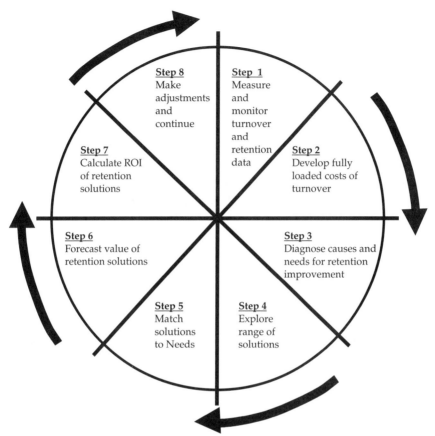

Figure 2-1. Strategic accountability approach.

approach. Each step has options and possibilities but needs to be addressed in some way for the process to be successful.

The approach is a discipline and a methodology. Staying on track is easy with this approach, because each different issue must be addressed before moving onto another issue. The approach brings structure and organization to the retention issue, rather than "shooting from the hip" or implementing solutions without analysis.

It is a continuous cycle of improvement. Starting with a problem ultimately leads to a reduction in turnover. The process continues until turnover is at the desired level.

Ultimately, the approach positions the organization in a preventative stance working to maintain the appropriate level of staffing and reducing the risk of turnover. Each segment of the strategic accountability approach is briefly discussed in the remainder of the chapter.

MEASURE AND MONITOR TURNOVER DATA

Specific issues need to be addressed to properly monitor and measure turnover. Six key issues are explored here.

Appropriate Definition of Turnover

For many organizations, turnover is voluntary; for others, it results from resignations and terminations based on unsatisfactory performance. The clearest definition to use is avoidable turnover. A few organizations actually call this kind of turnover "regrets"; employees left (voluntarily) or had to leave (involuntarily). It is important for the definition to match the definition in benchmarking studies, industry reports, or trade publications. While this seems simple, problems can easily develop because of the different classifications of turnover. Most professionals would agree that deaths, disabilities, and retirement should not be included in the turnover rate. However, in an organization where early retirement is an option, this could be an issue that deserves consideration. The important point is to select the proper definition and use it appropriately to compare with others.

Turnover Rates by Various Demographics

A variety of demographics could be reported, showing the regions, divisions, branches, plants, as well as sex, age, and personal characteristics of the individual employees. Reporting by using too many demographics may confuse the issue. It is important to report demographics that appear to account for differences, thus enabling patterns to be developed and analyzed.

Reporting by Critical Job Groups

A job group may be important for benchmarking comparisons. Certain jobs are more critical than others, particularly in technology industries. Employee groups that design, develop, or deliver products and services are essential to the lifeblood of the organization, requiring special skills that are often in short supply. These individuals need to be monitored and tracked separately, if possible.

Report Turnover with Costs

Although actual turnover rates and percentages are reported either monthly or yearly, additional reporting of actual costs can be more effective. Since the actual cost of turnover appears in different cost statements, it is important to bring the total cost of turnover to the attention of the senior management team, revealing the true impact of turnover in the organization. The fully loaded cost of turnover should be developed, even if it is only an estimate. Cost formulas should be used to detail the cost of the turnover. Senior managers should agree on the assumptions, formulas, methods, and comparison values used to develop the cost of turnover, which is usually expressed as a percentage of annual salary. This agreement is not difficult to achieve. For example, most senior managers agree that it costs 1.5 times the annual pay for turnover of a sales representative (relationship manager, client partner, and so on). To determine the actual cost of each turnover, simply multiply the annual pay for that individual by 1.5. More than likely, this approach will attract the senior team's attention and, subsequently, their support for implementing solutions.

Compare Data with Benchmarking Targets

Turnover data should be compared in three or four ways.

1. A comparison within the industry is recommended. Trade associations often have turnover data or access to benchmark studies for the industry. This comparison shows how the organization stacks up with others in similar situations.
2. If possible, a custom-designed benchmark project should be developed in which the organization is compared with best-practice firms. This approach has the advantage of using benchmarking studies identified with best-practice organizations. This comparison involves a more select group.
3. A comparison with history is critical. Trending is important: Is employee retention going up, down, or stable? Comparing with last year, the year before, or last quarter are all-important considerations.
4. A comparison with expectations, particularly from the division manager, senior team, or plant manager, is essential. What is expected? What is tolerated? What should the rate be? These comparisons provide an excellent opportunity to have a

dialogue with the senior team and understand when a measure is not working adequately from their perspective.

Develop Trigger Points for Action

When using benchmark data and other comparisons, trigger points for action must be developed. When should an alarm sound? Is it a rising trend or a sudden spurt? Is the measure going up when it should go down? Each of these could signal action necessary to begin exploring causes and creating solutions.

DEVELOP FULLY LOADED COSTS OF TURNOVER

The impact cost of turnover is one of the most underestimated and undervalued costs in the organization. It is often misunderstood because it does not reflect the actual costs of a turnover statistic, and it is not regularly reported to the management team who then are not aware of the actual cost. In addition, it can be alarming to management when fully loaded costs are calculated for the organization for an entire year. In one technology-based organization, the full costs for turnover were estimated to be almost $2 billion, in a firm with revenues in the $20 billion category. This data is frightening when you consider the total impact on the organization.

In some turnover cost studies, only the costs for recruiting, selection, and training are considered. These are easily calculated and, consequently, inappropriately reported as the total cost of turnover. In reality, other costs should be included to generate a fully loaded cost profile. Table 2-1 provides a more comprehensive listing that includes twelve categories.

Table 2-1
Recommended Categories for Accumulating Turnover Costs

Exit costs	Lost productivity
Recruiting costs	Quality problems
Employment cost	Customer dissatisfaction
Orientation cost	Loss of expertise/knowledge
Training cost	Management time for turnover
Wages and salaries while training	Temporary replacement costs

Exit costs

The cost of employees leaving the organization, including termination expenses, severance arrangements, or even litigation connected to the departure. This category could be significant when the departure is involuntary.

Recruiting costs

The cost to attract candidates to the organization, sometimes involving external resources and sign-on bonuses. In recent years, this category has increased significantly.

Employment

The cost of selecting the candidate and completing all the necessary steps to hire an employee.

Orientation

The cost for the social adjustment processes (i.e., initial orientation and socialization). This usually involves several days (sometimes weeks or months) for someone to be fully adjusted to the organization and its culture.

Job-related training

The total cost of the training needed to elevate the new employee to the level of productivity of the previous employee. In some situations, this is extensive; for others, it may be minimal.

Compensation while in training

The cost of the time for training, including the salaries, adjusted for employee benefits. This is a significant expense as employees are receiving compensation but not providing services to the organization.

Lost productivity

The cost of productivity lost because of disruption of service caused by turnover. Almost every departure translates into something not being accomplished. Productivity loss is an elusive figure but represents a tremendous cost.

Quality problems

The cost of errors, mistakes, and bottlenecks that can develop during the learning process. The cost of lost quality can be a significant issue in turnover.

Customer dissatisfaction

The cost of dissatisfaction of internal or external customers. The presence of new, unprepared employees on the job causes disappointments and concerns from customers, and sometimes a customer defection.

Loss of expertise and knowledge

The cost to replace lost expertise. In many knowledge industries, this highly variable cost can be extremely significant when a departing employee possesses a high level of expertise.

Management time for the turnover issue

The cost of the actual administrative time devoted to turnover problems. Supervisors, team leaders, and managers are involved in different steps of the replacement processes. This is valuable time that translates directly into cost.

Temporary replacement costs

The direct cost of temporary employees. In some situations, temporary replacements must be used while another employee is being prepared for the job.

In summary, a complete cost profile is recommended, covering all the different categories above. Because this is such a critical issue, an entire chapter is devoted to calculating the fully loaded cost of turnover for a specific job group.

DIAGNOSE CAUSES AND NEEDS FOR RETENTION IMPROVEMENT

Determining the cause of turnover is a critical and illusive issue. Some causes may be obvious, whereas others can be extremely elusive. Collecting appropriate data is often a challenge because of

Table 2-2
Tools to Diagnose Turnover Problems

Diagnostic tools
Demographic analysis
Diagnostic instruments
Focus groups
Probing interviews
Job satisfaction surveys
Organizational commitment surveys
Exit interviews
Exit surveys
Nominal group technique
Brainstorming
Cause-and-effect diagram
Force field analysis
Mind mapping
Affinity diagrams
And the list continues

the potential for bias and inaccuracies that surface during the data collection process. Several diagnostic processes are available. Table 2-2 shows an initial list of diagnostic tools available to use with turnover analysis, beginning with analyzing trends and patterns in particular groups and demographic categories to pinpoint the problem area. The tools range from a survey to a focus group to uncover the causes of turnover. Because of this critical issue, an entire chapter is devoted to this process.

Explore a Range of Solutions

Organizations are very creative in their approach to the turnover problem, resulting in hundreds of excellent solutions. Confusion may develop because of so many potential solutions to a problem. The critical issue is to ensure that the solution is feasible for the organization. Because of this, four chapters are devoted to these most important solutions. Figure 2-2 shows the various major categories of needs and solutions and the major influences on turnover. Table 2-3 provides a listing of the 24 typical solutions presented in this book.

Human Performance & Retention

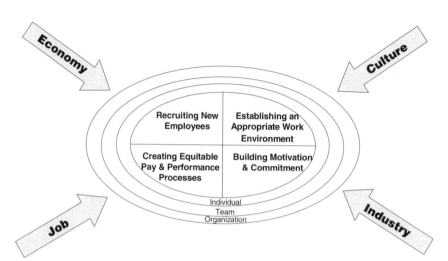

Figure 2-2. Major categories of needs for turnover problems.

The entire middle section of this book focuses on the range of potential solutions.

MATCH SOLUTIONS TO NEEDS

This step goes hand in hand with the issue of forecasting the value of solutions presented next. The development of the two issues should be parallel since the solutions selected for implementation are assumed to meet specific needs, making the forecast of the antici-pated value imperative. When attempting to match solutions to need, five key issues are considered as follows:

1. *Avoid mismatches.* The solution selected for implementation must specifically address the need that has been identified. More importantly, this process will ensure that the need has been identified in enough detail to make the solution most obvious.

2. *Discourage multiple solutions.* Adopting too many solutions is probably worse than taking on too few. Focusing on key solu-tions that will add the most value is important. Consequently, the forecasting step should be developed simultaneously with the selection of solutions. Realistically, an organization can

Table 2-3
Typical Solutions for Managing Employee Retention

Category	Need	Solution
Chapter Six: Solution Set: Recruiting New Employees		
1. Image	To work in an organization with a positive public image	Maintain a strong, positive organizational image
2. Market performance	To work in an organization with a solid performance future	Improve and maintain profitability and performance
3. Recruitment	To be attracted to a specific organization	Recruit good employees that fit the organizational culture
4. Selection	To be selected fairly and offered a job in a timely manner	Manage a fair, equitable selection program
5. Job fit	To have an appropriate job that meets expectations and skill requirements	Place employees in a job that matches skills and talents
6. Orientation and initial training	To adapt quickly to the job, team, and organization	Provide a formal orientation, socialization, and training experience
Chapter Seven: Solution Set: Establishing an Appropriate Work Environment		
7. Job satisfaction	To be satisfied with key aspects of the job	Design a job and work environment to meet employee needs
8. Workplace design	To have an attractive, comfortable, productive work setting	Create professional, attractive work areas that support job functions and promote efficiency and productivity
9. Safety	To feel safe at work	Sustain a viable workplace safety program
10. Job security	To have a secure job; to feel confident about employment continuity	Maintain a viable workforce stability and security process

Table 2-3
(*Continued*)

Category	Need	Solution
11. Culture	To work in a culture that supports individual values, respect, and dignity	Create and sustain a culture that provides individual values and respect
12. Life balance	To work in a climate that supports a balance between work, family, and personal interests	Create family support and life balance programs
13. Diversity	To be recognized as individuals regardless of differences	Build and support a fair and equitable diversity program

Chapter Eight: Solution Set: Creating Equitable Pay and Performance Processes

Category	Need	Solution
14. Pay	To be paid fairly and equitably	Use a pay system that is fair, equitable, and competitive
15. Benefits	To have competitive benefits to meet individual needs	Offer economically feasible employee benefit programs tailored to individual needs
16. Rewards and recognition	To be rewarded and recognized for contribution	Implement a rewards and recognition program tailored to individual needs
17. Job performance	To know performance expectations for success and growth	Implement a performance management process

Chapter Nine: Solution Set: Building Motivation and Commitment

Category	Need	Solution
18. Quality of leadership	To have a leader who is respectful and one who inspires employees	Provide leadership mentoring, development training, and development
19. Empowerment	To be involved in job decisions and allowed to take actions on job issues	Implement and manage an empowerment program
20. Teamwork	To be part of a supportive, productive team	Create team-building programs; build effective, productive teams

Table 2-3
(*Continued*)

Category	Need	Solution
21. Ethics and trust	To work in a trusting and ethical environment	Implement an ethics program; treat people fairly, openly, and honestly
22. Organizational commitment	To be attached to the company, the team, and to other employees	Create team-building programs that improve employee commitment at all organizational levels
23. Professional growth and career advancement	To develop a variety of skills and competencies To have the opportunity to grow and prosper with the organization	Offer a variety of training and development programs to improve skills; implement a career management system

tackle only a few solutions because each solution requires the time and effort of many individuals—sometimes all employees. Adopting too many solutions creates an air of confusion and takes precious time and energy away from other important issues.

3. *Select a solution for a maximum return.* Understanding the payoff of a solution will help guide the selection process. The discipline of this step is simple: implement a solution only if the perceived return is acceptable. This is critical in developing a few solutions that will provide the best return.

4. *Verify the match early.* Accumulating data expeditiously from appropriate individuals can "red flag" a problem. If a cause has been clearly identified, a solution can swiftly address the need. Feedback data, collected simultaneously with implementation, provide information to make quick adjustments.

5. *Check the progress of each solution.* Periodic progress reports provide data to ensure a solution is adding the appropriate value that it should. Sometimes this requires collecting continuous feedback from appropriate stakeholders using a variety of data, both tangible and intangible. The key issue for stakeholders is: Is it working for them and providing the desired results?

FORECAST THE VALUE OF RETENTION SOLUTIONS

Developing a forecast for the value of a solution allows the team to establish priorities, work with a minimum number of solutions, and focus on solutions with the greatest return on investment. A difficult, challenging, and, sometimes risky issue, forecasting is an expert estimation of what a solution should contribute. As much data as possible must be accumulated to back up the estimate and build credibility around the process. The payoff value can be developed if the percentage of expected turnover reduction can be related to it. For example, if the No. 1 cause of turnover is actually addressed with a solution and removed, what percentage of the turnover would actually be eliminated? Sometimes employees can provide input for this issue as data are collected to identify the causes of turnover. This step may require several "what if" decisions with employees while making various assumptions about the data. This step also may involve building on previous experiences to the extent possible. In some cases, the experience of other organizations can be helpful.

Ideally, the forecast should contain an expected return-on-investment (ROI) value. However, a more realistic approach is to offer a range of possible ROI values, given certain assumptions, removing some of the risk of making a precise estimation (Phillips, 2003). This step is perhaps one of the most difficult, but necessary, parts of the process. Because of the difficulty, a chapter is included to develop forecasted values for solutions.

CALCULATE ROI OF RETENTION SOLUTIONS

Another often-neglected step is the actual calculation of the impact of a turnover reduction strategy. This step often is omitted because it appears to be an add-on process that may be unnecessary. If accumulating solutions is the measure of success of turnover reduction or prevention, the impact to those solutions may seem to have no value. From a senior executive's point of view, accountability is not complete until impact and ROI data have been collected, at least for major solutions. The ROI process described in this book generates six types of data about the success of a turnover reduction strategy, as follows:

1. Reaction to and satisfaction with the solution
2. Skill and knowledge acquisition

3. Application and implementation progress
4. Business impact improvement
5. Return on investment, expressed as an ROI formula
6. Intangible measures not converted to monetary values

This strategy also includes a technique to isolate the effects of a turnover solution.

The ROI process has achieved widespread applications for the evaluation of all types of programs and solutions. It involves a series of steps collecting the six types of data at different time frames and processing the data in a logical, rational approach, as shown in Figure 2-3 (Phillips, Stone, and Phillips, 2001). This ROI process is comprehensive and accurate and can provide assessment of the impact of any turnover reduction strategy. However, because of the time and effort required, the process should not be applied to every turnover reduction program. Only those solutions considered to be expensive, time consuming, high profile, and closely attached to the goals of the organizations should be considered for this type of analysis. Because of its importance, a chapter is devoted to the calculation of ROI for turnover reduction strategies.

MAKE ADJUSTMENTS AND CONTINUE

The extensive set of data collected from the ROI process will provide information to make adjustments and changes in turnover reduction strategies. The information reveals success of the turnover reduction solution at all levels from reaction to ROI. It also examines barriers to success, identifying specifically what kept the solution from being effective or prevented it from becoming more effective. It also identifies the processes in place that enable or support a turnover reduction solution. All of the information provides a framework for adjusting or repositioning the solution so that it can be revised, discontinued, or amplified. The next step in the process goes back to the beginning—monitoring the data to ensure that turnover continues to meet our expectations . . . and the cycle continues.

FINAL THOUGHTS

This chapter explores a unique and necessary way to manage retention—implementing a strategic accountability approach. The approach has many inherent advantages and is highly recommended

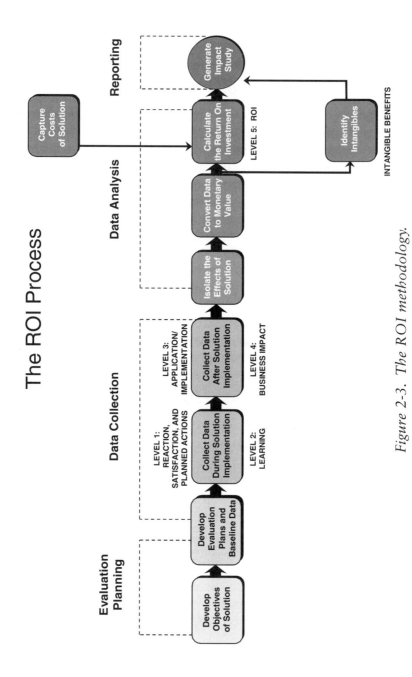

Figure 2-3. The ROI methodology.

when prevention or reduction of turnover from its current level is a concern. It is comprehensive, disciplined, and focuses on results throughout the process as retention is tackled in a productive and efficient way.

REFERENCES

Dell, D., and Hickey, J. *Attracting and Keeping Top Employees.* New York: The Conference Board, 2002.

Herman, R. *Keeping Good Employees.* Winchester, VA: Oakhill Press, 1999.

Phillips, J.J. *Return on Investment in Training and Performance Improvement Programs,* 2nd Ed. Boston: Butterworth-Heinemann, 2003.

Phillips, J.J., and Phillips, P.P. "Why Retention Is a Serious Problem . . . Still." *Retaining Your Best Employees,* in *In Action Series.* Alexandria, Va., American Society for Training and Development, 2002:1–15.

Phillips, J.J., Stone, R.D., and Phillips, P.P. *The Human Resources Scorecard: Measuring the Return on Investment.* Boston, Butterworth-Heinemann, 2001.

Phillips, J.J., and Phillips, P.P. "A Strategic Approach to Retention Improvement." *Retaining Your Best Employees,* in *In Action Series.* Alexandria, Va., ASTD, 2002.

Steel, R.P., Griffeth, R.W., and Hom, P.W. "Practical Retention Policy for the Practical Manager." *Academy of Management Executive,* 2002; 16(2):149–162.

FURTHER READING

Chambers, H.E. *Finding, Hiring, and Keeping Peak Performers: Every Manager's Guide.* Cambridge: Perseus Publishing, 2001.

Dibble, S. *Keeping Your Valuable Employees: Retention Strategies for Your Organization's Most Important Resource.* New York: John Wiley & Sons, 1999.

Griffeth, R.W., and Hom, P.W. *Retaining Valued Employees.* Thousand Oaks, Calif.: Sage Publications, 2001.

Johnson, M. *Talent Magnet: Getting Talented People to Work for You.* New York: Prentice Hall, 2002.

McConnell, J.H. *Hunting Heads: How to Find and Keep the Best People.* Washington, D.C.: Kiplinger Books, 2000.

McKeown, J.L. *Retaining Top Employees.* New York: McGraw-Hill, 2002.

Michaels, E., Handfield-Jones, H., and Axelrod, B. *The War for Talent*. Boston: Harvard Business School Press, 2001.

Sears, D. *Successful Talent Strategies: Achieving Superior Business Results through Market-Focused Staffing*. New York: Amacom, 2003.

Wells, S.J. "Catch a Wave: Strategy, Staffing Flexibility, and Retention Issues Float to the Top When the Economic Surf's Up." *HR Magazine*, April 2002.

Yates, M. *Keeping the Best: and Other Thoughts on Building a Super Competitive Workforce*. Holbrook, Mass.: Bob Adams Publishers, 2001.

CHAPTER 3

Measure and Monitor Turnover and Retention Data

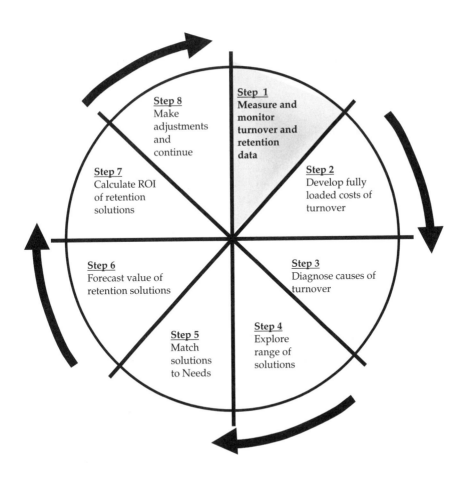

This chapter is the first step of the strategic accountability approach to managing retention and logically begins with measuring and monitoring turnover. This simple step is not as easy as it may seem. Determining the precise definition of turnover is critical and other measures, such as intention to leave and turnover costs, should be considered a part of the measurement strategy. Although the organization's turnover rates are critical, they must also be considered in the context of the economic climate and expectations of the senior team. A comprehensive approach to measuring and monitoring enhances the likelihood that the retention issue will be understood and proper action taken.

DEFINITIONS

When discussing turnover and what is considered to be an appropriate rate of turnover, several issues must be addressed. First is the misconception that a very low turnover rate (near zero) is the most acceptable. It is virtually impossible and undesirable to achieve a continuous zero turnover rate in an organization. Extremely low turnover rates can be dysfunctional and unhealthy, particularly when new thinking and fresh ideas are needed. Also, extremely low turnover rates for extended periods can add tremendous costs as incumbent employees reach higher salaries. The electric utility industry has been addressing this problem for decades. In recent years, the industry has gradually forced employees out, often with huge severance packages, simply because turnover rates were not high enough. In the early 1990s, many telecommunication companies, particularly the baby Bells in the United States, faced this same situation. This pattern also has evolved in other major organizations, including General Motors, General Electric, and IBM. In some cases, turnover is injected into the system as management policy. For years, General Electric has had a policy of terminating the bottom 10 percent of its employees, the lowest performers. Obviously, this adds to the annual turnover rate (Welch, 2001).

Another issue concerns the definition of the word *employee* in the retention issue. For the purposes of this book, employee refers to all paid workers and excludes volunteers. In some organizations, this is not an issue because there are no unpaid volunteers; in others, there are. The American Red Cross, for example, depends heavily on volunteers to serve in traditional employment roles. The turnover of the volunteers may be an issue, but this book focuses directly on paid employees, although much of the material may be helpful in voluntary situations.

Defining the acceptable rate of turnover is another concern. After the specific type of turnover is defined, the economic climate considered, the expectations detailed, and capabilities considered, a turnover rate above a certain level becomes excessive and will trigger action. More importantly, monitoring leading indicators to the actual turnover rate is better. Turnover may be defined in many ways and five different types of turnover calculations are described here. The employee-of-choice definition utilizes the first, third, and fifth category (Fitz-Enz and Davison, 2002).

Total Turnover Rate

The definition of total turnover is the total number of employees leaving the organization during the month divided by the average number of employees during the month. Some calculations use the number of employees at mid-month in the denominator. However, this can be slightly misleading because of the surge of employees who leave at the end of the month (many professional employees prefer to leave at the end of the month). This category includes all the reasons for an employee's departure, regardless of the performance of the employee or unavoidable situations that created the departure. In reality, this standard value has little practical meaning because there are so many unavoidable reasons for turnover. The value also includes functional turnover, where a certain number of employees are purposely removed from the organization. Still, it does provide the absolute value, showing the total rate of exit of employees in the organization.

Voluntary versus Involuntary Turnover

Voluntary turnover usually refers to those employees who initiate the departure from the organization. It is defined as the number of employees who voluntarily leave during the month divided by the average number of employees during the month (or number at mid-month). At first glance, this appears to be the appropriate definition. However, a question often arises as to whether a departure is *actually* voluntary—the employee could be pressured into resigning. The practical issue of voluntary versus involuntary coding may be a problem. An employee may actually leave voluntarily, but then the departure is coded as a performance termination, escaping the scrutiny of the volunteer issue.

Avoidable versus Unavoidable Turnover

The next definition is based on the concept of avoidable turnover. This turnover rate is defined as the number of employee departures that are avoidable, divided by the average number of employees during the month (or number at mid-month). This calculation requires the analysis of turnovers that could have been avoided in some way. Figure 3-1 shows how the concept of avoidable turnover translates into specific types of departures. Obviously, the unavoidable turnover should not be considered as a controllable retention issue. For example, it is difficult to prevent an individual from leaving because of the relocation of a spouse, a home care issue, or a desire to care for children after a maternity leave. The avoidable categories include both voluntary and involuntary issues. In most situations, the focus of attention would be the voluntary, avoidable category and most of this book focuses on this category. However, the other avoidable category, involuntary, deserves some attention. Terminations for substandard performance, layoffs, early retirement encouragement, and resignations in lieu of terminations, could, for the most part, be prevented. Consequently, they should be included in the statistics.

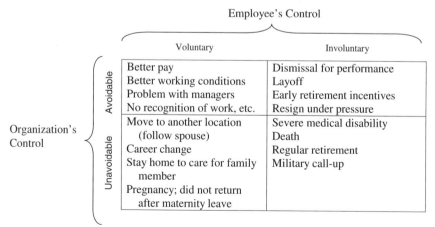

Figure 3-1. Avoidable versus unavoidable turnover. (Adapted from Griffin and Hom, 2001.)

Dysfunctional versus Functional Turnover

In previous definitions, the quality of the employee's performance is not taken into consideration. The issue becomes critical when high-performing employees leave the organization versus those considered to be low performers. Some organizations intentionally weed out the low performers, creating turnover. On the other extreme, the departure of a high-performing individual can be a devastating blow to the organization. Figure 3-2 shows the concept of functional versus dysfunctional turnover (Hom and Griffeth, 1995). Employees with a negative rating are either terminated for substandard performance or quit because they see the inevitable consequences of their performance. This is called *functional turnover*. When an employee leaves after receiving a positive rating, it is considered *dysfunctional* turnover and should be the primary focus of attention for the organization.

Cisco Systems, which has a reputation for attracting and keeping the best talent, uses the above approach to turnover (Beck, 2001). According to the vice president of human resources at Cisco, two questions are addressed when analyzing turnover data: Are the low performers being moved out of the organization to create a better team? Of the volunteer turnover, how many of those are high performers? Both issues are critical to retain the best employees in the organization.

Consequently, the definition of dysfunctional turnover is the ratio of the number of high performing employees who leave during the

Figure 3-2. Dysfunctional versus functional turnover. (Adapted from Hom and Griffeth, 1995.)

month divided by the average number of employees during the month (or the number at mid-month). This turnover rate can be developed for actual performance levels. For example, consider an organization with five levels (or categories) of performance evaluation for employees, typical of most performance review systems. This could range from 1 for unacceptable performance to 5 for outstanding performance. If voluntary turnover is tracked along performance ratings, the percentage of high performers leaving can be quickly pinpointed. This essentially modifies the definition. Turnover at performance level 5 is the number of employees leaving the organization with a rating of 5 divided by the average number of employees during the month with a performance rating of 5 (or at mid-month). This is an excellent way to examine turnover and focus attention on the critical issue that many organizations today face—retaining high-performing employees.

Early Turnover

A critical time in an employee's tenure with an organization is usually with the first few days, weeks, and months of employment. It is during this period that mismatches are identified and frustrations intensify. An employee may decide to leave if other opportunities are available. This early turnover is often a function of improper selection systems, ineffective orientation systems, and inadequate socialization processes to adapt the employee to the organization. To understand this issue completely, an early turnover measure should be developed. This measure is defined as the number of employees leaving in the first 60 days of employment divided by the number of new employees hired in the same period. The time period for the length of employment could vary from a shorter time frame, 30 days for entry-level unskilled employees, to a longer period for technical and professional employees (90 days). Monitoring and understanding this specific turnover rate provides an opportunity for early attention to an important issue.

Setting Retention Targets

Collectively, the five measures listed previously should be appropriate for monitoring turnover data. Two other issues of monitoring will be discussed later. They are intention to quit and turnover costs. Total, avoidable, and early turnover are the measures typically collected by employers of choice (Fitz-enz and Davison, 2002). A more appropriate measure may be dysfunctional turnover rate.

In addition to selecting the appropriate definition, it is important to set the targets or triggers for action. Triggers can be set at different levels, depending on when and where action is needed. The maximum acceptable rate for the turnover is often the first trigger. A value above this rate is unacceptable and triggers significant analysis, action, or both. A value below that rate is accepted as minimum; however, organizations often set lower targets as desired or stretch goals. Some organizations striving to be employers of choice set their turnover rates at a value below the maximum acceptable rate. These organizations focus much attention on attracting and retaining employees. In still other situations, a few organizations desire to be the best at this issue. When considering their position in the industry and other best-practice firms, a lower rate is often set that is considered to be a best practice, world-class, or a top 10 percent standard for the industry. This represents truly exceptional performance, achieved by only a few organizations. This becomes a stretch goal for the entire organization. Figure 3-3 illustrates these three trigger points that drive action. Specific actions to address the

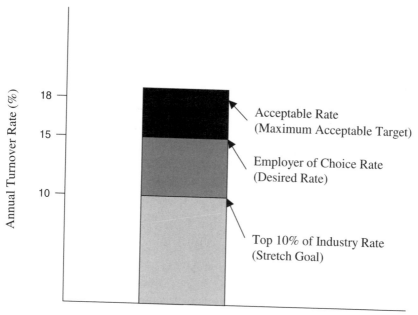

Dysfunctional Turnover Rate for All Non-Management Employees

Figure 3-3. Targets for turnover rate.

retention issue can occur when rates hit either target. Other labels may be used, such as satisfactory, above average, and exceptional. The important challenge is to achieve success at different target levels.

ECONOMIC CLIMATE AND NATIONAL DATA

One of the first places to start in a turnover and retention analysis is to examine the current economic situation. To a large degree, the economic climate drives the availability of other opportunities, and thus can inhibit or exacerbate the turnover issue. Several economic statistics should be monitored routinely to gain a sense of the state of the economy and the impact on the labor market. The following is a sample of the key indicators for the U.S. economy (Wells, 2002). Similar measures are available in other countries.

Gross Domestic Product

Change in the gross domestic product from the previous year or the previous month provides some indication of the state of the economy. These measures, available from the Bureau of Economic Analysis, indicate that the economy is growing, stagnant, or slowing. This measure attempts to reflect the total amount of goods and services provided by a country in a given year.

Stock Market Changes

The stock market reflects a number of variables that can have an impact on employment and the labor market. Changes in stock market indices reflect corporate earnings, economic leading indicators, and the general business climate. In the United States, the Dow Jones Industrial Average, the New York Stock Exchange Composite Index, the NASDAQ, Standard and Poor's 500, and the Russell 500 Index are all measures that reflect the state of business from the private sector. Consistently advancing indices usually spell trouble for the labor market in the near future; declining indices may signal that the labor market will not be as tight.

Consumer Confidence Index

This key index, released monthly by the Conference Board, measures consumer sentiment by surveying people about their confidence in the economy. Questions explore consumer job security and willingness to spend money.

Index of Leading Economic Indicators

The Conference Board's leading economic indicators, regarded as a barometer of economic activity over 3 to 6 months, is designed to signal peaks and troughs in the business cycle. It is derived from 10 leading indicators, 4 coincident indicators, and 7 lagging indicators. Because it covers a wide scope of measures, from stock prices to building permits to interest rates, it presents a broad picture of the economy and helps to confirm suggestions of either recovery or recession. The index usually signals a change if it is positive or negative for 3 months in a row.

Help-Wanted Advertising Index

The Conference Board tracks help-wanted advertising volume monthly in 51 major newspapers across the country. Because ad volume has proven to be sensitive to labor market conditions, the index provides a gauge of change in the local, regional, and national supply of jobs. The index is released toward the end of every month for the previous month.

Weekly Hours Worked

Another important measure is the average weekly hours worked for all private, nonagricultural industries. Available from the Bureau of Labor Statistics, this information indicates how the workweek is developing. If it is increasing, it reflects a very tight labor market; if it is decreasing, a loosening market. The measures are presented in hours per week and generally hover under 40, but with some fluctuation.

Total Civilian Employment

Available from the Bureau of Labor Statistics, total civilian employment is the estimated total employment. In 2002, total civilian employment was approximately 135,000,000 in the United States. An upward movement of this number means that there is much job growth occurring and individuals are entering the labor market. More job growth usually translates into more opportunities and turnover could increase. Declining or stable civilian employment indicates that jobs are becoming scarcer and turnover may decrease.

Layoffs

In almost any type of economic climate, organizations announce layoffs of employees. Even in periods of high growth, layoffs occur as some industries are restructuring, merging, combining, or reinventing themselves. Consider, for example, the actual layoffs announced in the second quarter of 2001 in the United States during a time when most experts characterized the economy as slowing and in a recession. According to the Bureau of Labor Statistics, 350,000 employees were laid off. In the second quarter of 1998—during a period of high economic growth—employers laid off 402,000 workers. Layoffs are usually heavier in times of economic decline, and the number of actual workers laid off for more than 30 days is an important number to track. Although it can be misleading, this number can be helpful in understanding the general economic climate.

Jobless Claims

Other figures from the Bureau of Labor Statistics is the number of individuals receiving jobless benefits (unemployment compensation) and the number of new claims filed during the week. These numbers reflect the impact of layoffs and employee migration, indicating that the individuals may be having a difficult time securing employment. When this rate is considered in conjunction with layoffs, it can begin to reflect how individuals are struggling to find jobs. For example, if levels of job layoffs are high, but jobless benefit claims are relatively low, individuals are able to find jobs quickly. In recent years, the economy experienced high productivity, growth, and labor shortage at the same time.

Unemployment Rate

Perhaps the most critical measure is the annual unemployment rate. Figure 3-4 shows this rate from 1990 to 2002. This rate is of tremendous importance to organizations as they attempt to address the retention issue. Some economists argue that full employment occurs when the economy experiences 6 percent unemployment rate. At that rate, the labor market is loose enough that employers can

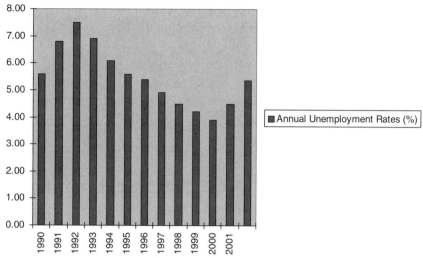

Figure 3-4. Annual unemployment rates in the United States.

find suitable candidates and the jobs are not so plentiful that employees with high mobility are being enticed to move frequently. During the late 1990s and early 2000s, the economy experienced low levels of unemployment, including rates around the 4 percent mark (Bernstein, 2001).

National Turnover Data

Some organizations publish national turnover data reflecting annual turnover rates for all organizations using projections based on small samples. The Bureau of National Affairs, for example, publishes monthly turnover rates as a percentage of average workforce by number of employees, industry, region, and overall for all organizations. Employment organizations and professional groups attempt to publish data for the industry as a whole. The Society for Human Resource Management publishes annual turnover data based on a small sample, reflecting the actual turnover by organizations, grouped by the number and type of employees.

Collectively, these measures provide a sense of the overall climate, primarily on a national basis. Although the data presented here reflect the economic indicators and labor data in the United States, similar types of data are available in industrialized and emerging nations. The management team (and the retention management team) must have an adequate understanding of the current economic climate and, more importantly, changes in the climate, particularly from those measures considered to be leading edge and related to retention and turnover.

BENCHMARKING TURNOVER

While meaningful by itself, turnover data collected by the organization need to have some basis of comparison. Comparing the data with a variety of types of organizations and groups is useful. Five possibilities emerge.

National Reports

Some organizations have developed national turnover studies that attempt to benchmark employee turnover. Different types of organizations that collect the turnover data use techniques to ensure that the data are accurate, fair, and useable. Perhaps the best known is the Human Resources Effectiveness Report developed each year by Saratoga Institute. This report contains a variety of turnover measures, including many of those defined earlier in this chapter. Saratoga takes the extra steps to provide quality control and data auditing to provide a very consistent and reliable report (Fitz-enz and Davison, 2002).

Although the firms involved in the studies may not reflect best practices, they do provide a measure that is important to understanding the actual turnover rates by particular industry segments. Participating organizations pay for their involvement and often take the responsibility more seriously and provide more accurate data. These measures are often more accurate than government data and voluntary data provided through a professional organization.

Industry Associations

Because retention is sometimes a critical issue within an industry, many trade and industry groups have begun to track turnover data, collecting it directly from the members and reporting it back to them. For example, the National Restaurant Association, concerned about high turnover rates in its industry, publishes reports, studies, and data concerning the turnover in that industry. The Direct Marketing Association publishers information about turnover in call centers.

Industry reporting provides benchmarks, which are necessary to compare with other operations in similar situations.

Occupational or Field Data

In some situations, the professional society or organization reflecting a professional field will collect turnover data, particularly in professional and technical areas. For example, the Institute of Electrical and Electronics Engineers collects data about the engineering shortages in the electrical and information science fields and publishes it regularly in its bulletins and other communication.

Regional or Local Data

Some cities, states, and regions collect turnover data in the local area. Business and economic development authorities, chambers of commerce, metropolitan development boards, and even chapters of the Society for Human Resource Management are great sources for regional and local turnover data—sometimes even by industry. This relates turnover to the local employment scene, where it becomes an important issue. It reflects the actual applicant pool for the organization, which is sometimes more relevant than national data.

Customized Benchmarking Study

Perhaps the most accurate way to obtain comparison data is to develop a custom-designed benchmarking study. This may appear to be an expensive and time-consuming process, but it may be worthwhile if retention and turnover are considered critical issues and appropriate comparison data are a major part of the process. Figure 3-5 shows the basic steps to develop a benchmarking project. As the

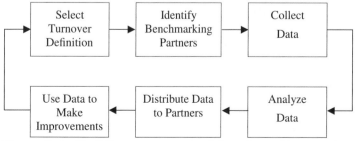

Figure 3-5. Building a customized benchmarking project.

figure underscores, the process is cyclical: collecting data, reacting to it, and continuing to collect more data.

Step One: Develop the appropriate definition of turnover. This step ensures that the specific measure that is most critical to the organization can be captured. This approach is particularly helpful when national data sources do not reflect the desired turnover definition.

Step Two: Identify benchmarking partners. Perhaps the most critical part of the process, this step develops the desired group for comparison. The group may be competitors, noncompetitors in the same industry, or organizations in the same geographic locations competing for the same employees. The group may include organizations in the United States, multinational organizations, or organizations based in other countries. The important point is to define those organizations where it makes the most sense for comparison. Comparison organizations often are those with best practices, although the concept of best practices can be an elusive term.

Step Three: Collect the data. The most economical and credible method is use of a survey, followed up with a telephone interview. As the data collection process begins, it is important for the partners to fully understand definitions, data desired, the confidentiality of data, and the use of the data. Response rate should not be a problem because partners make a commitment to provide data when they agree to participate.

Step Four: Analyze the data. The data should be summarized by individual firms (identified by a code) and for all partners. This comparison provides incentive for partners to become involved with the project. Most human resource executives will participate in benchmarking projects if they can find value with the project, as they obtain data from other organizations in the benchmarking survey.

Step Five: Distribute the information to partners. Prompt, on-schedule distribution is critical to providing current data. The data are reported in a variety of ways that can be helpful to the partners.

Step Six: Use the data to make improvements. This approach to benchmarking provides the best comparative data available and should be used as a basis for setting targets and triggering actions for improvements.

Although this approach takes time, it has several advantages. It is more valuable than other national or regional data available because it focuses directly on the most desired organizations for comparison. Also, the data are more accurate because the quality is controlled by the organization initiating the survey. Additional information on developing a benchmarking project can be found in other references (Phillips, 1997).

Monitoring Turnover and Retention Data

Monitoring turnover and retention data is the step that measures the current performance. Trends and patterns are quickly observed and addressed when action is needed; however, before monitoring, it is essential that definitions are clearly developed and data collection systems are in place to capture data in appropriate categories. Two general categories of internal turnover data exist for analysis—organizational and individual.

Organizational Data

When collecting organizational data, eight breakdowns are suggested:

1. Organization-wide, showing the entire organization.
2. Different divisions, particularly if the divisions are vastly different or represent companies within the organization.
3. Geographic regions, if the organization is national.
4. Functional units, such as sales, marketing, manufacturing, engineering, research and development.
5. Major departments, such as design, sales support, supply chain management.
6. Work units, such as call centers and technical support.
7. Occupational groups, such as nursing, engineers, software specialists.
8. Specific jobs, such as customer service reps, mechanics, x-ray technicians.

These breakdowns show where the turnover is occurring, even by job groups. This is an important step to obtain an understanding of problems and successes.

Individual Data

In addition to showing where turnover is occurring by location, other demographic data can be helpful in understanding the causes of turnover. The recommended groupings are as follows:

1. Tenure—the length of service of departing employees (or tenure of remaining employees)
2. Age breakdown of employees (or age of remaining employees)
3. Gender of departing employees (or gender of remaining employees)
4. Race and national origin of departing employees (or origin of remaining employees)
5. Educational levels of departing employees (or education of remaining employees)
6. Family status (married, single, single head of household, having children, etc.) of departing employee (or family status of remaining employees)

These breakdowns are important to determine how the workforce is changing and where the turnover rates are highest. The measures in parentheses are the retention countermeasure, reflecting the status of remaining employees. Together they provide useful tools for analyzing particular issues, understanding the causes, and ultimately developing solutions. Figure 3-6 shows how tenure is used to spot problem areas. Breaking points can usually be outlined in three areas: a new employee crisis, promotion crisis, and boredom crisis (Branch, 1998). Monitoring turnover by tenure can keep the focus on breaking points, taking action as needed. Also, by projecting tenure data, it is possible to predict when these issues may come into play.

By creatively breaking down the data (which can readily be accomplished with today's human resource information systems), it is possible to conduct the first step of analysis. Trends and patterns readily appear, and the potential causes of turnover quickly emerge from the data. For example, high levels of turnover with single mothers may indicate child care issues that need to be addressed. This issue is revisited in Chapter 5 (Diagnosis) because it is the first step in understanding where turnover is occurring and with which groups and at what time.

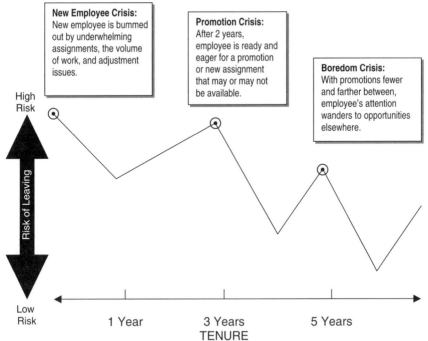

Figure 3-6. Employee breaking points. (Adapted from Branch, 1998.)

ADDITIONAL MONITORING

In addition to monitoring turnover data and comparing the data with a variety of benchmark sources, consideration of two additional measures is helpful. The first is a leading-edge indicator of turnover and the second highlights the impact of turnover.

Intention to Leave

Researchers have been attempting to identify leading-edge indicators of turnover. Historically, job satisfaction has been the best measure. Low rates of job satisfaction would usually translate into turnover. Although this relationship still applies in many circumstances, in several situations satisfied employees leave for a variety of other reasons; satisfaction data alone are not necessarily a valid leading-edge indicator. Organization commitment is a better indicator, because it measures the degree to which an employee identifies with, connects to, and supports the organization. Organization commitment data are not always readily available or collected universally. However, the most important linkage may be with the employee's *intention* to leave.

Academic research and credible evidence from corporations suggest a strong link between employees who express an intention to leave and actual employee turnover. The strength of the correlation may vary in organizations, but intention to resign is one of the strongest leading indicators of employee turnover in corporations (Griffeth and Hom, 2001). Intent to leave is measured by asking survey respondents, usually taken in the annual employee survey, how strongly they agree or disagree with this statement: "I intend to look for a new job in the next year." This simple statement can have a significant correlation with actual turnover as shown in Figure 3-7. This measure is recommended because it is easy to collect in traditional employee feedback or opinion survey data, even if the survey focuses on job satisfaction. However, the data must be collected independently, anonymously, and treated confidentially so the employees are willing to provide accurate responses to the questions.

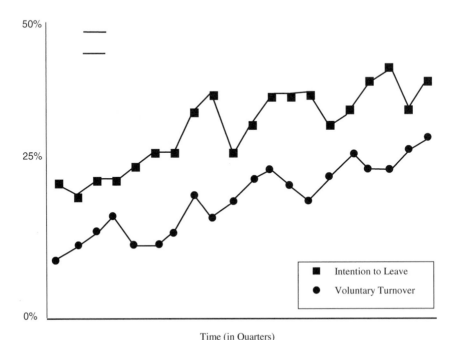

Time (in Quarters)

Figure 3-7. The correlation between intention to leave and actual turnover departure. (Corporate Executive Board, 1999.)

Turnover Costs

It is important to develop a fully loaded cost for employee turnover and report it to executives. Too often, executives who must monitor turnover data do not have a grasp of the total impact turnover on their own organization. The fully loaded turnover costs are developed, using the cost categories and procedures described in the next chapter. Turnover costs should be routinely reported along with turnover data. This can be easily accomplished by developing an agreement as to the cost of turnover, expressed as a multiple of employee compensation. In certain job groups, it is relatively easy to develop this value; for others it is more difficult, and the value varies with the job. For example, for software designers, turnover cost may be as much as three times annual compensation; for sales representatives, it could be one and a half times annual compensation; for fast-food employees in a restaurant chain, the value could be half the annual compensation.

After this agreement is reached, the costs can easily be calculated routinely on reporting mechanisms to show the cost of turnover along with turnover data for a particular job group. Ideally, turnover costs should appear on operating reports to show the management team the full impact of turnover. This will receive attention and drive action. Sometimes turnover is ignored because turnover costs were not known. Today, hundreds of cost studies have been developed, providing an accurate picture of the approximate cost of turnover. Using this reporting mechanism, approximate costs are sufficient. An important point is to determine the approximate amount early, prior to the actual reporting.

DISTRIBUTION OF INFORMATION

Turnover data must be distributed to the management team and other interested parties so that appropriate action can be taken. Three time periods are recommended: monthly, quarterly, and annually. The monthly report contains two major categories of data: current turnover performance and turnover costs. The quarterly report is more comprehensive and should stimulate action and build support for retention solutions. Six specific areas should be addressed in this report.

1. *Description of the current employment climate.* Using national data, including economic and labor information, the current

state of affairs is described. This is a perfect lead into current performance.

2. *Current turnover performance.* Divided in a variety of ways, as outlined in this chapter, the data focus on the very critical issues. The retention countermeasure may be appropriate.

3. *Turnover costs.* At the current level of turnover performance, the fully loaded costs of turnover are presented by unit, department, region, or division. This will grab the attention of every executive.

4. *Comparison data.* A side-by-side comparison with turnover data from a benchmarking source, whether from organizations in a benchmarking project or other national, regional, and local data sources, is presented. This type of comparison is important for many executives who use benchmarking data for other issues.

5. *Issues and trends.* When analyzing the economic climate, current performance, and comparative scenarios, specific issues and trends that deserve recognition or attention are highlighted. This information creates the need to make adjustments and improvements, if necessary.

6. *Planned action.* As a result of the trends and issues, planned actions are detailed. The specific actions may vary, such as identifying the underlying causes of turnover or the implementation of specific solutions to reduce turnover. In either case, it is important to translate measurement into action.

The annual review should include the above issues, plus success with solutions and leading indicators, such as the intention to leave, job satisfaction, and organizational commitment data. Figure 3-8 shows a profile of information that should be considered in three reporting formats. Collectively, these issues should be addressed in any reporting mechanism. The important point is to focus the appropriate amount of attention to this critical issue.

Responsibility

Historically, the turnover and retention issue has been perceived to be a human resources problem. That perception is rapidly changing. Most management teams readily accept retention as a strategic issue and recognize it as their responsibility. As part of the retention strategy, it may be helpful to include tactics to clarify the responsibility for retention and turnover. Although the human resource staff

Reporting Options

Topic	Presentation	Monthly in a Report	Quarterly in a Summary	Annually in a Meeting
1. Current economic climate			X	X
2. Turnover (or retention) data in all categories		X	X	X
3. Turnover costs		X	X	X
4. Benchmark data			X	X
5. Issues and trends			X	X
6. Planned actions			X	X
7. Success with solutions				X
8. Leading indicators				X

Figure 3-8. Recommended reporting formats and content.

must collect and assimilate data, perform appropriate analysis, and make comparisons, it must also create action items, coordinate and implement solutions, and show the value of solutions. The management team, however, is ultimately responsible for making it all work, and they often need to be reminded of their critical role. Because of this emphasis, turnover data must be included with the manager's operating data as part of the operations report. It becomes a routine part of the manager's performance indicators needed to manage the business effectively.

An important test of the shift in responsibility occurs when senior executives are actively exploring and examining the retention issue. The answers to several questions define the extent of the shift: Who reports on the retention issue? Who describes the steps taken when turnover is unacceptable in certain job groups? Who accepts the responsibility? If the senior team is addressing these issues in executive meetings, they have accepted retention as their responsibility. If all of the comments and questions are deferred to the human resource executive, the shift has not occurred.

Responsibility for retention is a critical issue—one that seems obvious, given the role and influence of top managers. However, in practice, the shift in responsibility does not take place as often as it should. Although human resource executives must accept responsibility from every aspect of their control, ultimately, the responsibility and accountability must rest with the operating departments because so many of the issues and causes of employee turnover *originate* in operating departments. When managers clearly see that it is their responsibility, they will become more involved with the process, initiating solutions and taking a more aggressive role to ensure that the solutions are successful.

Final Thoughts

This chapter is the starting point of the strategic accountability approach to managing retention. Measuring and monitoring turnover is essential to bringing the appropriate attention to the issue and taking constructive action. Understanding the employment climate is fundamental to developing an understanding of retention. Also, having acceptable targets, based on precise definitions of turnover that are meaningful to the organization, helps bring the process clearly into focus. A variety of ways to collect and categorize data were described in the chapter. These are all aimed at bringing the proper resources and attention to this critical issue so that action is taken and the senior management team accepts responsibility for managing retention.

References

Beck, B. "Cisco Recruitment and Retention Secrets." *Link and Learn Newsletter*. Boston: Linkage Inc., 2001.

Bernstein, A. "The Human Factor." *Business Week*. August 27, 2001:118.

Branch, S. "You Hired 'Em. But Can You Keep 'Em?" *Fortune*. November 9, 1998:248.

Corporate Executive Board. *Salient Findings on the Career Decisions of High Value Employees*. Washington, DC, 1999.

Fitz-Enz, J., and Davison, B. *How to Measure Human Resources Management, 3rd Ed.* New York, NY: McGraw-Hill, 2002.

Griffeth, R.W., and Hom, P.W. *Retaining Valued Employees*. Thousand Oaks, CA: Sage Publishing, 2001.

Hom, P.W., and Griffeth, R.W. *Employee Turnover*. Cincinnati, OH: South-Western, 1995.

Phillips, J. *Accountability in Human Resource Management*. Boston: Butterworth-Heinemann, 1997.

Welch, J. *Jack: Straight from the Gut*. New York: Warner Books, 2001.

Wells, S. "Catch a Wave: Strategy, Staffing, Flexibility, and Retention Issues Float to the Top when the Economic Surf's Up." *HR Magazine*, April, 2002:31.

FURTHER READING

Branham, L. *Keeping the People Who Keep You in Business: 24 Ways to Hang on to Your Most Valuable Talent.* New York: Amacon, 2001.

Herman, R.E., and Gioia, J.L. *Workforce Stability: Your Competitive Edge.* Winchester, Va.: Oakhill Press, 2000.

Johnson, M. *Winning the People Wars: Talent and the Battle for Human Capital.* New York: Prentice Hall, 2000.

McKeown, J.L. *Retaining Top Employees.* New York: McGraw-Hill, 2002.

Saks, A.M., Schmitt, N.W., and Klimoski, R.J. *Research, Measurement, and Evaluation of Human Resources.* Scarborough, Ontario, Canada: Nelson Thomson Learning, 2000.

Sears, D. *Successful Talent Strategies: Achieving Superior Business Results through Market-Focused Staffing.* New York: Amacom, 2003.

CHAPTER 4

Develop Fully Loaded Costs of Turnover

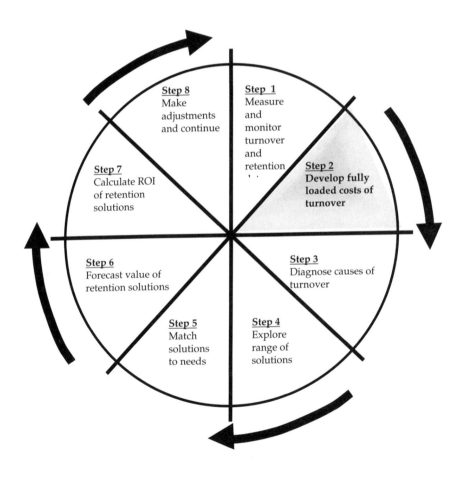

Step 8
Make adjustments and continue

Step 1
Measure and monitor turnover and retention

Step 2
Develop fully loaded costs of turnover

Step 7
Calculate ROI of retention solutions

Step 6
Forecast value of retention solutions

Step 3
Diagnose causes of turnover

Step 5
Match solutions to needs

Step 4
Explore range of solutions

This chapter explores the financial impact of turnover, outlining specific costs that should be captured and economical ways in which they can be developed. One of the important challenges is to decide which costs can be developed from cost statements and which costs need to be estimated. Some costs are hidden and, consequently, never counted. The conservative philosophy is used to account for all costs—direct and indirect. Several checklists and guidelines are included.

IMPORTANCE OF COSTS

A Silicon Valley high-tech company specializing in the delivery of total enterprise solutions signed a $30-million contract to install and maintain a new, state-of-the-art business enterprise software solution (Ware, 2001). Not long into the project, the lead manager unexpectedly resigned. He was the master engineer experienced in the design and installation of the product, as well as the initial reason the client signed the contract. Recruitment of a new project leader dragged on. It was difficult to find an individual with the sufficient skills to complete the job on schedule. As expected, the promised delivery date passed, forcing the client to cancel the contract. An enterprising reporter picked up the story and published it in the local business journal. A Wall Street analyst interested in the company's performance read the story. Wall Street immediately downgraded the company's rating, which led to a sharp plunge in its stock price. As employees' option prices eroded, the company suffered from a flood of turnover, which further damaged customer relationships and prolonged other time-sensitive projects.

As this story illustrates, the cost of unwanted and avoidable turnover can be catastrophic. Although most managers are aware of the destructive nature of the loss of a valued employee, few managers actually understand the true cost of turnover. The problem revolves around three important issues.

1. The costs are not contained to any one location or one report.
2. The costs are not routinely reported to managers.
3. Most of the costs are actually hidden. They are difficult to develop.

These obstacles have caused many organizations to place a less-than-desired emphasis on developing and reporting the actual costs.

The following situation underscores the apparent lack of understanding about the true cost of turnover. In April 2001, Cisco Systems' business strategy was affected by a serious slowdown in the company's sales figures. The company reported it would write off $2 billion in excess inventory and lay off 8,500 full-time and temporary employees, 5,000 of whom had been hired between November and March of that year. (Thurm, 2001) Some analysts estimate that the cost to bring the 8,500 employees on board could total $1 billion. The write-off did not include the $1 billion sunken costs involved in the acquiring and developing those employees. According to the *Wall Street Journal*, John Chambers, Cisco's Chief executive, and other Cisco executives ignored or misread crucial warning signs. The sales forecasts were too ambitious, overstating Cisco's backlog after misleading information was provided by its internal order network. Still, the company continued to aggressively expand, even after business slowed in some of their divisions. If John Chambers had had a full understanding of the actual costs and the devastating consequences of turnover, the decision to acquire all those employees may have been very different. The more the chief executive officers understand the full impact of costs, the decision to increase or decrease staff size will be considered more carefully.

Monitoring turnover costs is an essential step in managing retention. Observing costs as they occur makes it easier to bring issues to management's attention. Cost monitoring not only reveals the status of direct expenditures, but also provides visibility of the impact of turnover and its consequences. In addition, monitoring costs on an ongoing basis is much easier, more accurate, and more efficient than trying to reconstruct events retrospectively.

From all viewpoints, turnover is a costly process that now commands the appropriate attention of many. This chapter provides all the information needed to develop a fully loaded cost of turnover.

How to Develop Turnover Costs

The first step in monitoring turnover costs is to define and discuss several issues about a cost control system. The key issues are presented.

Costs Are Difficult to Develop

Capturing all the costs of turnover is challenging. To be thorough, the figures must be accurate, reliable, and realistic. Although most organizations develop *some* costs with ease, the true cost of turnover is often an elusive figure, even in some of the most progressive organizations. Direct charges can be developed easily; it is more difficult to determine the indirect or hidden costs. Fortunately for most items, the major costs are known and tools are available to capture or estimate other costs. The result can be an accurate, complete, and credible profile of cost.

Why Report All Costs?

More organizations are struggling to understand the full impact of costs. In one retail store chain with more than 400 locations, turnover was considered a major problem. The turnover rate for the permanent employees was hovering around 100%. With 25,000 full-time permanent employees and 50,000 part-time, seasonal employees, the company decided to capture a more accurate value for the cost of turnover. To obtain an objective view, the firm engaged the services of an external consulting firm experienced in developing cost impact studies. The project involved developing all of the costs of turnover, including the hidden costs, which were obtained as estimates with input from a variety of individuals. As an initial exercise, the principal consultant obtained information directly from human resources (HR) managers representing recruitment, employment, benefits, compensation, training, organization development, employee relations, and compliance. The managers were all asked to provide an estimate of the annual, fully loaded cost of turnover for the 25,000 permanent employees. The estimates ranged from $2 million to $12 million. When the final costs were reported, the results were staggering. The total fully loaded cost of turnover was $180 million—greatly exceeding their estimates. Incidentally, the HR staff did not question the credibility of the value, preferring to focus their attention on what they could do about the problem. Unfortunately, they never got the opportunity. The company was forced to file for Chapter 11 bankruptcy; turnover was one of the key issues leading to their demise (Phillips, Stone, and Phillips, 2001).

If the organization had taken the time to develop the fully loaded cost of turnover, and reported it routinely to senior management, the disastrous situation may have been avoided. With knowledge of these costs, management is aware of the magnitude of the problem and can initiate and support solutions. The huge difference between the estimates from the HR managers and the actual "agreed to" turnover value lies in the indirect or hidden costs category. Where direct costs are usually in the cost accounting system, although difficult to develop with ease, the hidden costs are almost never considered. However, they can be developed using assumptions and estimation processes.

Fully Loaded Costs

A recent survey developed by Development Dimensions International (DDI) shows that companies are aware that the replacement cost is redlining for professionals and managers. DDI has included additional costs beyond the traditional replacement categories (IPMA News, 2000). As shown in Figure 4-1, turnover costs in this study include not only the replacement, but also exit costs and hidden costs, amounting to $107,970 for the total cost for hire. However, this fails to include other critical issues, such as the time it takes for the individual up to the desired productivity and competency levels or the disruptive nature of the exit employee being replaced. These must also be included to develop a fully loaded cost profile.

Although some debate exists as to which cost categories should be included few would argue that the majority of turnover cost goes unreported in an organization. For all the reasons described previ-

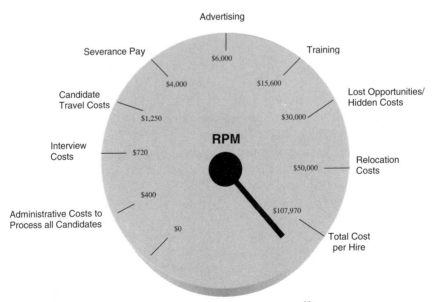

Figure 4-1. Turnover costs are redlining.

ously in this chapter, the senior team and the operating executives must have a clear picture of the total impact of turnover. Calculating the fully loaded cost is the only way to capture the total impact.

The approach described in this chapter follows several steps and is developed in a logical, organized manner so that the total impact is clearly understood. Each cost item is identified in a specific cost category. For items where an estimate is required, the actual costs are adjusted. The controller or chief financial officer should review and approve the cost data. When a fully loaded cost is calculated and reported, the process should be able to withstand even the closest scrutiny of its accuracy and credibility. The only way to meet this challenge is to ensure that all costs are included.

Reporting Total Costs

Reporting turnover costs can be a simple task because the costs are typically expressed as a percentage of the wages and salaries of the employees in a particular job group. This figure is determined after a detailed cost study is conducted or a similar study conducted in another area is used as a basis. The percentage can be fixed for a group (i.e., the sales force) or a specific job (i.e., client relationship manager). If a cost study in another industry has concluded that the cost to replace a client relationship manager averages 150 percent of annual compensation, this amount can be offered as a beginning point in determining the final value. If there were some concern about the cost being too high, perhaps a lower number would be appropriate, maybe 120 percent or even 100 percent. After agreement on the figure, the turnover cost is then reported on statements along with the actual costs. In the retail store example, 45 percent of the average sales associate's salary was included as a cost of one turnover statistic. It is important to reach an acceptable figure without expending excessive time and resources to develop the cost.

The Danger of Reporting Costs Without Solutions

It is sometimes risky to communicate the costs of turnover without presenting a solution or, at least, an action plan to develop a solution. Unfortunately, some organizations get caught in the following trap. Because some of the costs can be retrieved from the accounting systems, they are reported to management on request. Although they are not necessarily fully loaded, the costs are still staggering. The next obvious question from the senior management team is, "what can be done about it?" This often pressures the HR group or others to quickly find solutions, sometimes overreacting and throwing solutions and money at the problem without fully diagnosing it. A decision to report fully loaded costs should include a methodology to fully understand the causes of turnover and develop feasible solutions to address the issue. The strategic accountability approach in this book provides the framework to address this issue credibly. The fully loaded costs are presented to the management team to secure support to tackle the issue and implement solutions.

Developing and Using Cost Guidelines

For most turnover cost situations, it may be helpful to develop guidelines for the HR staff or others who monitor and report costs, detailing the philosophy and policy on costs. These guidelines show which cost categories are included in turnover and how the data are captured, analyzed, and reported. Standards, unit costs, guiding principles, and generally accepted values should be included in this document, which can range from a one-page brief in a smaller company to a 50-page document in a large, complex organization. The simpler approach is better. When completed, cost guidelines should be reviewed and approved by the finance and accounting staff. The final document provides direction in collecting, monitoring, and reporting turnover costs. When turnover costs are discussed in a formal setting or report, costs are included in a summary form or table, and the cost guidelines are referenced in a footnote or attached as an appendix.

Typical Cost Data

Fortunately, many detailed turnover cost studies have been developed in organizations and published in the literature. Of all employee-related variables (e.g., turnover, absenteeism, sick leave, accidents, grievances, and complaints), turnover is studied more extensively because of its significant cost and impact in organizations. Studies are published in academic and research journals, industry and trade publications, and business and professional publications. Consulting firms, industry associations, and business support groups routinely publish turnover cost studies, particularly in those situations when retention is a critical issue. Because so much is published, many organizations do not need to use resources to conduct a fully loaded cost study. Table 4-1 presents some selected

Table 4-1
Turnover Costs Summary

Job Type/Category	Turnover Cost Ranges (Percentage of Annual Wage/Salary)*
Entry level—Hourly, nonskilled (e.g., fast food worker)	30–50
Service/production workers—Hourly (e.g., courier)	40–70
Skilled hourly (e.g., machinist)	75–100
Clerical/administrative (e.g., scheduler)	50–80
Professional (e.g., sales representative, nurse, accountant)	75–125
Technical (e.g., computer technician)	100–150
Engineers (e.g., chemical engineer)	200–300
Specialists (e.g., computer software designer)	200–400
Supervisors/team Leaders (e.g., section supervisor)	100–150
Middle managers (e.g., department manager)	125–200

*Percentages are rounded to reflect the general range of costs from studies. Costs are fully loaded to include all of the costs of replacing an employee and bringing him/her to the level of productivity and efficiency of the former employee.

turnover cost data captured from dozens of impact studies. The data are arranged by job category, ranging from entry-level, nonskilled jobs to middle managers. The ranges represent the cost of turnover as a percentage of base pay of the job group. The ranges are rounded off for ease of presentation. The costs included in these studies are fully loaded to include exit cost of previous employee, recruiting, selection, orientation, initial training, wages and salaries while in training, lost productivity, quality problems, customer dissatisfaction, loss of expertise/knowledge, supervisor's time for turnover, and temporary replacement costs. The sources for these studies follow these general categories:

- Industry and trade magazines where the costs have been reported for a specific job within the industry.
- Practitioner publications in general management, HR management, human resources development, and performance improvement.

- Academic and research journals where professors, consultants, and researchers publish the results of their work on retention.
- Independent studies conducted by organizations and not reported in the literature, but often available on a website or through membership arrangements. These are research-based groups supported by professional and management associations. In addition, a few consulting firms develop and report on cost impact studies.

This list is not intended to be all-inclusive but illustrates the availability of current studies and tremendous impact to the cost of the actual turnover data. Unfortunately, finding a specific study is sometimes difficult and can tax the search skills of even the most adept Internet browser.

Cost Monitoring Issues

Status of Cost Development

One of the most important tasks is defining the specific costs to be included in turnover costs. This task involves decisions made by the HR staff and usually approved by management. In many instances, the finance and accounting staff may also need to approve the list.

As emphasized earlier, costs are not developed to the extent needed in organizations. A major study of 968 senior HR managers reveals the status of calculating turnover costs. (Becker, Huselid, and Ulrich, 2001) Managers were asked to respond in one of three ways, as follows:

1. We don't measure any element of turnover costs.
2. We use a subjective estimate or intuition.
3. We use a formal procedure.

The results indicated that roughly 44 percent do not measure turnover costs, 43 percent use a subjective estimate or intuition, and a formal procedure was used in only 13 percent of the cases. The HR staff has a long way to go to develop the cost data needed to address this critical issue. The process outlined in this chapter should provide the appropriate tools to tackle this issue.

Sources of Costs

The sources of costs vary in an organization. The HR information system will provide some of the cost data, particularly those items involving recruiting, selection, employment, employee processing, separation costs, and other expenses related to termination. The training and development or learning management system should provide data for the training and orientation costs. Compensation and benefits records can provide more detail regarding the benefits for employees as they are enrolled in, and removed from, benefit plans and the subsequent administrative cases involved. Beyond the HR records, much of the data are housed in other parts of the organization. In some cases, sales, productivity, and quality records may reflect the impact of turnover as the disruptions are clearly identified. In other cases, they must be estimated using input from the team leaders and managers in areas where turnover is excessive.

Sometimes, managers who have to address turnover issues are the most credible sources of data, particularly when estimates are needed. For some hidden costs, it may be necessary to include input from other sections and functions, such as quality, process improvement, marketing, and the customer relations staff. Virtually any department or function adversely affected by the disruptive nature of turnover is a valid source to help substantiate the impact of turnover.

The Timing of a Turnover Statistic

The timing of turnover statistics significantly affects the costs. For example, if a new employee leaves after only 1 week on the job, the total cost of the turnover statistic is low, depending almost totally on the costs involved in recruiting, selection, employment, orientation, and training during the initial week of employment. At the other extreme, a specialized, high-performance employee who remains on the job for 5 to 10 years has probably made a contribution that offsets the cost of recruiting, training, and other transition activities. The greatest turnover cost occurs when a new employee leaves the organization just before becoming fully competent in the job. Up to that point, the organization has invested heavily in a variety of processes to bring the individual to the desired level of performance. This specific time can vary considerably, ranging from 1 week for employees with simplistic skills and repetitive functions to 2 years for specialized employees who need to understand the organization's specific processes, products, and capabilities. To develop costs for a specific job group, an average must be established using several different situations and scenarios. Knowing if the next turnover prevented would have been an expensive one or an inexpensive one is impossible to predict. The average cost reflects the impact or cost of several turnovers.

The Employment Cycle as a Reference

Another important way to develop turnover costs is to consider the cycle of an employee as he or she enters and exits an organization. Figure 4-2 shows the employment cycle of a 6-month employee

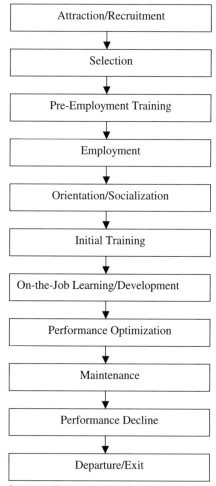

Figure 4-2. The employment cycle for a 6-month employee.

who left just after becoming fully competent on the job. The attraction/recruitment, selection, pre-employment training, and employment expenditures occur before the employee actually begins the work cycle. Orientation, socialization, and initial training are often downtime activities for the new employee and represent significant expenses because the employee is now receiving a salary. On-the-job learning and development represents a net loss to the organization as the employee is still learning the job, yet receiving a salary equivalent to that of a fully competent employee. It is not until the employee has reached the desired or optimum level of performance that compensation is in line with contribution. In addition, additional maintenance costs are necessary to ensure the individual is adapting to the organization. These costs are usually more significant for newer employees compared with those with longer service periods. A decline in performance occurs in two key exit situations: involuntary and voluntary. Involuntary terminations occur when an employee's performance begins to deteriorate (for a variety of reasons) and the coaching, counseling, and discipline fail to salvage the employee. When employees make a voluntary decision to exit and begin seeking other opportunities, performance usually declines. Employees are mentally checked out, often distracted, and a drop in performance may be intentional if the departure is because of a mismatch in the employee job placement or assignment. Either voluntarily or involuntarily, the employee leaves, often incurring exit costs.

This cycle clearly underscores the wide range of activities associated with the employment experience, but it does not consider the other disastrous effects of turnover as unexpected vacancies result in disruptions and operational problems. In most settings, this disruption and lack of service continue until the new replacement employee is fully competent. Nevertheless, the major components of the cause of turnover are outlined in this cycle of employment.

Types of Costs

Five different types of turnover costs are usually captured. **Direct costs** are those directly charged to the turnover issue. For example, recruiting costs should be directly charged to turnover costs as a total cost divided by the number of recruits.

In other times, **indirect costs**, not directly related to turnover, are allocated in some way to the total costs. For example, the overhead in the HR staff should be allocated to all HR functions and the overhead for the functions related to turnover are included in the turnover costs. For example, if 40 percent of the HR staff time is devoted to recruiting, employment, orientation, initial training, and separation, then 40 percent of the HR department overhead should be directly charged as overhead in costs of turnover.

Another category is **prorated costs** where certain costs are prorated for certain time periods. For example, a new college graduate is recruited and participates in 6 months of formal classroom training and job rotation schedule. The initial development cost for that program should be prorated for the expected life cycle of the program and included in the turnover costs. The life cycle would be the time from the initial development of the program until a major revision is initiated. This is usually a 2- to 3-year period.

A fourth type of cost is **estimated costs**, usually from experts who have credibility with the cost item. For example, supervisors and team leaders are usually in a position to estimate the cost of an employee's abrupt departure. The cost for the inconvenience and disruption is very subjective and should be estimated with an adjustment for error.

The final cost category is **linking costs**, which are costs that are very difficult to convert to monetary value but are linked to other measures that are more easily converted to monetary value. For example, turnover may be directly linked to customer dissatisfaction, which is linked to sales. The profit margin on sales provides an approximate value for the disruptive nature of the customer service function.

In summary, all five types of data should be considered and captured for a fully loaded cost profile. The values listed in Table 4-1 contain the five types of measures.

Employee Benefits Factor

When an employee's time is required to address a turnover issue, the costs must represent total compensation. This means that the employee benefits factor should be included in the total analysis. This number is used in other costing formulas and usually is readily available. It represents the cost of all employee benefits expressed as a percentage of their payroll. In some organizations this value is as high as 50 percent to 60 percent, whereas in others it may be as low as 25 percent to 30 percent. The average in the United States is 38 percent (*Nation's Business*, 2002).

Classifying Costs

Because so much has been developed and written about turnover costs, various classification schemes are often devised. Figure 4-3 shows one classification scheme, which places turnover costs into two major categories. This classification characterizes turnover costs as an iceberg, with the tip of the iceberg being the visible turnover

Turnover Iceberg

"Green Money," or Visible, Turnover Costs

Last paycheck, accrued vacation, separation pay, increased unemployment tax, continued benefits, advertising and recruiter fees, interview expenses, printing, assessments, criminal/credit/reference checks, temporary/contract employees, sign-on bonus, medical exams, drug tests, relocation, salary, orientation materials, formal training

"Blue Money," or Invisible, Turnover Costs

Processing benefits, contacting unemployment office, calculating changes in unemployment tax, notifying Payroll and other departments, lost productivity of exiting employee/ peers/supervisor/subordinates, exit interview(s), transition meetings, first/second/ third interviews, advertising creation and placement, ordering forms, scheduling, scoring assessments, coordinating with hiring manager, orientation setup and teardown, orientation materials, recruiter selection, resume screening, orientation participants' salaries, informal training, one-on-ones

Additional hidden costs: low morale, loss of organization knowledge, loss of client relationships, disrupted departments, missed deadlines, chain-reaction turnover

Figure 4-3. Turnover costs.

costs labeled "Green Money." A major part of the iceberg under the water is the category called "Blue Money," which is the invisible cost of turnover (Ahlrichs, 2000). This concept is useful because it places emphasis on the large amount of cost often labeled "hidden" or "indirect." The iceberg example is useful to communicate the growth of hidden costs.

More detail is needed to develop the calculations for all costs. Figure 4-4 shows the major cost categories presented in this book. Turnover costs have been divided into four major categories, three of which are relatively easy to develop. The first category is departure/exit costs, which includes those costs connected with leaving the organization, whether voluntary or involuntary. The concept of reducing turnover for involuntary departures is important if the exit could have been avoided. (This issue was explored in Chapter 3.) The second major cost involved is that of actually replacing the individual and includes recruitment, selection, employment, and the administrative overhead associated with those issues. This is a very significant cost for most organizations. The third cost category is initial orientation, socialization, training and development. Included in this is the formal and informal preparation and training for the individual to assume the initial job and become fully competent in the work. The fourth category, perhaps the largest and most difficult to measure, is hidden costs—the consequences of turnover that include productivity and quality problems, disruption of service, loss of knowledge and expertise, and loss of client relationship. Total fully loaded costs are not complete until all categories in the classi-

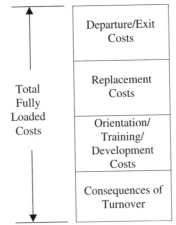

Figure 4-4. Major cost categories.

fication scheme have been developed, even if some have been estimated. Each major cost category is now described in more detail to provide a framework for analyzing and understanding the fully loaded costs in an organization.

Departure/Exit Costs

Table 4-2 presents the details of the four major cost categories. Departure/exit costs, those incurred when an employee leaves for avoidable reasons, represent significant investment in time and direct expenditures. Eight cost items are included in this category.

Exit interview costs. This category involves all the costs for the exit interviews, including the downtime of the departing employee and the interviewer. Also included are the costs of the materials, processing, analysis, and reporting the data.

Administrative time. All the time associated with the entire issue of separation, departure, and exit should be included. Essentially, this category is the HR staff time for completing paperwork and addressing the issue.

Management time. This category is the time allocated by the management group, direct supervisors, and other managerial stakeholders to address the turnover issue. This includes not only their individual participation, but also the time spent in meetings discussing the issue. Some management time is always involved in any departure, but some situations require more than others.

Benefits termination/continuation. The cost to continue benefits for a period of time must be included. The cost to remove employees from benefit programs or administer benefits in the future is also included. Some benefit programs, such as a 401(k), may require company maintenance after an employee has terminated.

Paid continuation/severance. This category of costs can be significant, depending on policy. Company policy may entail salary continuance, even with voluntary separations. Preventable, involuntary separations often result in much larger severance arrangements, sometimes consisting of packages extending over an entire year.

Table 4-2
Cost Accumulation Categories

Departure/Exit Costs _____

Exit interview costs _____
Administration time _____
Management time _____
Benefits termination/continuation _____
Pay continuation/severance _____
Unemployment tax _____
Legal expenses (if applicable) _____
Outplacement (if applicable) _____

Replacement Costs _____

Recruitment/advertising _____
Recruitment expenses _____
Recruitment fees _____
Sign-up bonuses _____
Selection interviews _____
Testing/pre-employment examinations _____
Travel expenses _____
Moving expenses _____
Administrative time (not covered above) _____
Management time (not covered above) _____

Orientation/Training Costs _____

Pre-employment training _____
  Development _____
  Delivery _____
  Materials _____
  Facilities _____
  Travel (if applicable) _____
  Overhead (administration) _____
Orientation program _____
  Development _____
  Delivery _____
  Materials _____
  Facilities _____
  Travel (if applicable) _____
  Overhead (administration) _____

Table 4-2
(*Continued*)

Initial training		_____
Development	_____	
Delivery	_____	
Materials	_____	
Facilities	_____	
Time off the job	_____	
Travel (if appropriate)	_____	
Overhead (administration)	_____	
Formal on-the-job training		_____
Development	_____	
Job aids	_____	
Delivery	_____	
Management time	_____	
Overhead (administration)	_____	
Consequences of Turnover		_____
Work disruption	_____	
Lost productivity (or replacement costs)	_____	
Quality problems	_____	
Customer dissatisfaction	_____	
Management time	_____	
Loss of expertise/knowledge	_____	

Unemployment insurance. The employer pays this tax to a state or local agency, enabling the departing employee to obtain unemployment benefits. This provides income while the employee is seeking new employment and is usually appropriate for those who involuntary leave. In some states in the United States, these benefits are also available in cases of voluntary departures.

Legal expenses. Some departures, particularly involuntary terminations, may result in litigation for the company. In some situations a voluntary departure generates legal expenses (e.g., a sexual harassment complaint). Notably, only a few separations actually involve legal actions. To determine an average value, the total costs are spread out over the total number of departing employees.

Outplacement. For employees who leave involuntarily, outplacement is sometimes included as part of a severance package. This includes counseling and support services to assist the employee in obtaining a new job. Again, this usually applies only to the involuntary terminations and is applicable only to those avoidable situations.

The departure and exit costs are significant and often omitted from turnover cost analysis. As previously indicated, these expenses are incurred even in voluntary termination and should be included. In certain situations, this can be a critical part of the turnover issue, particularly if employees leave voluntarily because they are dissatisfied with the organization to the point that they are considering litigation.

Replacement Costs

As Table 4-2 illustrates, recruitment costs are perhaps the most visible cost directly related to turnover as employees are recruited and employed to replace the departing employees. Ten major cost categories are contained in the replacement costs.

Recruiting/advertising. Expenditures directly related to attracting new employees are included. Image-building ads and materials, direct letters, and other communication tools are typical.

Recruitment expenses. This category includes direct expenses involved in recruiting, such as travel to visit job candidates, conducting job fairs, and expenses to inform applicants about the organization prior to the actual application process.

Recruitment fees and bonuses. One of the most significant expenditures for highly specialized employees and managers is the recruiting fees paid directly to third-party agencies. It is not uncommon for these fees to be equal to 1 year of the new employee's salary or more.

Employment bonuses. Bonuses may be paid for the employee to join the organization. Payments may include cash, expense allowances, vacation time, stock, stock options, or a new computer. Obviously, not all new employees enjoy such bonuses, but in more situations, specialized employees and managers are offered these items as incentive to join the organization.

Selection interviews. This category includes the expenses associated with the interview process, including the interviewer's time, materials, and other expenses directly related to the interview.

Testing/pre-employment examinations. This item includes the cost of administering and analyzing any type of pre-employment test. Physical examinations, drug screening, and other pre-employment hurdles are included.

Travel expenses. All company-reimbursed travel expenses for the candidates to interview for the job and cycle through the pre-employment process are included. This includes airfare, ground transportation, lodging, meals, and other direct expenses.

Moving expenses. All moving expenses are included in this category, including fees for the relocation firm. In a competitive recruiting situation, employees are sometimes offered relocation expenditures, including the direct costs of moving. Most professional, technical, and managerial employees have moving expenses.

Administrative time. The time for administrative staff support, including overhead, and other expenses allocated to the replacement functions are included here. To avoid duplication of cost, time allocated in any categories listed previously should be factored out.

Management time. This category is the time managers spend in this process, from planning a recruitment strategy for a particular individual, to conducting interviews and making the final job offer. If previous categories account for management time, it should be excluded from this category.

Overall, replacement costs are relatively easy to ascertain but may require some adjustments in cost reporting to ensure that the costs assigned to a specific individual or type of employee can be easily separated.

Orientation and Training Costs

As presented in Table 4-2, orientation and training costs are divided into four categories and include formal and informal pre-employment and post-employment training and development. These categories may represent the most extensive part of the training and development budget. For example, a major aircraft manufacturer will spend weeks training a new employee before the actual job assignment. A large banking organization recruits new college graduates for a variety of professional assignments. A 6-month training program is typical prior to actually being assigned to the job. In each situation, training is significant and the fully loaded costs must be included in turnover costs.

Pre-employment training. Some organizations conduct pre-employment training as a screening tool in the new employee process. For example, a major automobile company in the southeast United States has a special facility designed to train individuals to perform basic job functions. The pre-employment training becomes a screening tool using the results in the selection process, allowing only the best candidates to advance to employment. This approach is very advantageous for the employer because the candidate is not on the payroll and the training is conducted on the participant's own time. In some situations, local government provides pre-employment training to support businesses or as an incentive to lure a business to the area. In these cases, the fully loaded costs of the pre-employment should be included because the total cost is there, even if local taxpayers share it. Six major categories should be included in pre-employment training.

Development—The development of the training program should be considered on a per-participant basis. The estimated number of participants who will be involved in the program during its life cycle is divided into the cost of developing the program, yielding a development cost per participant. The life cycle is determined by estimating the time from the initial development (or last major revision) and the next major revision.

Delivery—The delivery costs are those costs directly allocated to the actual instruction or facilitation. Major items are the facilitator's time and direct coordination expenses. Meals or refreshment costs are also included.

Materials—The materials are the consumable items in the training, which include reference guides, manuals, books, and other handout material used or retained by the participants. Equipment rental is included in this category.

Facilities—The cost of the facility for the training center is included, which is usually the total cost divided by the number of participants trained during the life of the facility (which usually is quite long). If a designated on-site training room is used, the equivalent rental price would be appropriate.

Travel (if applicable)—This category includes the cost of travel for the instructor or any other travel related to the actual training. Participant travel should be included if travel costs are reimbursed by the organization. Since participants are not employees, travel costs may not be an issue.

Overhead/administration—This category is the cost of administrative time not included previously, but allocated in some convenient way.

Orientation/socialization program costs. The costs for the orientation and socialization are both formal (e.g., training sessions and meetings) and informal (e.g., self-study materials and on-the-job coaching). The costs can be captured using the same six categories of pre-employment training plus time off the job:

Development—This category includes the cost to develop the program, which should be prorated on a per-person basis, using the expected life cycle of the program. The life cycle would be the expected duration of the program before a major revision is considered.

Delivery—The costs directly related to the delivery of the program are included. Examples are the time of the individual facilitating the program and any other direct expenses, such as equipment rental and meeting costs. Meals and refreshment costs should be included.

Materials—This category includes the costs for handouts, such as manuals, documents, books, annual reports, and other materials provided in orientation. These materials are designed to improve understanding of the organization and the new employee's role in it.

Facilities—This category is the cost for the room where the orientation occurs, whether a rented facility or an on-site conference room. To have the cost fully loaded, allocating the cost for this space is important. The amount can be estimated by pricing a comparable meeting room at a local hotel. Facilities costs would also include any direct meeting room expenses.

Travel—In some cases, a new employee may travel to a different location for orientation and have these expenses reimbursed by the company. On other occasions, the person providing the orientation may travel for this presentation. Either way, the expenses should be included.

Time off the job—When employees are involved in off-the-job activities, the value of the time should be included. The cost is the estimated (or actual) wages or salaries, adjusted upward for the employee benefits factor.

Overhead/administration—The expenses not directly involved in the program, but allocated in some convenient way, would be included.

Initial training. Initial training has several major cost categories and varies considerably with the individual, type of job, and objective of the program. Several key areas are represented.

Development—This category is the cost for developing the training program, usually prorated by cost per participant. The estimated number of participants involved in the program during the life cycle is divided into the development cost to obtain the cost per new employee. The life cycle is determined by estimating the life of the program from its initial development to the next major revision.

Delivery—The costs of the instructor, direct coordination, and meeting room expenses, such as refreshments and meals, are included.

Materials—This category includes direct training materials, including workbooks, manuals, books, and other consumables, used during the training and distributed to the participant.

Facilities—Direct cost of the meeting room should be included, even if part of the organization's facilities. In most situations, using the cost to rent a comparable training room at a nearby hotel will suffice.

Time off the job—This category may be very significant. It is the time for the participants to be involved off the job, including the direct wages or salaries for the time in training, adjusted for the employee benefits factor.

Travel (if appropriate)—Actual travel expenses for the new employees to attend training are included. This category also includes airfare, hotel, meals, ground transportation, and other related travel costs.

Overhead/administration—The expenses not directly involved in the program, but allocated in some convenient way, are included.

Formal on-the-job training. In addition to formal classroom training, some employees receive formal on-the-job training. The supervisor or team leader may coordinate this job site training. In some cases, a training coordinator for the local area may coordinate the training. In other cases a coach or mentor may be involved. This training is important and often represents a significant expense. Five areas are usually involved.

Development—This category is the cost to develop the program, which should be prorated on a per-person basis, using the expected life cycle of the program. The life cycle would be the expected duration of the program before a major revision is considered.

Job aids—This category includes specific job aids developed to teach the job or parts of the job. The expense of this cost category could be prorated over the potential use of the job aid using the life cycle as the time until the job aid is redesigned.

Delivery—This category includes the actual time of the on-the-job coordinator, team leader, mentor, coach, or others who are actively involved in delivering the training.

Management time—Time of management group involved in job teaching or coaching—not counted in the above categories— should be included.

Overhead/administration—The expenses not directly involved in the program, but allocated in some way, should be included.

Consequences of Turnover

Some argue that the most significant costs of turnover are those hidden costs that represent the consequences of unexpected employee departure. These costs underscore the importance of having a capable staff in the work setting at all times. In some cases, particularly in direct customer contact jobs, the costs can be staggering. Consider the customer service area where employee turnover can adversely affect service delivery. As shown in Figure 4-5, two critical consequences affect customer service: the staff shortage created by the often sudden departure of employees, and the problems created when inexperienced employees are learning new skills to competently serve the customer. Either process translates into unacceptable customer service, which leads to customer dissatisfaction and, ultimately, to a decline in sales. Customers do not buy as much as they did or no longer frequent the organization, convincing others

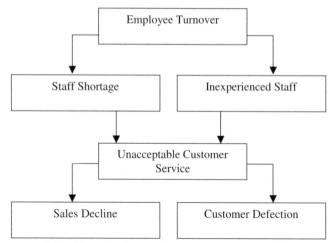

Figure 4-5. Customer service consequences of turnover.

to do the same or discouraging them from going there in the first place. This model has been supported and validated in many organizations and often called the service profit chain (Heskett, Sasser, and Schlesinger, 1997).

The specific cost categories in this area can be grouped into six categories.

Work disruption. This category includes the actual costs associated with having the workplace disrupted by staff shortages or inexperienced staff. This amount can range from being an inconvenience to the complete inability to deliver appropriate levels of service.

Lost productivity (or replacement costs). This category is the actual work lost because the previous employee is absent or the new employee is not fully prepared. It is easy to envision this loss in a production or sales environment, but it exists in essentially all types of jobs. An alternative to this cost would be the actual replacement costs if temporary labor were used until other employees are fully prepared for their jobs. This cost is significant and would have to be developed directly from estimates or records in the organization.

Quality problems. This category is the cost for the errors, mistakes, rework, and rejects directly related to the turnover issue. In most cases, it is directly related to the new, inexperienced employee on the job.

Customer dissatisfaction. As discussed previously, customer dissatisfaction can be a significant expenditure. The amount of this cost will be an estimate from management in the area where employees are leaving. A chain of impact or linkage arrangement can also be developed (Figure 4-5). An estimate should be included, particularly for those employees directly involved in customer service.

Management time. This cost is the time used by management to address the turnover issue or focus on problems as the consequences of turnover. This figure includes any time not allocated previously and usually involves operational issues and problems stemming from staff shortages and inexperienced staff.

Loss of expertise/knowledge. In the knowledge industry, enormous cost is connected to replacing an individual who has accumulated a significant amount of expertise with the products, processes, and projects in the organization. In some cases, it may take sometimes years to recoup this investment. In this category, a rough estimate is generated to reflect the costs (or time) to develop the lost expertise.

The consequences of turnover are tremendous, representing perhaps one of the largest categories of turnover cost. This part is often discussed but rarely calculated. Using estimates and opinions are more important than having no data at all. If estimates are chosen, an error adjustment process is suggested as discussed in Chapter 12.

General Considerations

Several important issues must be considered in summarizing the development of turnover costs.

Collect costs, even if they are not required or immediately used. Too often the HR staff neglects to accurately collect and report the turnover costs because they are not requested or no action is taken with them when presented to the senior management team. Cost control is an important management function and necessary to properly manage retention. Eventually these costs will be requested by the senior team and used in their analysis of the issue. It is best to develop them before they are actually requested.

Costs may not be precise. As highlighted in this chapter, costs are not always exact. With so many hidden costs and cost allocation possibilities, it is difficult to develop a completely accurate picture of turnover costs. Lack of precision should not discourage the HR staff from attempting to monitor and collect turnover costs. A reasonably accurate cost estimate is better than no estimate. More importantly, the senior executive team who reviews cost data is aware of the inaccuracy of information at their level. They also know that many of the data items they work with on a daily basis are based on expert inputs and not actual calculations.

Use external studies. Fortunately, many external studies on the cost of turnover have been developed. These studies should be used to the extent possible to avoid the time and expense of developing cost turnover studies for all major job categories. Although it is helpful to develop the fully loaded cost for a particular key job group, it is also important to be mindful of the availability of resources. Most organizations cannot afford to develop their own detailed impact studies for all major job groups. Consequently, the staff is forced to rely on other input. External cost studies are available and should be used whenever possible.

Use a practical approach. The cost for an ongoing monitoring cost system of turnover is significant and may not be practical for many organizations. Using more estimates and external studies may be an option. The trade-offs of accuracy versus feasibility in maintaining a system must be weighed. Of all the categories presented in this chapter, most can be monitored and allocated directly to the cost of turnover. If major systems modifications are needed to develop more accurate data, the costs may exceed the utility of these reporting systems. As an alternative, other informal processes must be used to develop a fully loaded cost profile within the budget constrains of the organization.

Develop a standard. Unfortunately, external standards do not exist in terms of which cost should be included or how the cost should be defined and calculated. Until a standard is developed, a fully loaded cost profile should be used with a conservative approach to making estimates and adjustments. When used consistently, these become the internal standard. The approach presented in this book can be used as a standard for reporting the fully loaded cost of turnover.

Use caution when reporting costs. As discussed in this chapter, it is important to communicate cost carefully. The target audience should know when estimates are involved. The actual methodology used to determine the cost should be detailed, including the methodology used for obtaining estimates. The data should be compared with any external data as a benchmark comparison, if possible. Costs should always be presented in the context of how a solution can be or has been developed so that when a problem is detailed, it can be rectified. If possible, costs should be included with the routine turnover reporting, not just when a serious problem occurs.

FINAL THOUGHTS

The message in this chapter is very simple: turnover is expensive—more so than most individuals realize. The importance of costs and cost tracking has been clearly outlined and presented in detail. The various issues involved in accurately reporting, monitoring, and communicating costs are included. The heart of the chapter focuses on the different categories of cost so that a more accurate, fully loaded cost profile can be developed to include not only the direct cost of turnover, but indirect and hidden costs as well. Finally, the overall guidelines and general considerations for using cost data have been outlined.

REFERENCES

Ahlrichs, N.S. *Competing for Talent.* Palo Alto, Calif.: Davies-Black Publishing, 2000:12.

"Annual Employee Benefits Survey" *Nation's Business*, January 2002.

Becker, B.E., Huselid, M.A., and Ulrich, D. *The HR Scorecard.* Boston, Mass.: Harvard Business School Press, 2001:94.

Heskett, J.L., Sasser, E., Jr., and Schlesinger, L.A. *Service Profit Chain.* Boston, Mass.: Harvard Business School, 1997.

IPMA News, "Turnover Tachometer" *IPMA News.* Alexandria, Va.: International Personnel Management Association, December 2000:3.

Phillips, J.J., Stone, R.D., and Phillips, P.P. *The Human Resources Scorecard.* Woburn, Mass.: Butterworth-Heinemann, 2001.

Thurm, S. "Behind Cisco's Woes Are Some Wounds of Its Own Making." *Wall Street Journal*, April 18, 2001:1.

Ware, L.B. "Employee Retention and Performance Improvement in High Tech Companies." *Performance Improvement*, February 2001:23.

FURTHER READING

Becker, B.E., Huselid, M.A., and Ulrich, D. *The HR Scorecard.* Boston, Mass.: Harvard Business School Press, 2001.

Boulton, R.E.S., Libert, B.D., and Samek, S.M. *Cracking the Value Code.* New York: Harper Collins Publishers, 2000.

Cascio, W.F. *Costing Human Resources.* Cincinnati, Ohio: South-Western College Publishing, 2000.

CHAPTER 5

Diagnose Causes of Turnover

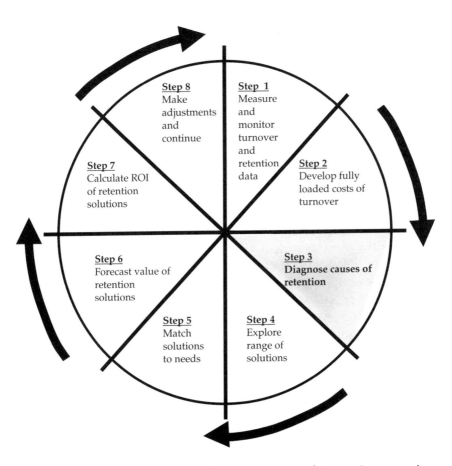

Step 8
Make adjustments and continue

Step 1
Measure and monitor turnover and retention data

Step 7
Calculate ROI of retention solutions

Step 2
Develop fully loaded costs of turnover

Step 6
Forecast value of retention solutions

Step 3
Diagnose causes of retention

Step 5
Match solutions to needs

Step 4
Explore range of solutions

This chapter addresses one of the most critical issues in managing retention: determining the exact cause of excessive turnover. Too often, retention issues focus on solutions and employee needs without taking the steps to uncover the specific problems or issues in the organization. The consequences can be disastrous, as reported in earlier chapters.

A variety of tools are needed to thoroughly and accurately analyze the exact causes of turnover so that the potential solutions can be matched to the particular cause. The chapter begins with fundamental issues that must be addressed to focus directly on the content of the chapter. Analyzing records is the first step to understanding where the problems are located. However, this is only evidence; additional analysis is needed for the actual connection to a particular cause. The diagnostic tools in this chapter are comprehensive and include the use of questionnaires, surveys, interviews, focus groups, and other analytical techniques. The chapter concludes with the process to reach conclusions about the actual causes of turnover.

The Dilemma of Analysis

Analysis is often misplaced, misunderstood, and misrepresented. The process conjures up images of complex problems, confusing models, and a plethora of data with complicated statistical techniques. In reality, analysis need not be so complicated—simple techniques may uncover the causes of turnover.

Analysis is not often pursued to the necessary detail for five reasons:

1. **Employee needs appear to point to a solution.** When employee needs are examined, several potential solutions are connected to the need. However, the solutions may not be appropriate. For example, the need for supportive supervisors does not always translate into a training solution. If employees characterize supervisors as unfair, it does not mean that the supervisors need training. Maybe supervisors know how to treat employees fairly and with respect but are most required or encouraged to do so. Consequently, training is not necessarily the appropriate solution.

2. **Solutions appear to be obvious.** Some solutions appear obvious when examining certain types of data. If the base pay of a particular employee group is lower than a competitor's pay for the same group, the obvious solution is to increase the base pay. However, many employees indicate that pay is not the principal reason for departure. Low turnover rates can be achieved in organizations providing a lower than average salary. In each case, the causes must be thoroughly analyzed.

3. **Everyone has an opinion about the cause of turnover.** Almost every individual (or groups of individuals) who wrestles with the retention issue has an opinion about the actual causes of turnover. In a recent study of turnover causes in a manufacturing plant, the multiple reasons for turnover were identified. The cause of turnover, as perceived by the plant manager, was completely different from the reasons offered by the supervisors, and still very different from the causes pinpointed by the individuals who were leaving. Because everyone has an opinion, it is tempting to use the highest ranking input (e.g., plant manager) and move forward with a solution.

4. **Analysis takes too much time.** Turnover analysis takes time and consumes resources; however, the consequences of no analysis can be more expensive. If solutions are implemented without determining the cause, time and resources may be wasted—and the results can be more damaging than doing nothing at all. If incorrect solutions are implemented, the consequences can be devastating. When planned properly and pursued professionally, an analysis can be completed within any organization's budget and time constraints. The key is to focus on the right tools for the situation.

5. **Analysis appears confusing.** Determining the causes of turnover may appear to be complex and confusing. However, some analysis are simple, straightforward, and achieve excellent results. The nominal group technique, described later in this chapter, is a simple, inexpensive process that can accurately determine the causes of turnover—maybe more than any other tool presented in the chapter.

With these misconceptions about analysis, the challenge to use more analysis becomes apparent. This is a critical step that cannot be omitted; otherwise, the process is severely flawed from the beginning.

Building Insight: Connection Between Employee Needs, Causes, Situations, and Solutions

Before beginning a specific analysis technique, it is helpful to review the relationships between the needs of employees, the causes of turnover, specific solutions offered, and the context in which employees often make the decision to leave. When employees have particular needs on the job, the challenge of the employer is to meet those needs in some way or face the consequences. If employees' needs are met, an employee stays. If a need is not considered strong enough, an employee may decide to adjust or adapt to the situation rather than leave the organization.

Extensive research has been conducted about the relationship between employee needs and employee turnover. Perhaps the most analyzed connection is the relationship between job satisfaction and turnover. Job satisfaction involves a variety of issues (see Table 5-6). Job satisfaction has been declining in organizations since 1995 (Shea, 2002).

The second most analyzed group of factors are those labeled organization commitment, where there is an attempt to understand the extent to which employees are committed, even emotionally attached, to the organization. Measures include the degree to which employees identify with the organization's mission, vision, and values; the extent to which employees have meaningful and challenging work; and the freedom to grow and develop within the organization. These two measures—job satisfaction and organization commitment—have enjoyed extensive research, including meta-analyses conducted to show the impact on turnover. A meta-analysis is an attempt to combine different studies to reach a conclusion about relationships (Hom and Griffeth, 1995, and Griffeth and colleagues, 2000).

Although employee needs must be met, other factors also drive retention. For example, the concept of job alternatives becomes an issue in retention. When employees believe that they can find a better job elsewhere, the likelihood to leave increases. The decision can be greatly influenced if employees think they can obtain a new job with ease or within a short time. The actual search for another job is yet another factor. This includes the steps to which employees engage in job search activities, such as sending out resumes, reading advertisements, participating in interviews, and discussing job possibilities with friends and relatives. Job search behavior has an important connection to the actual intent to leave and departure.

In recent years, additional research has been conducted on the extent to which employees feel attached to their position—job embeddedness. Employees have a greater tendency to stay with the organization if their job is a good fit, they are comfortable with their work group, or feel that leaving would require a sacrifice. Table 5-1 shows some of the recent research linking all of these issues to intent to leave and actual turnover (Mitchell and colleagues, 2001).

Table 5-1
Relationships Between Turnover and Major Factors

| | Hospital Chain | | Grocery Store Chain | |
	Voluntary Turnover	Intent to Leave	Voluntary Turnover	Intent to Leave
Job satisfaction	✗	✗	✗	✗
Organization commitment		✗	✗	✗
Job alternatives			✗	✗
Job search behavior	✗	✗	✗	✗
Job embeddedness	✗	✗	✗	✗

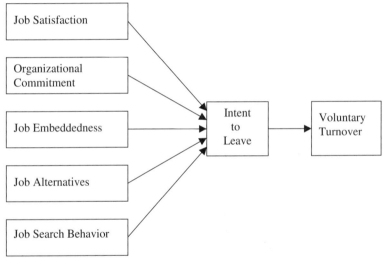

Figure 5-1. Employee job factors related to turnover.

The data show two separate studies, one involving a hospital chain, the other a grocery store chain. The researchers were able to identify significant correlations with many of the variables in the table. For example, in the grocery store chain, job satisfaction, organization commitment, job alternatives, job search behavior, and job embeddedness are all directly related to the intent to leave and voluntary turnover. The same is true for the hospital chain, with the exception of job alternatives and organization commitment, which did not correlate with voluntary turnover.

The relationship outlined in Table 5-1 is depicted in Figure 5-1 where job satisfaction, organization commitment, job embeddedness, job alternatives, and job search behavior all are linked to intent to leave and intent to leave is linked to voluntary turnover. Although this relationship does not apply in every organization in every context, it provides a general understanding of the connection between these job-related factors and actual turnover in the organization.

This means that there are some very strong relationships between what employees need at work, their perceptions of their jobs, their perceptions of the job market, and their actions to seek jobs and voluntary turnover. These relationships provide some indication as to the reasons for turnover, but they do not point to the particular reasons why employees intend to leave or are leaving a specific organization. In essence, these factors and their relationships form the overall framework to understand the complex nature of employee turnover.

Some research efforts take a more simplistic approach. The Gallup organization published a major study involving thousands of employees in which 12 questions were identified that would link to employee turnover in some way (Buckingham and Coffman, 1999). These questions, shown in Table 5-2, are simple issues, but power-

Table 5-2
Key Questions to Ask Employees, According to Gallup

Key Employee Questions

*1. Do I know what is expected of me at work?

*2. Do I have the materials and equipment I need to do my work right?

*3. At work, do I have the opportunity to do what I do best every day?

 4. In the last 7 days, have I received recognition or praise for doing good work?

*5. Does my supervisor, or someone at work, seem to care about me as a person?

 6. Is there someone at work who encourages my development?

 7. At work, do my opinions seem to count?

 8. Does the mission/purpose of my company make me feel my job is important?

 9. Are my co-workers committed to doing quality work?

10. Do I have a best friend at work?

11. In the last 6 months, has someone at work talked to me about my progress?

12. This last year, have I had opportunities at work to learn and grow?

*Correlation with turnover.

fully connected to turnover in many organizations. The research shows that questions 1, 2, 3, and 5 show the strongest direct relationship to turnover.

Still other research focuses on developing an employer of choice. It is assumed that an employer of choice would be able to attract and retain employees easier than those not considered to be an employer of choice. The definition of an employer of choice depends on who is advocating the particular research study or publication. Table 5-3 shows one approach that details the shift that must take place in organizations to develop an employer of choice (Ahlrichs, 2000).

Still more confusing are the various reports that yield the secrets to reducing turnover, often presented as the solutions found in a particular organization or across several organizations. These reports are generated by consulting firms, research groups, industry groups, and professional organizations concerned with the retention issue (Salopek, 2000).

Although these relationships and analysis may be confusing, it is important to note that they merely develop a framework for con-

Table 5-3
Paradigm Shift to an Employer of Choice

| Shifting to an Employer of Choice | |
Then	Now
Lean and mean	Lean and nice
No time to train	Invest in training
Hire experienced people	Hire people who can learn
Career development is the employee's responsibility.	Career development is the responsibility of the organization and employee.
If you don't like it here, leave!	If you don't like it here, why?
You should be grateful just to have a job.	Thank you—your contribution matters!
Anyone off the street could do your job.	Only *you* will do!
(If someone gives notice) Don't let the door hit you on the way out.	(If someone gives notice) If you must leave us, we hope you will stay in touch and tell us why you're leaving.
It's not personal; it's just business.	It's all personal.

Adapted from Ahlrichs, 2000, p. 228.

sideration and identify an initial point in analysis. It is essential for an organization to focus and determine the exact cause of turnover. Every organization is unique—the exact causes of turnover in one organization are not necessarily duplicated in another. The remainder of this chapter focuses on the steps needed to determine the specific causes of turnover.

Starting Point: Analysis of Turnover Data

The starting point in any analysis is the examination of turnover records. This includes reporting data along different categories and around various job characteristics. For example, turnover among single mothers younger than age 25 may indicate a work/family balance issue and suggest that on-site child care could be a solution. As illustrated in Figure 5-2, however, the records merely indicate a problem with a particular group; it does not necessarily identify the cause of the problem, nor does it define a solution. Additional analysis is needed to confirm or refute the problem and identify a potential solution. This point is important because the first step of analysis is often where the solution is inappropriately applied, immediately following the examination of turnover records.

The turnover data can be analyzed in many ways: by job group, region, variety of personal characteristics, and job status. Data must be collected so that key questions can be answered, such as those listed in Table 5-4. As the table reveals, in a comprehensive analysis of turnover records, many issues point to a problem area and potential causes.

Developing an appropriate database to dissect turnover is critical. Many human resource information systems (HRIS) provide multiple options for capturing, dissecting, and analyzing data. Not only do they slice the data into the kinds of category shown in Table 5-4, but they also build relationships between the data and other factors, such as the relationship between turnover and salaries, expressed as a percent of the competitive rate. Another example is the relationship between job satisfaction and turnover. The analysis of the turnover

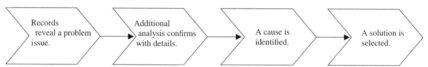

Figure 5-2. Analysis of records leads to more analysis.

Table 5-4
Key Questions Addressed Directly from Records

Key Questions	Example
Which major job group contains the most turnover?	Professional
Which specific job category contains the most turnover?	Senior client partner
Which specific function contains the most turnover?	Sales & marketing
Which specific department contains the most turnover?	Direct sales
Which specific area/region contains the most turnover?	West Coast
What is the timing of most turnover statistics?	Early summer
What is the tenure of most turnover statistics?	Less than 6 months
What is the age of most turnover statistics?	25–30 years
What is the educational level of most turnover statistics?	Master's degree
What is the sex of most turnover statistics?	Male
What is the race or ethnic background of most turnover statistics?	Asian
What is the marital status of most turnover statistics?	Single
What is the family status of most turnover statistics?	Divorced parent

data, collected and presented in Chapter 3, serves as the beginning point of the analysis. Determining the cause(s) of turnover requires the use of additional techniques, many of which focus directly on the employees leaving or those who may leave.

Sufficient resources must be devoted to analyzing turnover records, examining solutions, and plotting strategies to retain key employees. It is sometimes more important (and efficient) to go directly to employees and ask them what motivates them to stay with the organization, who might lure them away, and what would cause them to leave. These are critical questions that must be asked in any type of analysis (Kaye and Jordan-Evans, 1999). The following sections focus on the principal ways in which employees are asked these key questions.

QUESTIONNAIRES AND SURVEYS

Questionnaires

The questionnaire is probably the most common and inexpensive instrument used to study turnover. Questionnaires range from brief reaction forms to detailed instruments. Questionnaires can obtain all types of data, ranging from subjective information about employees' feelings to business impact data for use in a return-on-investment (ROI) analysis. With this versatility and popularity, it is important for questionnaires to be designed properly to satisfy their planned use.

Types of Questions

Five basic types of questions are recommended. Depending on the purpose of the questionnaire, any or all of the following may be used:

1. **Open-ended question**—has an unlimited answer and should be followed by ample blank space for the response.
2. **Checklist**—offering a list of items, the respondent is asked to check the items that best apply to the situation.
3. **Two-way question**—has alternative responses, a yes/no, disagree/agree, or other possibilities.
4. **Multiple-choice question**—has several choices from which the respondent is asked to select the one most applicable.
5. **Ranking scales**—require the respondent to rank a list of items.

Questionnaire Design

An improperly designed or worded questionnaire is confusing, frustrating, and potentially embarrassing. Questionnaire design should be a simple and logical process. The following steps will help ensure that a valid, reliable, and effective instrument is developed.

Determine the information needed

The first step of any instrument design is to itemize the topics and issues to be addressed. Questions are developed later. It might be helpful to develop this information in outline form so that related questions can be grouped together.

Select the type(s) of questions

The type of questions must be determined—open-ended questions, checklists, two-way questions, multiple-choice questions, or a ranking scale. The planned data analysis and variety of data to be collected should be take into consideration.

Develop the questions

The next step is to develop the questions based on the type of question(s) planned and the information needed. The questions should be simple and straightforward enough to avoid confusion or leading the respondent to a desired response. Terms or expressions unfamiliar to the respondent should be avoided. Develop the appropriate number and variety of questions consistent with the validity and reliability issues (Phillips, 1997).

Check the reading level

To ensure that the target audience can easily understand the questionnaire, it is helpful to assess the questionnaire's reading level. Most word processing software contains features that will evaluate the reading difficulty by grade level.

Address the anonymity issue

Questionnaires should be anonymous unless there are specific reasons for individuals to be identified. Because a link usually exists between anonymity and accuracy, respondents should feel free to respond openly without fear of reprisal. When the questionnaire must be completed in a captive audience or submitted directly to an individual, a neutral third party should collect and process the data, ensuring that participants' identities are not revealed. When the identity must be known (e.g., to compare output data with the previous data or to verify the data), every effort should be made to protect the respondents' identities from those who may be biased in their actions.

Design for ease of tabulation and analysis

Each potential question should be viewed in terms of data tabulation, data summary, and analysis. If possible, the data analysis process should be outlined and reviewed in mock-up form. This step helps avoid inadequate, cumbersome, and lengthy data analysis caused by improper wording or design.

Test the questions

After the questions are developed, they should be tested for understanding, ideally on a group of typical respondents. If this is not feasible, the questions should be tested on employees at approximately the same job level as the potential participants. As much input and as many critical comments should be collected as possible. The questions should be revised as necessary.

Prepare a data summary

A data summary sheet should be developed so that data can be tabulated quickly for summary and interpretation. This step will help ensure a quick analysis and meaningful presentation.

Develop the completed questionnaire

The questions should be finalized in a professional format with proper instructions. After completing these steps, the questionnaire is ready to be administered.

Attitude Surveys

Attitude measurement is critical in retention solutions. Whether measuring job satisfaction, organizational commitment, or a variety of other retention-related issues, attitudes are important to understanding retention. However, measuring attitudes is a complex task. It is impossible to measure an attitude precisely, because the input may not represent a respondent's true feelings. The behavior, beliefs, and feelings of an individual do not always correlate. Attitudes tend to change with time, and several factors can form an individual's attitude. Nevertheless, it *is* possible to obtain a reasonable assessment of an individual's attitude about work and the organization.

Continuous measurements are required to show changes in attitudes. Attitude surveys represent a specific type of questionnaire with applications for measuring attitudes, perceptions, and intentions. Surveys are not the only way to measure attitudes. Interviews and focus groups may be appropriate in some situations and are discussed later in the chapter.

Survey Design

The principles of attitude survey construction are similar to those of the questionnaire, as discussed earlier. However, a few guidelines unique to the design of an attitude survey are presented.

Involve appropriate management

The executives involved in this process must be committed to taking action based on survey results. Include management early in the process, before the survey is constructed. Address management concerns, issues, and suggestions and attempt to win commitment.

Determine precisely the attitudes that must be measured

Although this step is obvious, it is easy to stray into areas unrelated to the subject. "Let's check their attitude on this" is a familiar trap. It may be interesting information, but it should be omitted if not related to the purpose of the survey.

Keep survey statements as simple as possible

Participants need to understand the meaning of a statement or question. There should be little room for differing interpretations.

Ensure that responses are anonymous

If feasible, respondents must feel free to respond openly to statements or questions. The confidentiality of their responses is of the utmost importance. If data are collected that can identify a respondent, a neutral third party should collect and process the data.

Communicate the purpose of the survey

Respondents tend to cooperate better in an activity if they understand its purpose. When a survey is administered, an explanation of its purpose and what will be done with the information should be provided. Also, participants should be encouraged to provide correct and proper responses.

Identify survey comparisons

Attitudes by themselves are meaningless. They must be compared to expected results, to changes over time, or to other groups. A group of employees may be compared to all employees, a division, or a department. For purchased surveys, information may be available on a regional or national scale and in similar industries. In any case, specific comparisons should be planned before administering the survey.

Design for easy tabulation

In an attitude survey, yes/no remarks or varying degrees of agreement and disagreement are the usual responses. Uniform types of responses make it easier for tabulation and comparisons. On a scale of strongly agree to strongly disagree, numbers are assigned to reflect their response. For instance, a value of 1 may represent strongly disagree and a 5 strongly agree. Some argue that a 5-point scale permits the respondent to select the midpoint range, not really making a choice. If this is a concern, an even-numbered scale is advisable.

Purchasing an Existing Survey

Many organizations purchase existing surveys to use in retention improvement. Purchased surveys can have several advantages. They can save time in development and pilot testing. Most reputable companies producing and marketing surveys have designed them to be reliable and valid for retention. External surveys also make it easy to compare the results with others. Benchmarking and norm comparisons are possible.

Timing and Focus of Retention Surveys

Surveys and questionnaires can be administered at a variety of different times. Table 5-5 shows the five most important time frames for conducting surveys. Routine, annual surveys are probably the most important. These are preventative data collection tools that indicate the status of employees and their perceptions of the organization and their jobs. The issues usually focus on job satisfaction and organization commitment.

Reaction surveys are captured when major actions are undertaken or events have occurred. These surveys are designed for preventing

Table 5-5
Timing and Focus of Retention Surveys

Survey	Focus	Timing
Routine surveys to identify trends and issues	Prevention	Annually
Reaction surveys after major actions/events	Prevention, evaluation	Immediately after event
Surveys to analyze problems and seek causes	Diagnostic	Immediately after problem uncovered
Exit surveys as employees leave the organization	Diagnostic	Just before, or immediately following departure
Impact surveys to measure success of a retention solution	Evaluation	Three to 6 months after solution implementation

problems or evaluating the impact of a particular action. For example, if several major change processes have taken place due to a company merger, it may be helpful to administer a survey soon after the integration has begun. This is an attempt to spot issues before they become problems. If the company has experienced a tremendous change in its business, major customers, or other significant event, it may be helpful to understand the extent to which the event or action is affecting the employees in the organization. As serious problems surface, surveys can help develop more insight into underlying issues, pinpoint the exact causes, and develop potential solutions.

Perhaps the most important use of surveys is the **exit interview survey**. Although the term *exit interview* is used, it is often conducted by a survey and is usually taken on the employee's last day or immediately following departure.

Finally, **impact surveys** are an effective way to measure the success of a solution. When retention problems are addressed and improvement has occurred, it may be helpful to capture the reactions to the solution implementation. Surveys and questionnaires are very flexible and perhaps the most useful tool in turnover analysis.

Survey Content

The specific issues addressed in a survey can vary with the organization, structure, and situation. Table 5-6 shows typical content issues for a retention survey. This is a collection of 20 issues devel-

Table 5-6
Typical Content Issues for Retention Survey

Survey Content

1. Salaries and base pay
2. Bonuses, pay for performance
3. Benefits and benefits package
4. Career development
5. Work expectations
6. Opportunity to excel at work
7. Opportunity to learn skills/knowledge
8. Resources to perform work
9. Appreciation for work
10. Recognition of individual contribution
11. Relationship with supervisor
12. Relationship with associates
13. Viability of organization
14. Organization's values and mission
15. Job security
16. Leadership
17. Burnout/stress
18. Flexibility in work schedules
19. Meaningful work
20. Work/life balance

oped as a composite of several surveys conducted by employer-of-choice organizations, the Society for Human Resource Management, and major consulting firms. In an organization, the number of issues addressed may be less than this number. The content of the survey must be directly related to what are perceived to be the key issues, particularly the issues derived from the relationships traditionally found in the literature and the problems identified in the analysis of the turnover records.

Improving Response Rates for Questionnaires and Surveys

The content items listed previously represent a wide range of potential issues to explore in a questionnaire or survey. Obviously, asking too many questions could cause the response rate to be reduced significantly. This is a critical issue when the questionnaire is the only data collection method for retention analysis. The following actions can be taken to increase the response rate.

Provide advance communication

When feasible, employees should receive advance notice of the questionnaire or survey. This minimizes some of the resistance to the process, provides an opportunity to explain the circumstances surrounding the analysis in more detail, and positions the survey/questionnaire as an integral part of data collection.

Have an executive sign the introductory letter

For maximum effectiveness, the letter sent with the questionnaire or survey should be signed by the top executive or by the senior executive responsible for the division, region, or location. Employees may be more willing to respond to a senior executive than to a member of the HR staff.

Communicate the purpose

Respondents should understand the reason for the questionnaire, including who or what has initiated this retention analysis. They should also know if the survey is part of a systematic process or a special analysis tool.

Let employees know they are part of the sample

If appropriate, employees should know that they are part of a carefully selected sample and that their input will be used to make decisions regarding a much larger target audience. This action appeals to a sense of responsibility and often encourages employees to provide usable, accurate data for the questionnaire.

Use anonymous input

Usually the questionnaire or survey should not identify the employee. Using anonymous input will increase the response rate and the input will be more candid.

Explain who will see the data

It is important for employees to know who will see the data from the questionnaire. The confidentiality and anonymity should be clearly communicated, along with the steps being taken to ensure confidentiality and anonymity. Employees should know if senior executives will see the combined results of the analysis.

Describe the data integration process

Employees should understand how results will be combined with other data, if appropriate. Often the questionnaire is only one of the data collection methods utilized. Employees should know how the data are weighed and integrated to provide the final report.

Keep the questionnaire as simple as possible

A simple questionnaire or survey does not always provide the full scope of data necessary for analysis. However, a simplified survey should be the goal as questions are developed and the total number and scope of the questionnaire is finalized.

Simplify the response process

The questionnaire or survey should be designed for easy response. If appropriate, a self-addressed stamped envelope should be included, or offer the option to respond via e-mail. In some situations, a conveniently positioned response box, provided near the work area, is advisable.

Utilize local manager support

Management involvement at the local level is critical to response rate success. Managers can distribute questionnaires, refer to them in staff meetings, follow up to see if they have been completed, and generally show support for completing the questionnaire. Later they are involved in the feedback of results and specific actions to address problems or issues.

Consider using incentives

In some situations, an incentive is provided to enhance response. This approach may be helpful when the survey is new or commitment is low. A variety of different types of incentives can be offered. When employees return the questionnaire, they receive a small gift, such as a T-shirt or mug. If identity of the employee is an issue, a neutral third party can provide the incentive.

In another category, an incentive is provided to make respondents feel guilty if they choose not to respond. One U.S. dollar (or other monetary equivalent) can be clipped to the questionnaire or a pen enclosed in the envelope. Respondents are asked to "take the dollar, buy a cup of coffee, and fill out the questionnaire," or "please use this pen to complete the questionnaire."

Use follow-up reminders

Follow-up reminders should be sent a week after the question-naire/survey is received and repeated 2 weeks later. The times could be adjusted depending on the questionnaire and the situation. In some situations, a third follow-up is recommended. The follow-up could also be sent via different media. For example, a questionnaire may be sent by regular mail, the first follow-up reminder provided by the immediate supervisor in a staff meeting, and the second reminder sent by e-mail.

Provide a copy of the results to the employees

Employees should always be given the opportunity to see the results of the survey, even if in an abbreviated form. More impor-tantly, employees should be told that they will receive a copy of the study when they are asked to provide the data. This promise often increases the response rate, as some individuals want to see the results of the entire group along with their particular input.

Collectively, these actions help boost response rates of question-naires and surveys. Using all of these strategies can result in response rates in the 70 percent to 90 percent range, even with a lengthy ques-tionnaire that might take 30 minutes to complete. Some companies report response rates of more than 90 percent .

INTERVIEWS AND FOCUS GROUPS

Interviews

Another helpful collection method is the interview, although it is not used as often as questionnaires or surveys. The HR staff, supervisors, or an outside third party can conduct interviews. Interviews can provide data that are not available in performance records or are difficult to obtain through written responses. Employees may be reluctant to provide input on a questionnaire, but they will volunteer the information to a skillful interviewer who uses probing techniques to uncover changes in perceptions and attitudes.

There are two basic types of interviews: structured and unstructured. Much like a questionnaire, the structured interview presents specific questions with little room to deviate from the desired responses. The unstructured interview is more flexible and can include probing for additional information. As important data are uncovered, a skilled interviewer can ask a few general questions that can lead to more detailed information.

Two major disadvantages of the interview are that it is time consuming and loses the sense of anonymity. Interviewers must be trained to ensure that the process is consistent. The primary advantage is that the interview process ensures that a question is answered and that the interviewer understands the responses supplied by the employee.

Interview Guidelines

The steps for interview design are similar to those for the design of the questionnaire or survey. A brief summary of key interview issues is outlined here.

Determine specific information needed

The topics, skills, issues, problems, and other needed information are identified.

Develop questions to be asked

Specific questions must be developed. Questions should be brief, precise, and designed for easy response.

Test the interview

The instrument should be tested on a small number of employees. The responses should be analyzed and the interview revised, if necessary.

Train the interviewers

The interviewer should have the appropriate skills, including active listening and the ability to ask probing questions, collect information, and summarize it in a meaningful form. If the employee is nervous during an interview and develops signs of anxiety, he or she should be made to feel at ease.

Provide clear instructions to the employee

The employee should understand the purpose of the interview and know how the information will be used. Expectations, conditions, and rules of the interview should be thoroughly discussed. For example, the employee should know if statements will be kept confidential.

Administer the interviews according to a scheduled plan

As with other instruments, interviews need to be conducted according to a predetermined plan. The timing, location, and the person conducting the interview are all relevant issues in developing a plan. For a large number of employees, a sampling plan may be necessary to save time and reduce the cost of the analysis.

Focus Groups

A focus group is a small group discussion conducted by an experienced facilitator. It is designed to solicit qualitative judgments on a planned topic or issue. An extension of the interview, focus groups are particularly helpful when in-depth feedback is desired. Group members are all required to provide their input; individual input builds on group input.

When compared with questionnaires, surveys, or interviews, the focus group strategy has several advantages. The basic premise is that when quality judgments are subjective, several individual judgments are better than one. The group process, in which participants often motivate one another, is an effective method for generating new ideas and hypotheses. It is inexpensive and can be quickly planned and conducted. Its flexibility makes it possible to explore a variety of retention-related issues.

Focus Group Applications

The focus group is particularly helpful when qualitative information is needed about the cause of turnover. Essentially, focus groups are helpful when information is needed that cannot be collected adequately with simple, quantitative methods. For example, these separate issues can be addressed in the focus group setting:

- Identify the reasons for the exit of other colleagues
- Identify the reasons why employees stay with the organization
- Identify the reasons why employees would leave the organization

In one organization involving a high-tech firm in Silicon Valley, there was some concern that a specific group of talented people was being targeted by "headhunters" and recruited by other firms. Recognizing the potential risk of losing these employees, the company formed focus groups and secured information on two major issues: what would keep employees from leaving and what would lure them away. As a group, they were able to yield insight into those two key questions.

Focus Group Guidelines

Although there are no set rules on how to use focus groups for turnover, the following guidelines should be helpful:

Ensure that management supports the focus group process

Because this is a relatively new process, it may be unfamiliar to some management groups. Managers need to understand focus groups and their advantages. This should raise their level of confidence in the information obtained from group sessions.

Plan topics, questions, and strategy carefully

As with any data collection, planning is the key. The specific topics, questions, and issues to be discussed must be carefully planned and sequenced. This enhances the comparison of results from one group to another and ensures that the group process is effective and remains focused.

Keep the group size small

While there is no magic group size, a range of 6 to 12 seems to be appropriate for most focus group applications. A group has to be large enough to ensure different points of view, but small enough to provide every participant a chance to communicate freely and exchange comments.

Ensure that there is a representative sample of the target population

It is important for groups to be stratified appropriately so that participants represent the target population. The group should be homogeneous in experience, rank, and influence in the organization.

Insist on facilitators with appropriate expertise

The success of a focus group rests with the facilitator who must be skilled in the focus group process. Facilitators must know how to control aggressive members of the group and diffuse the input from those who want to dominate. Facilitators must also be able to create an environment in which participants feel comfortable offering comments freely and openly. For this reason, some organizations use external facilitators.

In summary, the focus group is an inexpensive and quick way to determine the causes of turnover. For a complete analysis, focus group information should be combined with data from other instruments. Also, the focus group may be used in conjunction with other techniques described in the next section.

Nominal Group Technique

Target Audience

Perhaps one of the most useful and productive tools to determine the causes of turnover is to use a modified focus group process called the *nominal group technique*. With this process, a group of employees are asked to provide information on why their colleagues are leaving the organization. The key issue is to focus on the reasons why *others* would leave and not why *they* would leave. This repositions the data collection from a potentially threatening to a nonthreatening environment. The recommended audience is a representative sample of the target groups experiencing the highest turnover. The group size should be 8 to 12. A small number of samples would be appropriate for large target groups. The total sample size needed for statistical validity depends on several factors and can be accurately determined. However, this number may become expensive and unnecessary. One approach is to sample until trends and patterns begin to emerge. For example, in a target group with 1,000 employees doing the sample job, 5 to 10 samples would probably be sufficient. The key issue is to examine the results to confirm a pattern. Although the focus group process is inexpensive compared to some techniques, the issue may represent a balance of economics versus accuracy.

Facilitation

Normally, two facilitators are required for this process. Both should be trained to facilitate the nominal group technique. Both should be neutral to the organization (i.e., an independent third party) and removed from ownership of the issues that will be discussed. Employees must feel free to discuss issues; it is important for them to understand the confidentiality and anonymity of the input.

The session should be comfortable with ample space for two flip chart pads and a place to tape them on the wall. The process follows a series of steps, each of them very important.

1. *Explain the task.*
   As an introduction, the facilitator should explain the purpose of the meeting, stressing the importance of input from the group. The ground rules are covered, focusing on the mechanics of how they will provide information (i.e., the requirements for everyone's input, limit of time for input, confidentiality of information shared, and plans for sharing results).
2. *Employees are asked to think of reasons why their colleagues have left or may leave the organization.*
   It is important for them to understand that the focus is on others and not on themselves. A misunderstanding on this issue can cause employees to overact or clam up. If handled properly, employees will actually reveal why *they* would leave and that is what is needed.
3. *Employees are asked to make a list of why they believe employees are leaving.*
   At least five reasons are suggested; however, more can be listed if desired. On a provided blank piece of paper, employees

should include as much detail as possible so it is clear about the issue and how it relates to turnover.

4. *Lists are revealed, one item at a time, and captured on the flip chart.*
   Rotating through the group, employees reveal their first item. The second facilitator should capture the essence of each item on the flip chart, using as much clarity as possible. This may be captured on a screen, if a decision support system is used. After everyone has had a turn, they proceed to the second item, and so forth until all items are revealed. It is important that each item be captured accurately.

5. *As the lists are captured, the charts are taped to the wall.*
   The lists should be displayed clearly so that all the participants can refer to them often, thinking through the issues as the process evolves.

6. *Merge items on the list only if the meanings are the same.*
   Clarification may be required from the individual who offered the item. The combinations are helpful in terms of having a manageable list, but should not be forced for the sake of efficiency. If the issues are different, they should be listed that way. After this step, a smaller, merged and integrated list remains.

7. *Employees then list the 5 (or 10) most important reasons for turnover.*
   Using index cards, employees list the items—one on each card—using the wording on the flip charts on the wall. Employees are asked to focus on 5 (if the list is fairly short) or 10 (if the list is longer). In this step, employees have the opportunity to consider other issues in addition to their own items. The result is usually a blended list that reflects the input of the group and their own issues.

8. *The employees are asked to arrange their cards in order of priority.*
   The most important causes of turnover (or anticipated turnover) should be listed as No. 1. It must be stressed that the ranking is to be performed when considering the issue that is causing the most turnover, not the one that may be most important to the employee. This step helps downplay personal biases.

9. *Employees reveal their lists one at a time.*
   Rotating through the group, employees reveal their top priority item first, followed by the second priority, etc. Points are assigned to each item as follows: the No. 1 cause for turnover is assigned a value of 5 points, No. 2 equals 4 points, No. 3 equals 3 points, etc. (If there are 10 items on the list, the No. 1 cause is assigned 10 points, No. 2 equals 9 point, etc.)

10. *Assign the points.*
    As the items are assigned a point value, the number is written on the original flip chart sheet (taped on the wall) so that a total can evolve as the process is completed.
11. *Tally the points.*
    The points next to each item are totaled. The item with the most points is considered to be the No. 1 reason for turnover by this group. The item with the second highest number is the No. 2 reason for turnover, etc. As expected, the level of importance diminishes as the score diminishes.
12. *Develop the top 10 reasons for turnover.*
    The 10 items with the highest numbers are the top 10 reasons for turnover, from the point of view of those who are still with the organization.

Data Integration

The data usually can be integrated easily from one group to the next when the data items are similar. In most situations, the issues are clearly identified and well known. The combined data can be placed in a spreadsheet to show the results of different groups and the extent to which a pattern or trend is emerging. A trend will usually develop clearly as the issues causing turnover are identified.

The advantage of this process is significant. When facilitated properly, the data are objective, thorough, and thoughtful. Members of the group express their opinions about why others may leave the organization and why some left. Employees typically open up to the neutral third-party facilitators and ultimately reveal reasons why *they* would leave. This information is usually difficult to obtain due to the stigma attached to revealing why an employee would leave the organization. The process is very efficient and can be accomplished in a 1- to 2-hour time frame, depending on the size of the group and the number of reasons offered. If the group is confined to one geographic area, this can be an inexpensive process. The critical parts of this process are the trust that is established when employees realize that their names will not be attached to any of the information and the mechanics of the facilitation.

EXIT INTERVIEW (OR SURVEY)

One of the most utilized processes to uncover the causes of turnover is the exit interview, taken just before or after an employee leaves the organization. Exit interviews can be face-to-face interviews, a questionnaire, a brief survey, or even a focus group. An anonymous questionnaire, administered confidentially, usually gets the best results for the costs. In a recent survey conducted in the United States by the Society for Human Resource Management, almost 9 out of 10 respondents (87 percent) said that organizations conducted exit interviews to determine why employees are leaving. Of those, 98 percent administered them internally and more than 50 percent have initiated changes based on the information received (Society for Human Resource Management, 2000).

Issues

Exit interviews are notoriously inaccurate and unreliable; however, they need not be. When properly designed and implemented, exit interviews can provide excellent data to develop retention solutions. Exiting employees may be the best source of data to determine why employees are leaving. Three key issues represent challenges to conducting exit interviews.

The response rates

With an anonymous survey, the return rates may be very low. Departing employees do not feel obligated to provide data. The last thing they may want to do is help the organization after they have decided to leave.

The data may be incomplete, inaccurate, or both

Even when employees respond to the questions, their responses may not be complete or accurate. Since they are no longer attached to the organization, they may be unwilling to devote much time to this issue. Consequently, their responses are short, incomplete, and sporadic.

Data may be purposely biased

For fear of retaliation or negative references, the employee may provide misleading input. An employee may indicate that working conditions are fine, but he or she received an offer they could not refuse.

These issues pose critical challenges when conducting exit interviews (Adkerson, 2000).

Design Issues

The design of the questionnaire or survey is similar to the design issues discussed earlier in this chapter. Several key issues are emphasized as follows:

Keep it simple

Because of the above issues, the survey (or interview) should be brief and simple. Questions must be direct and designed for easy response.

Building trust

It is essential to establish trust with exiting employees so they will provide reliable feedback (or refrain from purposely exaggerating the feedback). This may be difficult in a climate where trust is nonexistent. A key issue is the explanation of how the information will be used and reported. If employees have seen no improvement from previous exit interviews, they will not trust the organization to do anything with future data. If they are aware of retaliation for those who have provided straightforward, candid responses, they will be reluctant to provide the same data. The individual conducting the interview, or administering the survey, must convince the departing employee to trust them to use the data appropriately.

Ensure confidentiality and anonymity

Along with building trust are the steps taken to ensure that the data are collected anonymously, if possible, and kept confidential. Demographic data, while helpful in analysis, should be kept to a minimum in questionnaires because it may identify the departing employee. Using a third-party data collection source can help ensure anonymous input and demonstrate how the data are treated confidentially in reporting, use, and discussions. An indication of who will actually have access to the data is critical to help with the confidentiality issue.

Set the stage for input

The individuals providing data need to know how they will benefit. This is a challenge with exit interviews because the respondent may have very little to gain personally and a lot to lose—if there is retaliation. As a first step in this process, it is helpful to inform the individual that his or her departure is regrettable and that the organization would like to keep in touch. This can be accomplished in several different ways. Some organizations establish alumni groups, planning periodic outings and activities. Others have an alumni newsletter. An "open-door" attitude lets them know they can return to the organization, assuming the opportunities are still there. This atmosphere might even encourage them to provide constructive criticism. Consider questions such as, "Would you like to make some changes in the organization? If you were to stay, what would you change?"

Consider an incentive

Incentives motivate some individuals to provide responses, but the incentive should not be so large that it appears to be a reward for leaving. The types of incentives discussed earlier in this chapter may be sufficient, with slight modification. Some organizations will send a "departure gift," as a small token of their appreciation for providing information on the exit questionnaire. A gift in the $25 to $50 price range may appeal to some individuals. Most departing employees would feel guilty accepting the gift and not providing data.

Appeal to the concern about colleagues

Another issue is appealing to their sense of responsibility for the left-behind colleagues. A typical question might be, "What can we do to improve working conditions for those you leave behind?" This small amount of empowerment provides departing employees with the opportunity to influence conditions for friends remaining in the organization.

Try Memo Posting

Some organizations have experimented with having employees post memos explaining why they are leaving. These memos could be posted on a bulletin board, the Internet, or a web site designed for this purpose. One extremely effective approach to turnover comes from the accounting firm of Plante & Moran, a 1,200-employee CPA firm. Whenever an employee leaves, they are allowed to place a memo on a bulletin board in the main break room. (In a tradition dating back 40 years, these departing memos are always written in green.) Employees explain (sometimes in excruciating detail) their decision to leave the firm (Zaslow, 2002).

Even those employees who are fired or laid off for economic reasons are allowed to write these memos. According to the HR manager, most memos are flattering; only two memos since 1982 have not been posted because of inflammatory or inappropriately provocative statements. The good news is that the company only experiences about 10 percent turnover. The approach of this firm is particularly impressive. It takes tremendous courage and outstanding leadership to allow people to write about why they are leaving. If this trust is established, nourished, and supported over time, it can be an amazing and rich source of data to determine why employees choose to leave.

Face-to-Face Interviews

Generally, face-to-face interviews are ineffective for obtaining candid information about why a person is leaving. Obviously, trust is a critical issue; this interview gives up anonymity and there may be much concern about who will see the data. These interviews may be appropriate in very trusting climates where the interviewer is a respected, trusted person. In other climates, the face-to-face interview is usually not worth the time it takes to conduct it, unless it is conducted by a trusted, third-party individual.

Timing

The exit interview data, whether obtained in a survey or face to face, should be collected as soon as possible after the decision has been made to leave the organization. It is quite common to mail questionnaires to home addresses, providing a stamped return envelope addressed to a third party. This removes the survey from the job environment and places some distance between the individual and the organization. The longer the wait, the less likely the individual can (or is willing to) recall all the issues that influenced the decision to leave. If feasible, it may be appropriate to administer the exit survey while the employee is still there. Otherwise, it should be sent as quickly as possible.

Using the Data

Exit interview data should be tabulated and summarized around key groups and issues. The data become an integral part of data collection for retention. Steps should be taken to ensure that data are in no way connected to an individual. For example, if a specific section has experienced only one departure in the last 3 months, it may be better not to include these data because they clearly connect input to that individual. It is probably best summarized and cut in ways that would make sense with the data (i.e., the job title and maybe the area of the company). Data should be integrated by job groups so that trends and patterns can emerge, particularly with changes over time. Some amount of voluntary turnover is always present; it only becomes a problem when it is excessive (Brotheron, 1996).

Post-Exit Interviews

Some organizations attempt to collect data 6 months after employees leave to determine the status of the employee and gain more insight into why they left. The results from post-exit interviews may vary from those in a traditional exit interview, underscoring flawed methodology in the exit interview process. Many possible explanations for differences exist. One organization, Agilent Technologies, offers three reasons for differences:

1. Individuals are less emotional 6 months after resigning and, consequently, offer more accurate information.
2. The individuals have had time to compare their new situations to the job they left and can be more objective.
3. The individuals no longer have to worry about a good reference from the manager, thus avoiding intentional bias (Griffeth and Hom, 2001).

Admittedly, this information is very difficult to obtain and gets quite involved. It may be worth the effort to attempt to collect this type of data. It will require use of multiple strategies to achieve a good response rate, utilizing essentially every technique described earlier in the chapter. In lieu of the post-exit interview process, it may be best to focus more attention on increasing the credibility and usefulness of the exit interview process, which is more manageable.

Basic Idea Generation Tools

The tools discussed to this point in the chapter are the principal tools that will yield insight into the causes of turnover. However, additional tools are available that can further help determine the causes of turnover. Most of these tools come from the quality and process improvement field and have proven useful in resolving retention issues. Several important tools to generate ideas about the cause of turnover are presented in this section (Harrington and Lomax, 2000).

Brainstorming

Brainstorming is perhaps the most widely recognized technique to encourage creative thinking. It has become an important tool for generating the causes of organizational problems, such as turnover. The process facilitation is similar to the focus group and those design issues and guidelines also apply to the brainstorming session. The goal is to generate as many ideas as possible with no restrictions. The groups are best kept small, usually in the range of 6 to 12 group members. The group focuses on the actual problem: excessive turnover.

The individuals invited to participate should be those who best understand the excessive turnover problem and are in a position to know the causes and corresponding potential solutions. The group should have a complete understanding of the problems, issues, and challenges. Providing advanced communication will help the individuals develop ideas prior to the meeting.

The ground rules for the process are fairly straightforward:

1. The individuals are encouraged to offer as many ideas as possible.
2. The ideas are not criticized by anyone, regardless of how they may be perceived.
3. All ideas are recorded.
4. All participants should have ample time to share their ideas.
5. Freewheeling is encouraged, even if the ideas seem to be "off the wall."

When input ceases to be produced as desired, a variety of techniques are available to stimulate additional creativity and ideas. Three are very helpful:

1. The participation is rotated through the group to enable one individual to build off the ideas of another. This also provides ample time for reflection from those who are not directly participating.
2. Using the concept of idea building, individuals are encouraged to add to or expand on previous ideas or to offer similar or even alternate issues as ideas.
3. Quiet periods can help people reflect and think through the problem, sifting through the data mentally and generating additional ideas. This period could last up to a half hour before it becomes pointless.

The data can be summarized in a variety of ways. Eliminating items, combining items, and reaching consensus on items are key steps in the process.

Cause-and-Effect Diagram

The cause-and-effect diagram is very useful for repetitive issues, when a problem and causes need to be identified. This process is sometimes called the fishbone diagram because of its appearance. The process follows the focus group and brainstorming formats, except the major categories of causes are identified first, with minor causes added. As shown in Figure 5-3, the diagram illustrates the problem (excessive turnover) along with the major-cause categories—eight in this case. The minor-cause categories, which can be considerable, are provided by the group using idea-generating processes such as those covered in brainstorming. Here, the focus is more specific and the group must be knowledgeable about the problem so that they can offer minor causes of the problem. The steps are very simple:

1. The groups are selected based on their capability to provide insight into the causes of turnover.
2. The groups are provided instructions and their role in the process is outlined.
3. The major cause categories are either identified or offered. They are offered if there is previous information to indicate the specific cause (from exit interviews or other data collection methods).
4. After some discussion, the most likely causes are circled. This takes place only after each item is critically evaluated and the

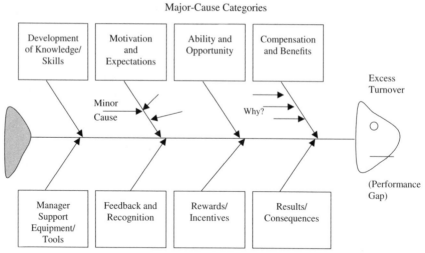

Figure 5-3. Example of a fishbone diagram.
(From Rothwell, 1999.)

group has reached a consensus as to which causes are most relevant. This process is more focused and, therefore, is more inclined to establish the real cause for the problem.

5. With the major-cause categories clearly identified and entered on the diagram, the individuals are asked to indicate the minor causes related to a major-cause category. These can be listed as minor causes, or sometimes just the "why" for the particular major cause category.

6. The fishbone diagram is then completed, showing the major and minor causes for the turnover problem.

Other Tools

A variety of other tools are available, primarily from the quality and performance improvement process, which can be used to analyze the cause of turnover. The following five tools might be helpful:

1. **Force field analysis** is a visual tool for analyzing the different elements that resist change (restraining forces) and those elements that wish for change (facilitating forces). This is a useful technique to drive improvement and retention by developing plans to overcome the restraining forces and make maximum use out of the facilitating forces.

2. The **mind mapping process** is an unstructured cause-and-effect analysis tool primarily designed for taking notes and solving problems. The problem (excessive turnover) is written on the center of a piece of paper and members of the group offer their suggestions or ideas as to the causes. These causes are drawn from the center as legs or lines. Branches are added to a line as additional causes or subcauses are generated. This is similar to the cause-and-effect process but might be more helpful with those individuals familiar with the mind mapping process.

3. The **affinity diagram** collects input from groups and organizes it according to the natural relationship with individual items. It has an extreme conceptual and logical simplicity that allows for a clear view of the largest and most complex problems. Basically, it is a way to structure and classify vague ideas. Consequently, it is helpful when a need exists to rationalize and focus on a complex, multifaceted problem, such as turnover (Galgano, 1999).

4. A **relationship diagram** is used when there is a need to build a map of the logical, sequential links among items that are interconnected and related to a central problem, such as turnover. It facilitates the solution of problems where causes interact, by dividing a problem into its basic components and isolating the relationships. The basic logic behind this tool is the same as the cause-and-effect diagram presented earlier.

5. The **tree-shaped diagram** systematically outlines the complete spectrum, paths, and tests that must be performed to achieve a particular goal, such as solving the turnover problem. The use of this tool changes some generalities into details by isolating the intermediate conditions that must be satisfied. The diagram leads to identification of the more appropriate procedures and methods to solve the problem.

These and other techniques may be helpful to analyze causes and relationships of other causes. The important point is to use a tool that works best for the organization in a specific setting.

FINAL THOUGHTS

This chapter explored how to determine the causes of turnover, one of the most critical steps in the strategic accountability approach to managing retention. Beginning with an explanation of the relationships of turnover to major variables, such as job satisfaction and commitment, the process of analyzing the specific causes in an organization are detailed. Analyzing the records is the beginning point. Several tools, both quantitative and subjective, are used to explore the actual causes. Questionnaires, surveys, interviews, and focus groups usually are the primary tools to identify the causes. Other useful tools were presented that may be helpful to understand the relationships between the problem and various causes. The output of this chapter is a list of the causes of turnover (arranged by priority), providing the organization with the top two or three (or, at the most, four or five) causes to undertake at any given time. Chapter 10 focuses on how to match a specific solution to a cause.

REFERENCES

Adkerson, D.M. *The Company You Keep: Four Key Tools for Employee Retention.* Brentwood, Tenn.: M. Lee Publishers, 2000.

Ahlrichs, N.S. *Competing for Talent: Key Recruitment and Retention Strategies for Becoming an Employer of Choice.* Palo Alto, Calif.: Davies-Black Publishing, 2000.

Brotheron, P. "Exit Interviews Can Provide a Reality Check." *HR Magazine*, 1996; 41(8):45–50.

Buckingham, M., and Coffman, C. *First, Break All the Rules.* New York: Simon & Schuster, 1999.

Galgano, A. *Company Quality Management.* Portland, Ore.: Productivity Press, 1994.

Griffeth, R.W., and Hom, P.W. *Retaining Valued Employees.* Thousand Oaks, Calif.: Sage Publishing, 2001.

Griffeth, R.W., Hom, P.W., and Gaertner, S. "A Meta-Analysis of Antecedents and Correlates of Employee Turnover: Update, Moderator Tests, and Research Implications for the Millennium." *Journal of Management*, 2000; 26:463–488.

Harrington, H.J., and Lomax, K.C. *Performance Improvement Methods: Fighting the War on Waste.* New York: McGraw-Hill, 2000.

Hom, P.W., and Griffeth, R.W. *Employee Turnover.* Cincinnati, Ohio: South-Western, 1995.

Kaye, B., and Jordan-Evans, S. *Love'Em or Lose'Em: Getting Good People to Stay.* San Francisco, Calif.: Berrett-Koehler Publishers, 1999.

Mitchell, T.R., Holtom, B.C., Lee, T.W., Sablynski, C.J., and Erez, M. "Why People Stay: Using Job Embeddedness to Predict Voluntary Turnover." *Academy of Management Journal*, 2001; 44(6):1102–1121.

Phillips, J.J. *Handbook of Training Evaluation and Measurement,* ed. 3. Woburn, Mass: Butterworth-Heinemain, 1997.

Rothwell, W. *ASTD Models for Human Performance Improvement.* Alexandria, VA: American Society for Training and Development, 1999.

Salopek, J.J. (2000). "Retention Rodeo." *Training and Development,* 2000:20–21.

Shea, T.F. (2002). "For Many Employees, the Workplace is Not a Satisfying Place." *HR Magazine,* October 2002:28.

Society for Human Resources Management Retention Practices Survey. Alexandria, VA: Society for Human Resource Management, 2000.

Walton, M. *The Deming Management Method.* New York: A Perigee Book, 1986.

Zaslow, J. "A Different Kind of Public Accounting: One Firm's Tradition of Goodbye Memos," *The Wall Street Journal,* August 1, 2002:D1.

Further Reading

Andersen, B., and Fagerhaug, T. *Root Cause Analysis: Simplified Tools and Techniques.* Milwaukee, Wis.: ASQ Quality Press, 2000.

Folkman, J. *Employee Surveys that Make a Difference: Using Customized Feedback Tools to Transform Your Organization.* Provo, Utah: Executive Excellence Publishing, 1998.

Griffeth, R.W., and Hom, P.W. *Retaining Valued Employees.* Thousand Oaks, Calif.: Sage Publications, 2001.

Gubman, Edward L. *The Talent Solution: Aligning Strategy and People to Achieve Extraordinary Results.* New York: McGraw-Hill, 1998.

Hale, J. *The Performance Consultant's Fieldbook: Tools and Techniques for Improving Organizations and People.* San Francisco, Calif.: Jossey-Bass/Pfeiffer, 1998.

Kraut, A.I., ed. *Organizational Surveys: Tools for Assessment and Change.* San Francisco, Calif.: Jossey-Bass Publishers, 1996.

Krueger, R.A. *Analyzing & Reporting Focus Group Results.* Thousand Oaks, Calif.: Sage Publications, 1998.

Kvale, S. *InterViews: An Introduction to Qualitative Research Interviewing.* Thousand Oaks, Calif.: Sage Publications, 1996.

Langley, G.J., Nolan, K.M., Nolan, T.W., Norma, C.L., and Provost, L.P. *The Improvement Guide: A Practical Approach to Enhancing Organizational Performance.* San Francisco, Calif.: Jossey-Bass Publishers, 1996.

Rea, L.M., and Parker, R.A. *Designing and Conducting Survey Research: A Comprehensive Guide*, 2nd ed. San Francisco, Calif.: Jossey-Bass Publishers, 1997.

Saks, A.M., Schmitt, N.W., and Klimoski, R.J. *Research, Measurement, and Evaluation of Human Resources*. Scarborough, Ontario, Canada, Nelson/Thomson Learning, 2000.

Sears, David. *Successful Talent Strategies: Achieving Superior Business Results through Market-Focused Staffing*. New York: AMACOM, 2003.

The Guidebook for Performance Improvement: Working with Individuals and Organizations. San Francisco, Calif.: Jossey-Bass/Pfeiffer, 1997.

CHAPTER 6

Solution Set: Recruiting New Employees

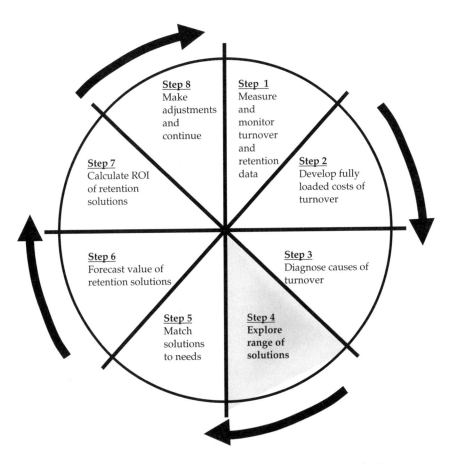

The previous chapter focused on the critical issue of diagnosing the exact causes of employee turnover. This chapter and the next three chapters identify the employee needs that cause turnover. Chapter 6 discusses employee needs that occur at the time an individual joins the organization. The corresponding solutions, which address these employee needs, provide suggestions on how employers can address turnover issues. Table 6-1 shows the first six categories along with the corresponding needs and solutions.

Employees are attracted to an organization for a variety of reasons, such as the organization's image, market performance, recruitment practices, and job assignment. How well these factors match the new hire's expectations can ensure whether that employee will fit into the organization and the job.

IMAGE

What creates an organization's image? It is more than the public's perception. It can be the leading indicator of whether a company will survive in the future (Marziliano, 1998). The image helps to

Table 6-1
Employee Needs and Organizational Solutions for Recruiting New Employees

Category	Need	Solution
Recruiting New Employees		
1. Image	To work in an organization with a positive public image	Maintain a strong, positive organizational image.
2. Market performance	To work in an organization with a solid performance future	Improve and maintain profitability and performance.
3. Recruitment	To be attracted to a specific organization	Recruit good employees who fit the organizational culture.
4. Selection	To be selected fairly and offered a job in a timely manner	Manage a fair, equitable selection program.
5. Job fit	To have an appropriate job that meets expectations and skill requirements	Place employees in a job that matches skills and talents.
6. Orientation and initial training	To adapt quickly to the job, team, and organization	Provide a formal orientation, socialization, and training experience.

convey the culture, success, and personality that distinguishes one company from its rivals. A good corporate image delivers its message through every available communication vehicle. Image helps people understand who the company is and who the company expects to be (Shoemaker and Lantos, 2000).

Need for Positive Organizational Image

Prospective and incumbent employees want to be associated with an organization that possesses a strong public image. An organization's image reflects not only on itself, but also on its employees. A positive organizational image creates pride for its employees. Employees feel that they are contributing to, and creating the image of, the organization. A tarnished public image, however, can contribute to turnover. Employees are reluctant to be a member of an organization that is not viewed favorably.

In a poll by Maritz Research, employees were asked if corporate image played a part in their decision to apply for and remain in their jobs. Approximately 49 percent responded that image did affect their decision to apply for their job, and 47 percent said that they also felt that they would remain with their company a year from the time of the poll (Dolliver, 2002).

The Media and Image

Image is integrated into organizational advertisements and media. For example, Apple Computer uses an apple as a symbol to help create its corporate image. Pillsbury uses a fat, small cartoon character called the Pillsbury Doughboy to help communicate its image. Celebrities are often used to help form an organization's image. Michael Jordan projects the super-athlete image for Haines underwear and Nike athletic footwear. Average, everyday people are used to portray organizational image, as with the Dell Computer guy or the United Parcel Service (UPS) delivery person. Even a color can help portray image, such as the color red to represent Campbell's soup products or blue to portray IBM. Demonstrated use of a product can also be a part of creating a positive image. Chrysler, Ford, Chevrolet, and Toyota create an image of excitement and fun when driving one of their vehicles. These characters, symbols, colors, and celebrities all contribute to the creation of organizational image. Ideally, employees view these images positively, relate to them, and identify with them. If employees do experience a positive identification with the organization's image, they will help to sustain it through remaining on the job—through their organizational membership.

Image Components

Understanding how to create a strong corporate image begins with clarifying its components. Addressing each component will help organizations improve their image. Table 6-2 presents seven components that comprise the recommended corporate image solution (Shoemaker and Lantos, 2000).

These seven components all work together to form the essence of the organization's image. Operationally, image is created and interpreted through answering questions that relate to the operational components listed above. The operational questions are:

1. Who is the organization talking to? (Customers, vendors, employees, partners, shareholders, competitors, etc. should be included in answering this question.)
2. What is the organization saying to these groups? (Addressing important issues and concerns can identify what is being communicated.)

Table 6-2
Components of Corporate Image Solution

Image Components	Discussion and Direction
1. Simplicity	Focus on a single important idea that can be developed over time and presented in a variety of creative ways.
2. Uniqueness	Develop a company theme that differentiates it from competition.
3. Appropriateness	Bring attention to the company and its qualities.
4. Continuity	Ensure that there is a consistent message and perspective of how the company is viewed.
5. Relevance	Address the company's target audiences.
6. Foresight	Reach target audiences before they can form a negative perception/attitude about the company or products.
7. Credibility	Match advertising claims with reality; make sure that what is touted in advertising can be delivered.

3. How does the organization say what it wants to say? (What are the symbols, methods, and communication vehicles used?)

Organizations can improve retention by considering the seven components and ensuring that the organization has answered the three operational questions. When employees experience the organization's image as positive, they feel validated and are more likely to remain in the organization.

One organization that understands this concept is Omnicom, a New York City services company with 43,000 employees. The advertising and marketing giant reached revenues in 1999 of $5.2 billion. Its ad agencies include the market leaders such as BBDO and DDB and have developed memorable campaigns for Pepsi, Visa, and Budweiser. Although Omnicom's image is not as well know as its clients, within the advertising community it is very strong. Omnicom experiences an 18 percent turnover rate, which is nearly half the industry average. To create their own image, they have focused on several image components, including simplicity, appropriateness, continuity, and relevance. Their dedication to internal communication and cooperation has contributed to a positive corporate image. An executive vice president at Omnicom states that cooperation is a buzzword that also helps maintain the company's outstanding employee retention strategy (Stein, 2000). For Omnicom, image is another way of retaining its top talent.

Market Performance

Organization with strong positive images are able to perform well in the marketplace, in part, because they have public support that helps to sustain financial performance. Successful market performance is both the means and the end to a successful retentions strategy. Without successful market performance, there is no need for employees and the organization ceases to exist. A strong performance in the marketplace requires not only attention to purely financial matters, but also a greater emphasis on employee retention.

Need for Strong Market Performance

Employees need their organization to perform well in the marketplace because it helps ensure their positive future. Market performance creates a promise that the company will be able to provide for its employees. Employees who perceive that they are a part of a successful organization are more likely to stay. The senior vice president of Dell Computer Corporation states, "You need a great business first—this attracts talent. We have and will transform the industry. People want to be a part of that. When it comes to retention, what's important is how well the company is run. We are very well managed." This statement articulates the close relationship between image and market performance (*HR Focus*, 2000).

A study conducted on 142 branches of a large automobile finance company validated this concept. Aggregate employee attitudes, such as satisfaction, teamwork, quality emphasis, and customer focus, were related to customer satisfaction, employee turnover, and measures of branch financial performance (Ryan, Schmit, and Johnson, 1996). The study supports the relationship between positive financial performance and a lower employee turnover. Employees are more likely to remain with an organization that is performing well.

Types of Organizations

Measuring market performance varies by the nature of the organization. Three types of organizations differ in how they gauge market performance. These are public organizations, privately held organizations, and public sector entities. The organizational solution to achieve strong market performance is different for each organizational type.

Publicly Held Organizations

A publicly held organization (i.e., traded on the stock exchange) has clear financial indicators that reflect its market performance through stock price, profit, loss, annual reports, and public perception. The higher the profits and lower the losses, the stronger the market performance.

A positive example of an organization that has strong market performance and set out to create a reputation as a market leader is Goldman Sachs, located in New York City. With more than 15,000 employees, the organization prides itself in hiring the best, making the best deals, and producing the best financial leaders. The company attracts superior MBA graduates and has made it a point to concentrate on employee needs. Treasury Secretary Robert Rubin was an employee of Goldman Sachs. "As a professional services business, our ability to recruit the best people is directly related to our stature in the market," says the global head of human resources at Goldman. In 1999, Goldman was the leading tech investment bank, raising 20 percent of all initial public offering (IPO) dollars, and is a top employer of choice for aspiring banking employees. The head of HR believes that the organization knows how to retain its employees, and that moving to a competitor, for Goldman workers, would be taking a step down (Stein, 2000).

Privately Held Organizations

Privately held companies have different market performance criteria because they are not required to make their financial situation known. Some key indicators for a privately held organization are:

- Growth indicators (expansion, new products, services, etc.)
- Budget increases (used instead of annual reports, which are not required for privately held organizations)
- Improved staffing levels (hiring new employees, temporary employees, and consultants)
- Bonus structures and profit sharing distributed to both management and employees.

When employees experience the above factors of growth, expansion, and bonuses, they perceive the organization is successful in the marketplace. An example of a successful privately held organization retaining talent is TDIndustries. Located in Dallas, TDIndustries installs infrastructures in buildings and employees 1,368 employees with revenues of $205 million. Nearly 14 percent of the employees have been employed for more than 10 years. TDIndustries also provides excellent benefits for its employees and treats them as true partners, which is accurate because the employees own the company (*Fortune*, 2002).

Public Sector Organizations

Public sector organizations have different market performance indicators. Unlike publicly traded companies, there are usually no profits or revenues. Public sector organizations are judged by image, not success with key performance indicators. Whether they are federal, state, or local entities, the public's perception of them determines their success. Opinion, in turn, drives budget allocations for these organizations.

Some public sector organizations rely heavily on customer satisfaction surveys to gauge public support and market performance. For example, police departments, fire departments, and military organizations were held in high esteem following the events of September 11, 2001, and the subsequent anthrax attacks in the United States. Immediately after the September 11 disaster, the City of New York was flooded with hundreds of employment applications despite the obvious risks on the job. Because of the performance of the organization and its employees, applicants wanted to work in an organization that was held in such high esteem.

Recruitment

Searching for and finding qualified, talented employees is a continuous process for every organization. Recruiting budgets continue to grow. Keeping the talent pool infused with productive employees is a critical organizational goal. For the individual, being recruited by the right organization is a critical individual need.

Need for Effective Recruiting

People need to be hired by an organization that is attractive to them. When individuals are in the job search process, they investigate organizations for a variety of reasons. The organization may be close to their residence, or they may have friends working in the company. Job seekers may like the pay and benefits or the kind of job the organization offers. They may also want to join an organization because of the potential for professional growth and career advancement.

Even in times of high unemployment, there can be a lack of qualified employees for particular industries. "We approach recruitment as if the employee is in a buyer's market," says the director of human resources for Loews Philadelphia Hotel. "We're selling ourselves as an employer" (Hensdill, 2000).

Organizations use a variety of recruitment initiatives and try to stay on the leading edge by taking advantage of new technologies. Standard recruitment solutions include newspaper advertisements, internal employee referrals, open houses, college recruiting efforts, use of search firms, sponsorship of job fairs, use of internship programs, and working with business schools and technical schools. The following solutions identify some of the customary corporation responses for recruitment.

Internal Referrals

Employee referrals are a highly effective means for attracting and keeping employees. If the current employees understand the organization's desired behaviors, referrals from those employees should yield excellent, long-term results. Some employee referral programs include bonuses of up to $3,000 per individual hired, whereas other organizations offer referral gifts. Such gifts can range in value and price from a small company catalog gift to a vacation package at a location of the employee's choice (Sabol, 1999). One organization that has successfully used an employee referral program is Health Group of Alabama (in the laundry industry). The organization actively encourages its employees to refer potential employees to the company by giving a $80 bonus. Once the new employee success-fully completes a 90-day probationary period, the employee who referred the new employee receives another $80, and if the new employee stays with the organization for a full year, the referring employee receives a $155 payment. The program is only a few months old, but the organization has experienced a steady increase in referrals and a high percentage of the new employees make it past the 90-day probationary period (Frederick, 2002).

Another organization that understands the importance of an employee referral program is SARAH, Inc. This small social service agency attracts good people and maintains a remarkably low turnover rate. The agency is based in Guilford, Connecticut, and has a staff of 110 people who provide services for about 450 clients on an annual basis. SARAH has been able to find the right people and contributes much of its ability to find and keep good staff to their employee referral program. However, SARAH does not rely solely on its employee referral program. The organization also has excel-lent benefits, tuition assistance, a comprehensive training program, and a team of 25 to 30 people willing to work for the company on a temporary basis. Although many of SARAH's employees could find higher-paying jobs in the area, SARAH has the most consistently low turnover rate in the area. Among the 168 agencies like SARAH in Connecticut, their turnover rate is the lowest. Others in the indus-try are experiencing turnover as high as 50%, but SARAH's turnover rate has consistently been in the low single digits (*Staff Leader*, 2002).

Open House Recruiting

Open house recruiting refers to any employer-sponsored meeting open to the public. A well-orchestrated open house serves as a useful tool in the recruiting process for attracting employees in all educa-tional and experience backgrounds. The open house reaches some of the most desirable, yet sometimes unreachable, prospective employees—those who are genuinely undecided about joining a company. It gives new applicants the opportunity to interact with other employees in the company in an informal atmosphere. It also allows the employer an opportunity to assess the way a prospective employee acts in a relaxed, unstructured setting. Open houses take place in the actual workplace and are an excellent way for candidates to see the area in which they might work and experience some of the organization's culture.

Job Fairs

Job fairs are similar to open houses except they usually take place off site, away from the organization's place of business. Because of size constraints at their business sites, organizations often rent large rooms or convention center space to host the numerous people that will attend its job fair. A job fair can be conducted in the community where the organization exists, or it can be an event that takes place on the road at a convention or professional society. A job fair may be organized by industry, university placement services, or even through the state's employment offices.

The Chicago-based Hyatt International Hotel uses a professional development conference, a 1-day road show that teaches students how to interview and advance in the workplace and informs students about career opportunities within Hyatt. This conference is free and offers breakfast, lunch, and appetizers in the evening. In addition, the attendees get discounted rooms at nearby Hyatt Hotels. In a tight labor market, the road show conferences in Washington, D.C., San Francisco, and Atlanta attracted between 40 and 100 potential employees at each site. In addition to the 1-day road shows, Hyatt is addressing its retention problem through the use of a creative program that improves employee retention through interaction between employees. Hyatt's Chicago-based manager of staffing is creating a mentoring program in nine Hyatt hotels. During the first 10 months of employment, new entry-level employees are paired with a more-senior employee to assist them in adjusting to their new job and workplace surroundings (Hensdill, 2000). Hyatt discusses this benefit as part of its recruiting effort and uses it to motivate prospective employees to apply for employment.

The cost of replacing employees can be exceptionally high, especially in the hotel industry where employee turnover ranges from 60 to 300 percent. In response to this employment crunch, several hotels and hotel companies, such as Loews Philadelphia Hotel, have developed innovative solutions to help retain talented employees. Loews needed to attract 525 employees and decided to recruit employees in much the same way as it attracts guests. They used community job fairs, trade shows, and a career page on their Internet website to attract more than 600 applicants from various communities in Philadelphia. In one subsequent recruiting effort, Loews rented a space at Philadelphia's convention center to showcase job offerings through videos. Meeting rooms were set aside for prescreening interviews. The event cost Loews $40,000 and resulted in 2,500 interviews with an estimated 300 new hires (Hensdill, 2000). The job fair was a huge success for the organization.

Use of Recruiters

When candidates are identified by a recruiter, a significant screening process has usually taken place. The recruiter has the opportunity to interview several potential applicants and present these to the company's HR department. Following the recommendations of the recruiter, the organization interviews and selects the best-qualified applicant.

Newspaper and Internet Advertising

Although advertisements in newspapers, trade magazines, and other publications are a common method of recruitment, some newer methods include the use of web advertisements, video broadcasts, and job boards on Internet search engines. These Internet-based solutions provide organizations with numerous employee applications. Often there are so many responses to the technology-based recruiting efforts that organizations cannot keep up with the deluge of applications. However, the credit organization Capital One has successfully used an approach that relies heavily on the use of technology as part of its recruiting solution. Because of growth, the need for recruiting customer-service representatives at Capital One is significant; at times, an estimated 30 to 40 percent of entire workforce needed as new. In the past, the company used a pen-and-paper testing method as part of its recruiting solution. More recently, computerized testing replaced the pen-and-paper test. Implementing an on-line process that tests new applicants will save Capital One an estimated $3.7 million (Nicholson, 2000).

Recruiting Courtesy

Organizations should apply the same standards of courtesy to the on-line applicant as is customary for traditional mail-in applications. A letter of response should state that the application was received and outline the timetable for hiring. After an applicant has been eliminated from consideration, the organization should inform the applicant of its decision with a courtesy letter or e-mail. If there is a lack of communication, the applicant will be hesitant to apply to the organization in the future. Courteous organizational communication can help create a positive relationship that will motivate potential candidates to apply for positions announced at a later date.

INTERVIEWING AND SELECTION

Interviewing consists of the discussions held between prospective employees and the employment staff and decision makers in the organization. The discussions can be formal or informal, depending on the culture and goals of the employer. Often there are several stages of interviews before an employee is selected. The interview process is designed to help select employees who are the most talented and will best fit with the organization.

Need for Effective Interviewing and Selection

The most common way for employees to become members of an organization is through an interviewing process. Prospective employees need to experience an interviewing process that they consider fair and impartial. They want to be treated professionally and made to feel as though they are valued. Within the interviewing and selection process, organizations should remember that everyone who goes through this process should be treated with professionalism. During the interviewing process, the organization should be on its best behavior and create goodwill among all applicants. Even candidates who are not selected should be treated with respect so that they can relate a positive experience when asked about the selection process.

Fairness and Timeliness

The interview and selection process should be fair and timely. Fairness consists of many issues, such as standardized selection criteria, use of a written hiring process, decision making based on factual data, and consideration of all qualifications and work history. The organization should also take into consideration the talents, education, and verifiable skill sets of the prospective employee.

Prospective employees need to have an identifiable, verifiable selection process that gives the employee a sense of fairness and timeliness in the selection process. There is a natural time frame to the selection process that takes potential employees' schedules into account. A reasonable length of time should be used to make the selection. If the organization takes too long to select individuals, the applicants may tend to lose their motivation to be hired; the job itself may become less attractive. Also, candidates who are turned down may be part of the recruitment pool for the next position within the organization and need to feel that the organization's conduct was reasonable.

The Realistic Job Preview

The realistic job preview (RJP) is an excellent process to clarify expectations of the organization and employee. Costly turnover can be avoided by allowing organizations to specifically state what they want from new employees. The RJP allows the organization and the individual to step outside the immediate concerns to fill a position and obtain a job and look to their future relationship. Clarifying expectations is an effective, inexpensive retention tactic that gives employees realistic job expectations. This exercise allows candidates who are not the best fit for the job to withdraw themselves from consideration, thereby avoiding the inevitable turnover. This review process has been used successfully to increase retention.

Whether in a group interview with several individuals or a one-on-one interview, the RJP identifies the fit between the individual's characteristics and job requirements. Professionally trained interviewers usually conduct the RJP at the employer's facilities. The interviewer uses questions about characteristics, skills, abilities, and other job-related dimensions to assess the applicant's personality, demeanor, self-assurance, and response to difficult questions, openness, and self-disclosure. The primary objective is to determine whether there is a good fit between the organization and the candidate.

During the RJP, employers can preview the job and the organization to the prospective employee to help ensure success and establish realistic expectations. Unfortunately, many RJPs tend to lower initial job expectations while increasing self-selection, organizational commitment, job satisfaction, and performance (Premack and Wanous, 1985). A good job preview reduces unrealistic expectations and contains the following components:

1. *Job duties and responsibilities.* The organization should provide samples of work that show prospective employees the required tasks. If possible, applicants can observe incumbent employees who can discuss job duties.
2. *Empowerment levels.* The interviewers may authorize the employee to role-play at specific levels with regard to decisions, approvals, and autonomous actions related to job performance.
3. *The education and training program.* The organization presents the various phases of the orientation program and the formal education and training program, including learning assignments of the job.
4. *The basis for performance evaluation.* The interviewers will identify how employees will be evaluated in initial assignments, who will evaluate them, and what performance means in terms of pay increases and promotion.
5. *Successful employees in the target job.* The interviewer may introduce employees who are successful on the job. These employees may explain the qualities and characteristics of current employees and those who have been promoted to higher levels.
6. *Promotions and advancement opportunities.* The organization should discuss career path information so the candidate understands typical progression and promotion opportunities.
7. *Expectations.* The interviewer communicates the expectations of work performance. Work habits, attitudes, requirements, and goals are identified along with the consequences for failure to meet established goals.
8. *Determinants of success.* The interviewers should identify and compare the typical employee performance record against the performance evaluation criteria. This comparison identifies successful employment behaviors.

RJP discussions of organizational expectations need not be limited to the time of hire, but may be given throughout the employee's first year of employment. For example, if the organization has a need for individuals who can work in highly stressful situations, candidates should be told this during the RJP. Candid, frequent follow-up discussions will clarify and update obligations and expectations.

Written material about policies, pay, benefits, and so on should be given to the employee at the time of the job offer. Future employees need both verbal and written materials to solidify the job offer in their minds and to help answer a multitude of questions. During the RJP, the HR representative can anticipate questions and respond to them verbally and in writing. Additionally, the employee's new manager can identify who to contact in case a problem or issue takes place between the time the offer is made and the first day of work.

JOB FIT

Job fit refers to the similarity, or congruence, between what employees want to experience on the job and what the organization offers. The greater the job fit, the more satisfied employees will be and the longer they will remain in the organization. Job fit not only refers to the actual work being done, but also how well employees can interact with members of the work team and their ability to work within the organizational culture.

Need for Proper Job Fit

Proper job fit is defined as an employee's perceived compatibility or comfort with the organization and with the work environment (Mitchell et al., 2001). Employees who do not experience job fit tend to leave slightly sooner than employees who fit their job (O'Reilly, Chatman, and Caldwell, 1991). Several studies support the relationship between employees experiencing job fit and their decision to remain in the organization (Chan, 1996; Cable and Judge, 1996; Werbel and Gilliland, 1999).

Job Fit Criteria

Finding a good job fit requires that the new employees have a clear understanding of the job. The following criteria can be discussed during the job interview to help the job applicant increase understanding and improve job fit.

- *Job role* is a definition of the job in terms of the service provided or product being sold.

- *Job clarity* is the amount of certainty or risk required to be successful in the new position.
- *Job autonomy* addresses the questions of who supervises new employees' work and how much independence will they have to accomplish their jobs in a timely, productive manner.
- *Task importance* is the enumeration of the priorities (i.e., the essential performance tasks that must be done in order to meet job standards).
- *Task repetitiveness* is a definition of the similar tasks or functions inherent in the job.
- *Task variety* is a description of the various tasks or functions required to do the job.

Organizations can create extensive job descriptions that list all of these characteristics in detail. They can then pursue recruitment and selection processes to find the person or persons with the right fit. There are three components of job fit: person/organization fit (P/O fit), person/culture fit (P/C fit), and person/person fit (P/P fit).

Person and Organization Fit

P/O fit occurs when the new employee's work history and future job goals align with the specific job tasks required to deliver organizational products and services. P/O fit may include an assessment of personal work characteristics of the individual, such as the following:

- Flexibility
- Autonomy
- Attention to detail
- Innovation
- Being a quick study
- Resourcefulness
- Dependability

Care should be given to ensure that the same objective criteria are used in the assessment of all candidates for P/O fit. Behavioral questions that assess the applicant's experience in demonstrating these personal qualities are a good way to assess P/O fit.

How well an employee fits into an organization is critical if organizations are to avoid turnover. *Fit* is defined as an employee's perceived compatibility or comfort with an organization and with his or her environment. An employee's personal values, career goals, and plans for the future must fit with the larger corporate culture and the demands of the immediate job (job knowledge, skills, and abilities). The better the fit, the higher the likelihood that an employee will feel professionally and personally tied to an organization (Mitchell, Holtom, Lee, Sablynski, and Erez, 2001).

Person/Cultural Fit

P/C fit occurs when the new employee's personal goals and lifestyle fit the organization's culture (Hensdill, 2000). Often organizations are looking for employees who will show loyalty or dependability to their mission; this may be a measure of P/C fit. The organization should recruit people who are aligned with its corporate mission and vision statements, but more importantly, it should clarify how its culture is evidenced through employee behaviors and should select people who are aligned with its culture.

For example, news media organizations should understand that they are deadline-driven and seek persons that thrive on meeting deadlines. Another example is the culture of software creators who work long, but flexible hours, and thrive on creativity. When the culture of the organization is understood, it becomes easier to gauge whether candidates would be a good fit.

Research by DBM, a career transition, career management, and outplacement organization headquartered in Boston, found that more than 70 percent of executives who were let go from their organizations were not let go for performance issues, but because they did not fit the organization's culture (Smith, 1999).

As part of the selection solution, the manager should take into consideration how the new employee's personal work characteristics will fit with the culture of the work group. If possible, a group interview can be held to help assess compatibility.

Person/Person Fit

P/P fit refers to people experiencing peer cohesion as the new employee's personality aligns with the personality of the team members. The organization can ask itself the simple question: Will this candidate fit in with the people he or she will be working with? Or will the candidate contribute tension to the workplace? Such considerations may seem arbitrary, but meshing with the organization is very important. Employees are more inclined to leave a job if they never feel accepted by their colleagues. Organizations that develop team-building activities and promote cohesion among co-workers help avoid turnover.

ORIENTATION

Orientation is more than a time to meet and greet new employees. It is a program to foster a sense of nurturing and acceptance through introducing the organizational culture, image, and values to new employees. During this time, companies can put their best foot forward and make a lasting impression. Conducting orientation with professionalism makes a positive impact on turnover.

Need for Effective Orientation

Most people can remember their first day on the job and the associated excitement and stress. Whether orientation is in a formal classroom setting or on the job, it is a time when people begin familiarization with the job duties and the people involved with the work assignments. The stress involved in accepting a new job (whether as a new employee or an existing employee) is often difficult. Orientation helps new employees deal positively with stress by explaining their obligations to the organization and the company's obligations to them (Wanous, 1992). Being accepted and feeling a part of the new team or organization is also critical to a successful orientation program.

A study conducted at Corning Glass revealed that new employees who attended a positive orientation session were 69 percent more likely to remain with the company 3 years later than those who did not attend such a session. A comparable study completed at Texas Instruments found that employees who were well oriented to the company and their jobs achieved full productivity two months earlier than those who did not. Conducting effective orientation programs is not just a part of organizational initiation, it is also good for business because it helps new employees become more productive in a shorter time and keeps them on the job.

Orientation Programs

There is great diversity in orientation. Some larger companies offer orientation sessions that are run continually because of the steady volume of hew hires. Other organizations wait until they have enough new employees to create an orientation session. Smaller companies might not have formal orientation, but they provide a one-on-one discussion setting for new employees. Whether the orientation is large or small, formal or informal, the orientation solution helps benefit both the individual and the organization by providing a consistent framework from which the new employee can begin a successful career.

How intensive should an orientation be? How long should it last? How is this determination made? The answers rely naturally on the goals of the orientation. The orientation program itself should be designed and delivered with the culture of that particular organization in mind. The more training that is required, the longer the orientation. For example, the military's orientation program, known as basic training, lasts from 6 weeks to 3 months or more. The military's orientation program has multiple objectives that include attempting to change most aspects of the recruits' life habits, such as sleeping, eating, physical conditioning, skills, and behaviors. For some jobs in the private sector, orientation programs can last as little as 15 minutes or as long as 1 year. The length of orientation programs depends on several factors that include the following:

- Size and complexity of the organization (more complex jobs require more time in orientation and initial training)
- Complexity of the job and the company (especially with regard to standard practices, organizational policies, and procedures)
- Importance that the organization places on having a thorough orientation program (commitment from the organization to the orientation process)
- Resources available to schedule, conduct, and complete the orientation program (available training staff and training rooms)
- Specific objectives of the orientation process (more objectives require more time)

Orientation Outcomes

Well-designed orientation solutions begin by establishing learning objectives that focus on what new employees need to know and what the organization needs to communicate. The key components for a strong orientation solution are integral for a successful program. Orientation should draw on the following outcomes as program goals:

- Welcome new employees and assure them that they are an important part of the organization.
- Build a positive attitude about the organization and the work community, including identifying the organization's goods, services, and customers.
- Share comprehensive and historical information about the organization, including its history, mission, vision, values, and structure.
- Introduce new graduates to their work environment.
- Identify benefit packages, ways to use them, and the company's pay practices.
- Ensure that the appropriate forms and documents are completed so that the offer of employment can be finalized.
- Communicate the policies, procedures, rules, and standards.
- Clarify the general expectations of employee performance.

After developing the structure around desired outcomes, another consideration is to allow flexibility in the program to address various employee needs. Orientation programs should recognize that employees are different and have different needs.

Using pilot tests, that is, conducting the orientation program with existing employees, ensures that the program will be effective. The pilot tests help in the use of appropriate materials and delivery methods for orientation. Finally, soliciting candid input from newly hired employees who have gone through the orientation program can identify what they learned versus what they feel they need to learn during the orientation program. Feedback provides valuable insight into opportunities for improvement.

Orientation solutions should be monitored continually for effectiveness. Even a program that is effective when first implemented can become ineffective when the needs of the organization change. Monitoring ensures that current information and materials are presented. Since today's companies experience constant change, updates to training programs are regularly required.

Computer-Based Orientation Programs

Effective orientation can be used as a tool to retain employees, especially for high-tech companies with specialty jobs. Steinwall Inc., a precision custom thermoplastic injection molder in Minneapolis, Minnesota, has been addressing turnover issues since 1994. At that time, 69 percent of its employees stayed with the company less than a year. The president spent 8 years trying to reduce turnover with no success. Then the CEO invited employees to a brainstorming session where they decided that the company needed an effective orientation program. Breaking from the traditional classroom setting, the CEO created 20 hours of computer-based animation that explained the organization to new employees in a playful way. It worked—turnover was reduced to only 18 percent. The CEO stated, "Orientation is the only thing I changed. I didn't change my wage base. I didn't change my managers. I just changed the way managers brought people on board." (Toloken, 2000)

Companies, like people, only get one chance to make a first impression. Well-conducted orientation programs are one way in which good impressions can improve productivity and retention. The orientation program should reflect both what the company needs to share and what the employee needs to learn, taking both perspectives into account. Well-designed, flexible, organized programs that are also enjoyable for individuals succeed at giving people a head start in their new jobs. Those organizations that develop strong, effective orientation programs are more likely to retain employees.

FINAL THOUGHTS

This chapter discussed six basic employee needs that relate to the recruitment process. The first two needs concerned the employee's desire to work in an organization that had a positive public image and solid market performance. Solutions to meet these needs, such as developing a good corporate image and ensuring successful market performance, were discussed. The next two employee needs revolved around the recruitment and selection process. Specific solutions, such as open house recruitments, job fairs, and use of recruiters, were matched to the need of recruitment, while solutions such as the use of the realistic job preview and standardized selection criteria were discussed. The final section of the chapter dealt with job fit and orientation. Solutions to ensure that employees were placed in jobs that match their skills and talents, as well as solutions to help employees adjust quickly to the job, team, and organization, were presented. The next three chapters will continue the focus on employee needs and organizational solutions.

References

"Best Practices: Small Agency Wins Big in Finding and Keeping Good Staff." *Staff Leader,* July 2002; 15(11):6–7.

Black, B. "Healthcare's Talent Dimension." *Gallup Tuesday Briefing,* May 14, 2002; 1.

Cable, D.M., and Judge, T.A. "Person-Organization Fit, Job Choice Decision and Organizational Entry." *Organizational Behavior and Human Decision Processes,* 1996; 67:294–311.

Chan, D. "Cognitive Misfit of Problem-Solving Style at Work: A Facet of Person Organization Fit." *Organizational Behavior and Human Decision Processes,* 1996; 68:194–207.

Dolliver, M. "A Way to Attract Workers." *Adweek New England Edition,* June 2002; 39(26):52.

Frederick, E. "Your Best Source for Finding New Employees May Be Right Beside You." *American Laundry News,* April 2002; 29(4):4.

Greco, S. "As the Talent Turns." *Inc.,* June, 2001; 23(8):88.

Hensdill, C. "Employee Recruitment and Retention Tactics." *Hotels,* March 2000; 34(3):28.

Marziliano, N. "Managing the Corporate Image and Identity: A Borderline Between Fiction and Reality." *International Studies of Management and Organization,* Fall 1998; 28(3):3.

Mitchell, T.R., Holtom, B.C., Lee, T.W., Sablynski, C.J., and Erez, M. "Why People Stay: Using Job Embeddedness to Predict Voluntary Turnover." *Academy of Management Journal,* December 2001; 44(6):1102.

Nicholson, G. "Automated Assessment at a Large Company." *Workforce,* December 2000; 79:202–204.

O'Reilly, C.W., Chatman, J., and Caldwell, D.F. "People and Organizational Culture: A Profile Comparison Approach to Person-Organization Fit." *Academy of Management Journal,* 1991; 34:487–516.

Premack, S.L., and Wanous, J.P. "A Meta-Analysis of Realistic Job Preview Experiments." *Journal of Applied Psychology,* 1985; 70(4):706–719.

Ryan, A.M., Schmit, M.J., and Johnson, R. "Attitudes and Effectiveness: Examining Relations at an Organizational Level." *Personnel Psychology,* 1996; 49:853–882.

Sabol, J. "How to Attract and Keep Employees in a Tight Job Market." *Business Journal, Supplement HR Guide,* 1999; 13(40):9.

Shoemaker, C., and Lantos, G.P. "Marketing Corporate Image." *Journal of Consumer Marketing,* 2000; 17(4/5):459.

Smith, B. "New Hires Gone Bad: Minimize Hiring Mistakes." *Business Press,* July 30, 1999; 12(14):21.

Stein, Nicholas. "Winning the War to Keep Top Talent." *Fortune Magazine*, May 2000; 132–137.

"The 100 Best Companies to Work for." *Fortune Magazine*, February 4, 2002; 72.

Toloken, S. "Software Makes Orientation Fun, Effective." *Plastics News*, January 2000; 11(49).

Wanous, J.P. *Personnel Psychology*, Winter 1980; 33(4):853.

Werbel, J.D., and Gilliland, S.W. "The Use of Person-Environment Fit in the Selection Process." *Research in Personnel and Human Resources Management*, G. Ferris (Ed.). Greenwich, Conn.: JAI Press, 1999.

"World Class Advice from Three Market Leaders" *HR Focus*, August 2000; 77(8):1.

FURTHER READING

Ahlrichs, N.S. *Competing for Talent: Key Recruitment and Retention Strategies for Becoming an Employer of Choice*. Palo Alto, Calif.: Davies-Black Publishing, 2000.

Blanchard, K.H., and Bowles, S. *Gung Ho! Turn on the People in Any Organization*. New York: William Morrow, 1997.

Bossidy, L., Charan, R., and Burck, C. *Execution: The Discipline of Getting Things Done*. New York: Crown Publishing, 2002.

Brantley, M.E., and Coleman, C. *Winning the Technology Talent War: A Manager's Guide to Recruiting and Retaining Tech Workers in a Dot-Com World*. New York: McGraw-Hill, 2001.

Coffman, C., Gonzalez-Molina, G., and Clifton, J.K. *Follow This Path: How the World's Greatest Organizations Drive Growth by Unleashing Human Potential*. New York: Warner Books, 2002.

Hiring and Keeping the Best People. Boston: Harvard Business School Press, 1999.

Johnson, M. *Talent Magnet: Getting Talented People to Work for You*. Paramus, N.J.: Prentice Hall, 2002.

McConnell, J.H. *Hunting Heads: How to Find and Keep the Best People*. Washington, D.C.: Kiplinger Books, 2000.

Peters, G. *Waltzing with the Raptors: A Practical Roadmap to Protecting Your Company's Reputation*. New York: John Wiley & Sons, 1999.

Smart, B.D. *Topgrading: How Leading Companies Win by Hiring, Coaching and Keeping the Best People*. Paramus, N.J.: Prentice Hall Press, 1999.

CHAPTER 7

Solution Set: Establishing an Appropriate Work Environment

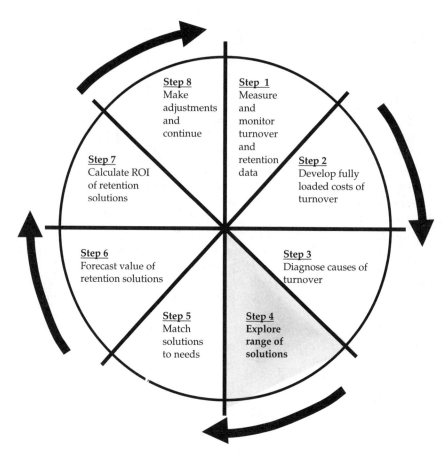

Employees need a work environment that they like and find appropriate. To satisfy this need, organizations can address a variety of solutions that focus on critical issues such as leadership, culture, job satisfaction, and life balance. Table 7-1 presents a complete list of these issues, as well as the employee needs and appropriate organizational solutions associated with these needs.

JOB SATISFACTION

Job satisfaction can be defined as the degree to which employees are content with the job that they perform. Historically, job satisfaction includes the following five factors:

Table 7-1
Employee Work Environment Needs and Organizational Solutions

Category	Need	Solution
Job satisfaction	To experience job satisfaction	Design a job that meets employee needs.
Workplace design	To have a functional, pleasant work setting	Create a professional, attractive work area that is functional and promotes efficiency and productivity.
Safety	To feel safe at work	Sustain a viable workplace safety program.
Job security	To have a secure job; to feel confident about employment continuity	Maintain a viable workforce stability and security process.
Culture	To work in a culture that supports individual values, respect, and dignity	Create and sustain a culture that provides individual values and respect.
Life balance	To work in a climate that supports a balance between work, family, and personal interests	Create family support and life balance programs.
Diversity	To be recognized as individuals regardless of differences	Build and support a fair and equitable diversity program.

- Satisfaction with the work itself
- Pay
- Opportunity for promotion
- Supervision
- Relationships with co-workers

High levels of employee retention have long been linked to job satisfaction.

Need for Adequate Job Satisfaction

A basic human need is the feeling of satisfaction in one's daily life, which includes work. Each of the five factors of job satisfaction is important to understanding the needs of employees; however, the factors may vary in importance by employees. For example, one employee might have a higher need for pay than for work satisfaction. Another employee may have a greater need for comfortable relationships with co-workers than for superior supervision. Combinations of the five factors translate into different job satisfaction needs for different employees. Some employees may need only one or two of the factors to experience job satisfaction and remain with the organization, whereas other employees might need all five or they become malcontent.

Four of the five job satisfaction factors are addressed in more detail elsewhere in this book (i.e., see Chapters 8 [Pay], and 9 [Teamwork, Professional Growth, and Leadership]). Because more detailed discussions of these four factors are provided in other areas of the book, only the factor of the work itself is discussed here in more detail.

The Work Itself

Imagine the feelings of anxiety you might feel if you were placed in a job without description of the end goal or the daily tasks. Questions such as "What should I do?" may fill the day without any perceptive progress being made. In contrast, well-designed jobs facilitate productivity and result in employee job satisfaction and retention. Good design includes giving employees proper tools and the end goal. As might be expected, the better the job is designed, the higher the productivity and the more satisfied the employee (Davenport, 1999). The following list of question aids in creating an effective solution for the work design:

- Is the job clear?
- Are the subprocesses clear and identifiable?
- Are there sufficient tools and resources to do the job?
- Does the work have task variety? Is the work repetitive? If so, how can the job be changed to allow for more variety?
- Does the work allow for some level of empowerment, input, and creativity?
- Are there incentives and rewards for goal achievement?

Measuring Job Satisfaction

Surveys, statements to leaders, and focus group discussions all indicate that high turnover is a prologue of things to come (Mathieu and Zajac, 1990). One job satisfaction survey is the Job Descriptive Index (JDI) that consists of 72 items that assess the five satisfaction factors. The JDI has been used to measure job satisfaction in more than 400 studies (Smith et al., 1989, and Nagy, 2002).

A simpler measure of job satisfaction is a single-item scale that asks one question for each of the five factors. The following is one example that uses direct questions on the single-item scale.

1. How satisfied are you with the work itself?
2. How satisfied are you with your pay?
3. How satisfied are you with your opportunity for promotion?
4. How satisfied are you with your leadership?
5. How satisfied are you with your relationships with your co-workers?

In a recent study, 207 full-time employees from a variety of organizations were polled using the JDI and the single-item scale. Both surveys predicted voluntary turnover (Nagy, 2002).

A third way to measure job satisfaction is by an open-ended questionnaire that uses a free-choice format consisting of carefully designed questions. The U.S. Department of Energy (DOE) used the open-ended questionnaire to survey 1,300 employees in two different groups: federal employees and contractors. The majority of employees responding to the questionnaire were satisfied with their jobs, and both groups identified the work itself as being an important retention factor (Tamosaitia, 2002).

Typical Solutions

Specific solutions to meeting job satisfaction needs are listed in Table 7-2 by factors. While these submeasures were not a part of the DOE study, organizing the solutions in the five areas identifies a practical application of job satisfaction solutions.

The security system distribution and marketing industry (SDM) has experienced high employee turnover. Their professionals regularly seek greener pastures, and competition with other alarm dealers and telecommunication and cable companies has increased the turnover problem. A recent discussion with 100 SDM companies and SDM employment-recruiting firms revealed that improving job satisfaction was a key solution to reducing turnover (Moss, 2000). In Table 7-3, two of the five job satisfaction factors were addressed in the solution.

Table 7-2
Solutions Identified by DOE Study

Job Satisfaction Factors	Recommendations for Improving Job Satisfaction
Work itself	• Recognize the desire for work independence and ensure that work programs encourage creativity. • Increase professional training.
Opportunity for promotion	• Review the job posting system on how people are selected for positions and use it consistently. • Discuss career progression, including job posting, training, career planning, and development.
Pay	• Provide monetary recognition to all employees. • Be cautious of potential benefit erosion. • Update and review salary comparisons.
Supervision	• Provide management training. • Reinforce values and actions desired by placing people who demonstrate desired performance characteristics in supervisory and management positions. • Guard against management creditability, which suffers from inconsistency, lack of interest in employee needs, and needs sensitivity in words and actions.
Relationships with co-workers	• Encourage teams through rewarding those who are obtaining good results.

Table 7-3
DSM Recommendations for Improving Job Satisfaction from 100 DSM Companies and Employment Recruiting Firms

Submeasurements of Job Satisfaction	SDM Recommendations
Work itself	• Equip blue collar employees with the same tools and computer equipment as used by white collar workers. • Allow employees to do the work they most enjoy. • Allow technicians to finish every job they start (technicians are process- and results-oriented).
Supervision	• Encourage leaders to ask employees how to be more efficient and productive. • Request leaders to visit technicians on site even when the job is going well. • Hold technical roundtable meetings with meals and refreshments provided. • Conduct one-on-one communication.

One recommended solution that was not a part of the SDM conference discussion involved rewards and commendations. The specific recommendation was to reward outstanding employees with week-long vacations and award banquets. The other three factors (co-worker relationships, opportunities for promotion, and pay) were not specifically mentioned as solutions during this conference (Moss, 2000).

Scheduling and Hours Worked

The restaurant industry has a concern over the lack of job satisfaction and mounting turnover, according to a survey of restaurant managers. Purdue University's Department of Restaurant, Hotel, Institutional and Tourism Management collected survey and anecdotal evidence from Purdue graduates who are leaving the industry. Job satisfaction for restaurant managers is adversely affected by the high number of hours worked and work schedules. Managers are often expected to fill in for hourly employees who fail to show up for their shift, resulting in an average workweek of 57.3 hours. In comparison, the average workweek for nonagricultural workers is

43.3 hours. Long working hours and poor scheduling for time off result in turnover (Berta, 2001).

The most successful companies in the restaurant industry schedule employees to work 5 days on and 5 days off to avoid burnout. Restaurants that have the lowest turnover and highest retention of employees use scheduling and time off as part of their retention solution (Berta, 2001).

WORKPLACE DESIGN

Workplace design describes the way the work area is organized and arranged. The work area should support employees' activities in a way that helps them be more efficient and productive. The design may be as varied as the many kinds of jobs that people perform.

Employee Need for Adequate Workplace Design

Investing in functional, well-designed workspaces not only creates an attractive, pleasing surrounding, but also helps retain employees and increase productivity. Organizations ignore workplace design at the risk of losing employees. Baby boomers and employees earning more than $35,000 are more likely to complain if they do not like their physical environment. Generation Xers and employees earning less than $35,000 are more likely to leave a job if they do not like the physical environment, rather than complain about it (*Facilities and Design Management*, 2000).

Because people spend a large portion of their lives at work, it is natural that they desire physical surroundings appropriate to their tasks. In a study on the impact of design on recruiting and retaining qualified employees, 21 percent of the respondents named the physical work environment as the top factor influencing whether a person will remain in a job or quit (*Facilities Design and Management*, October 2000.) Furthermore, employees who were pleased with their workspace were 31 percent more likely to say they were also satisfied with their jobs. Conversely, unsatisfactory physical workplaces contribute to employee dissatisfaction and turnover.

Employees who work in unsuitable work environments are often frustrated, reports the American Society of Interior Designers. Working in poor workplace conditions may lead to reduced productivity and the loss of high performers. The need for a work environment that is functional and aesthetically pleasing should also be addressed as a means to increase productivity. Employees who feel that their workplace supports their job and is aligned with the corporation's goals and image are more likely to be satisfied, work longer hours, and remain with their employer.

Functional Work Settings

An ideally designed workplace supports productivity, allows employees to communicate effectively, and is attractive. This does not mean that employees need the largest, or newest, or most expensive work surroundings. It does mean, however, that they need a functional, attractive environment in which to work. A workplace that supports functionality is the primary consideration because it provides employees with the tools, equipment, and space to accomplish their tasks. Employees also need to be able to communicate with leaders, other departments, and among themselves. Finally, employees enjoy working in a comfortable environment that is conductive to the type of work being performed. The most austere workplace can be highly functional, but unless organizations provide an aesthetically pleasing workplace, employee retention suffers.

Cramped workplaces limit productivity while spaciousness advances creativity. Space-with-a-message is what Ross and Baruzzini (R&B) sought when its business expanded beyond its workspace. A St. Louis–based design and building firm, R&B wanted a spacious workspace that would project a progressive, creative atmosphere, and identify the organization with innovative solutions to corporate workplace challenges. They chose to renovate an old vacant grocery store in a nearby suburb, Webster Groves. "This building type offered architectural opportunities including exposed trusses and an ocean of open interior space," according to their director of the architectural department. The result was a workplace design in which the company could maximize performance while feeling at ease (Richter, 2001).

Workplace designs often mirror the priorities of the organization. By placing productivity and communication first, SEI Investments of Oaks, Pennsylvania, embraced a bold, create-as-you-go design philosophy that distributes its workspace among 140 self-managed teams and lets each team arrange its space as it sees fit. All furniture is on wheels so that employees can create their own work areas, thereby building stronger team relationships (*Harvard Management Update*, 2000). The workspace design in the organization also promotes employee retention.

If an organization values communication, innovative designs can facilitate it. Several workplaces have been designed with "collision areas" where informal discussions occur and employees brainstorm new ideas. As organizations rely more on the innovations of their employees, the need for communication grows. In the last 4 years, more than 20 CEOs in Internet-related industries have rejected the traditional corner office for proximity to the team. Similarly, high-level managers of British Petroleum (the world's third largest energy company) work in offices with no walls or doors, no grand desk, no cherry-wood trim, and a more open environment. These executives prefer working side by side with the front-line employees to promote interaction between management and employees (Girion, 2001).

Another idea of the Washington, D.C.–based Greenwell Goetz Architects uses a model of "hoteling" in offices. A concierge in the reception area works like a concierge in a hotel by providing scheduling, arranging, and general information. The organization won the American Institute of Architects 2000 Honor Award for Outstanding Interiors. This workplace design is aimed at helping employees remain at work while the organization helps supply some of the services that employees typically would need outside the workplace.

Attractiveness

Each workplace is defined by its function. Whether the workspace is in a factory, warehouse, storefront, taxi cab, truck, or office, each space takes the form of its activity. Although attractiveness may be limited by the function of the work, even the most functional work-spaces can be designed to increase attractiveness. Even gravel pits can be lined with lawn and trees. Factories can have attractive sound-proof break areas. Warehouses can have color-coded aisles for variety and efficiency. Cabs of trucks and office cubicles can be personalized and made attractive so that employees experience an appeal for their surroundings.

Of course, a dazzling first (and lasting) impression is paramount to many organizations and their clients. The public relations firm, Parker Le Pla of Seattle, has an open-air workspace complete with trees, café tables, and a fountain. Personalized work areas line the outer walls so that everyone can have a view of the central park—and a corresponding outlook of comfort and stability. This organization's workplace design is aimed at providing an attractive space in which employees want to work and remain employed.

Safety

Safety is a hidden part of job comfort and satisfaction, yet it is only noticed when it is missing. The terrorist acts of September 11 have changed the way employees view on-the-job security, with more concern over the safety of the workplace. These safety concerns can be addressed by prevention, developing safety programs, training, use of consultants, and executive commitment to a safety program.

Need for Safe Work Environment

One of the basic needs of all people is to feel safe. After September 11, safety is more important than ever. More organizations realize that they must be proactive about safety and security. The American Society of Safety Engineers' president agrees, "In the past, a lot of the growth in the safety profession was regulatory driven, but today it just makes good business sense to protect people in the workplace." (*US Newswire*, 2002) Failing to provide an environment where employees can feel safe on the job is one of the fastest ways to lose good employees.

Part of the design of the September 11 attacks was to terrorize people at work. Understandably, people began experiencing anxiety and stress about safety. Postal workers were concerned over the heighten risks from anthrax, and many personal and business travelers stayed off airplanes. Many government and private organizations looked critically at their existing security infrastructure. The flight attendant's union quickly evaluated workplace safety and, on national network news, openly criticized the airlines for not being rigorous enough in creating new safety measures to guard against terrorism. America's strong response against terrorism was partly due to the understanding that safety and security are essential for workers to perform their jobs with confidence.

On-the-job accidents are nothing new. Prior to September 11, 16 workers lost their lives daily in on-the-job accidents in America. Every hour, 650 workers experience an injury or on-the-job illness. According to the National Institute for Occupation Safety and Health, in 1999, nearly 900 people were killed by violence in the workplace. The majority of these incidents occurred in high, risk industries, such as law enforcement where the workers assume a level of risk that comes with the profession. However, if employees perceive the workplace is less safe because of management problems, they are more likely to be dissatisfied and leave. People who feel unsafe at work also have higher intentions to quit (Hall, 2001).

Accident Prevention

Most safety and security organizations emphasize prevention. When employees feel the organization cares about them, they will be more likely to be satisfied and stay. Creating a viable safety program requires that the organization understands what employees value and what they perceive as the top threats to security and safety.

Safety in the workplace starts at the front door. One important solution to workplace security and safety is the implementation of background checks for all new employees and current employees who have not had background checks. This will eliminate individuals with criminal records or those who have been found to falsify statements regarding their backgrounds prior to potential violence. The organization should be open with their policy about background checks, substance abuse, and so forth in order to promote an atmosphere of safety.

Safety Programs

The final project of any safety program is a written safety and security statement. Employers who do not create and follow a written safety document have a potential civil liability. The punitive damages can be extreme. Federal Occupational Safety and Health Administration (OSHA) fines are leveled for failure to respond to signs that an employee may turn to violence in the workplace (Crawford, 2001). Implementing and following safety procedures, as a turnover solution, is an excellent way to protect investment in human capital.

Many organizations use a safety committee (or branch, division) to develop and implement safety programs and training. The safety committee can tackle policy statements, roles and responsibilities, program and meeting format, and memberships in safety groups. Safety committees can develop programs in hazardous materials, inspections, information areas, record keeping, and training.

The government of Polk County, Iowa, is an example of an organization that supports employee safety utilizing its human resources (HR) department, law enforcement, and records of safety losses and claims. The county's risk manager states that it is important to bring as many different experts to the committee table as possible

(Crawford, 2001). The result of the safer workplace will be employees who can feel confident about safety issues at work and less inclined to leave over safety concerns.

Safety Training

In one organization, an employee was installing a piece of sheet metal using a cordless screw gun to fasten it in place. As he secured the piece to the floor, a screw penetrated a 120-volt nonmetallic sheathed cable that electrocuted the employee (Hall, 2001). Every time someone dies at work, we ask ourselves, "What could have been done to prevent this accident?" Usually, the answer is *better training*. Training programs are one key solution to the employee's need for safety. One company that improved its safety record through training is Alliance Steel Construction Co. in Oklahoma City. They adopted training programs to show employees how to safely and properly operate equipment and perform job duties while reducing their personal safety risks. They also received training on such things as how to lift properly (Erickson, 2001).

Organized training for employees is valuable for reducing accidents. Training should be adapted to each organization's priorities and concerns, with courses in such areas as general safety principles, first aid and Cardiopulmonary Resuscitation, security, bomb scares, fire escape routes, machinery safety, level of dress, response to violence, and so on.

Use of Safety Consultants

Most companies are using safety professionals to full potential because people want safe work environments, according to the American Society of Safety Engineers (ASSE). A national ASSE membership survey shows an increase in the value of workplace safety by employers. This is due in part to concern over high employee turnover rates. The results of this survey was taken from a national survey of ASSE members. ASSE is a 90-year-old nonprofit organization that represents more than 30,000 occupational safety health and environmental professionals worldwide. Although the poor economy has resulted in some layoffs for safety professionals working within organizations, this trend is changing (*US Newswire*, 2002).

Safety consultants are expensive, and some experts charge as much as $1,000 per half day of consulting on implementing a safety program. However, the Oklahoma Department of Labor's OSHA

Program offers consulting free to companies with no more than 250 employees at the work site and no more than 500 employees in the entire company. The program is confidential, nonpunitive, and voluntary. While all companies in the state are required to adhere to OSHA's guidelines, those that can show that they are following a well-designed safety program are allowed to have 2-year exemptions from OSHA's general inspections. This program saved one company in Oklahoma, V.E. Enterprises in Ardmore, at least $100,000 in workers' compensation insurance costs because of their use of the free consulting and improvements in safety.

Executive Commitment to Safety

An organization's commitment to safety is apparent to employees, especially the company's response to incidents and accidents. In the aftermath of disastrous accidents or security breaches, organizations are judged by their response and their past behavior that may have contributed to the problem. Policies for organization's responses to safety issues should be concrete—in writing if possible. These policies may encompass such areas as accident investigation, disciplinary programs outlining sanctions, and a policy for employee reporting of unsafe conditions.

One way for organizations to promote safety is by adopting and enforcing zero workplace violence policies. Employees who see that a supervisor or company refuses to take action against a potentially violent employee will not remain with a company. Discharging employees who violate the zero tolerance policies is one way to help protect employees at work (Harris, 2001).

JOB SECURITY

Job security provides employees with a sense of stability from their jobs and the organizations they work for that allows them an opportunity to make plans, buy homes, and achieve a sense of confidence in their own future. If there is a lack of security—even a perception of insecurity—employees may leave the organization.

Need for Job Security

Employees need to feel they are working at a secure job that will be there for them in years to come. In an era of corporate downsizing, mergers, and acquisitions, job stability is a critical investment strategy in human capital. Lack of job stability diminishes the employees' sense of attachment and responsibility to the organization (Ashford, Lee, and Bobko, 1989). As a critical investment, stability should enhance retention of employees (Shaw, Delery, Jenkins, and Gupta, 1998).

Despite the extensive layoffs during 2001 and 2002, today's organization is faced with a future of fewer trained employees. This is because the supply of workers cannot keep pace with the demand. To respond to this worker shortage, organizations have a variety of options for increasing job security and, thereby, retention.

Various Levels of Job Security

Various levels of job security are found in organizations. The highest level, or full job security, is possible with the federal government and very few other organizations. Most organizations operate within the marketplace and are subject to profitability cycles. In many industries, job security is almost nonexistent. In place of security, the employee relies on the concept of *employability*, or the ability to quickly find another job. In industries where it may not be possible to keep good employees in the short term, there are strategies to treat the departing employees well enough to rehire them at a future date.

Although job security may be difficult, if not impossible, to find in the private sector, the U.S. government offers nearly full job security because the federal government is not as vulnerable to economic downturns as is the private sector. Aside from occasional reassignment, a government employee is fairly insulated from being laid off. Government employees have excellent benefits, pension plans, health care, and flexible work hours (Benjamin, 2002). "Government jobs are for people looking for secure employment with good salary potential," says the author of the *Book of U.S. Government Jobs*. Many individuals who desire such job security work for the government. However, other private organizations also offer high levels of job security.

Guaranteed Employment

A few organizations have provided full job security to employees. Southwest Airlines has not laid off one employee in its 31-year history, and AFLAC Insurance has had no layoffs in its 47-year history (Benjamin, 2002). Both organizations have experienced profits at a time when their competitors have not, and Southwest Airlines has a turnover rate as low as 9 percent for entry-level employees, which is far below the industry average (Stein, 2000). Another company that values job security is SC Johnson, which has never laid off a permanent employee in its 116 years. These organizations assign other work for employees to do during lean times (Benjamin, 2002).

Changing Employment Pay Rates

Faced with reduced demand for products and inevitable budget cuts, some employers avoid layoffs by keeping employees working at different jobs that may be lower paying than the job that the employee performs during strong economic times. In the company's 15-year history, Nucor Steel-Girder Plant in Indiana faced unprecedented challenges: orders fell 30 percent, and only 12 of the 390 employees are able to work at their usual welding jobs. Employees are given other work to do rather than being laid off. Nucor sends its welders to do other odd jobs and cleaning for $10 an hour. Although this wage is down from the $20 to $25 an hour that Nucor's welders earn, the company believes that its practice of providing job security will pay off in the long run. Nucor asks staff to put in lots of overtime during boom periods. Even though it costs $10,000 to $15,000 a day to keep the plant workers in Indiana busy, the HR vice president states, "We would only have a layoff if the survivorship of the company was at stake." (Benjamin, 2002)

Sabbaticals

Organizations can offer sabbaticals to employees in which both agree to resume their relationship in better times. When sabbaticals are partially paid, the employee will feel loyal to the organization, while the organization receives the benefit of retaining a trained employee in the future. Accenture, the former consulting arm of Andersen Worldwide, offers certain employees the opportunity to take a voluntary sabbatical. In 2001, the organization was forced to cut 600 support staff jobs but offered about 1,000 employees a partially paid sabbatical that paid the employee 20 percent salary, plus benefits, and let the individual keep the work phone number, laptop, and e-mail address. Employee Judie Jones jumped at the chance: "This gives me the security of knowing I'll have a job when I come back." Accenture hopes that the sabbatical program will ensure the needed talent when the economy turns around. Accenture's managing partner in charge of internal operations said, "This is a way to cut costs that gives us the ability to hang onto people we spent so much time recruiting and training." (Bernstein, 2001)

Employability

When organizations are not able to guarantee long-term employment, they are able to increase employee loyalty by supporting their employees' employability. Organizations can help employees ready themselves for their next job or role by providing training, assignments, and roles that help build employment skills. Organization can provide training for employees in new skills and coordinate the training to offer certifications and licenses. They can make available educational initiatives as tuition assistance (all or part), workshop training, and time off to attend classes.

In exchange for the employability security that an organization can provide its employees, employees will work harder and remain with the organization longer, according to a Kansas State University researcher (Oss, 2001). Companies that want to provide employability should concentrate on increasing the roles and responsibilities of its employees. Additionally, employee empowerment, training, and development should also be increased. Such actions create positions, which have employability security and also have enhanced job roles. "New supervisory skills, internal performance reporting, real-time employee communications infrastructure, new compensation systems, restructured employee education initiatives, and enhanced cost accounting capabilities are all necessary elements in moving the employer and employee relationship from one of job security to one of employability security." (Oss, 2001)

Severance Packages that Encourage Employee Return

When a layoff becomes inevitable, organizations can still look for ways to promote loyalty while easing the laid-off employees' burden. When other expenses are cut before jobs, employees sense organizational loyalty. Severance packages can contain more than money. Retention of health benefits, e-mail accounts, and so forth can help employees find new jobs and give them the impression that the organization wants them back. When Charles Schwab & Co., Inc.'s income began to deteriorate in the fall of 2000, it cut back on travel and entertainment expenses, followed by top-executive pay cuts of

50 percent for the company's two co-CEO's, 20 percent for executive vice presidents, 10 percent for senior vice presidents, and 5 percent for vice presidents. The company also encouraged employees to take unused vacation and to take unpaid leaves of up to 20 days. In February and March of 2001, three Fridays were designated as voluntary days off without pay. In the spring of 2001, Schwab did announce 2,000 layoffs, but to promote job security (even in the face of layoffs), the organization gave severance packages of $7,500 as a "hire back" bonus to any employee who will be rehired by the organization within 18 months. "We felt the markets will turn at some point, and the cost of hiring people back with the bonus is small compared to what it would be to pay for recruiting and retraining new employees," says the HR vice president (Bernstein, 2001).

Culture

Culture can be described as the identity of the corporation or the glue that holds an organization together. The culture of a firm is the sum of the company's values, support programs, policies, practices, and attitudes. Culture is different for different organizations. An advertising organization has a different culture than a tire manufacturer; a government agency has a different culture than a sole proprietorship. Even the branches of the military have different cultures that revolve around the same mission, to defend our country. Because one defense is from the ground while the other is from the sea, the Army, Navy, Air Force, and Marine cultures have become distinct from each other.

Organizational Culture

A positive culture helps employees stay with the organization. The organization must ensure that its working environment and culture meet employee needs. Social support and leadership are part of the culture solution, as well as ensuring that the employee can maintain a good work-life balance. Recognition and rewards, along with training and career progress, are part of creating a culture that is committed to the employee. Valero Energy of San Antonio, Texas, has developed a culture of caring and support for its employees and has been able to keep turnover rates low. An $8-billion dollar utility company with nearly 3,000 employees, Valero's mission statement encourages workers to be leaders in the community. Valero has donated $5,000 to employees who were recent flood victims, and its volunteer council organized teams to clean up flood debris. It donates heavily to the United Way sharing program. Valero hires candidates who fit into this philanthropic culture, based on rigorous assessment tests. The Valero management lets employees know they are appreciated. The CEO visits his facilities, eats lunch in the employee cafeteria, and makes himself available to his employees to promote a culture of caring. "People are smart," says the CEO, "they know when management is sincere." (Stein, 2000)

Need for Supportive Organizational Culture

Why does one organization succeed while another goes bankrupt? If both companies produce quality services at similar, competitive prices, the answer to this question may stem from the organizational culture (Joyner, 2001). The culture of some organizations and industries often drives employees away. Understanding corporate culture and using it as a retention strategy has become the subject of much research. Culture can be used as a key retention strategy. It helps employees feel connected to their company and their job. Progressive companies leverage their corporate culture to create a workforce whose values and skills align closely with the organization's driving purpose.

Understanding and using the company culture can make the difference between success and failure (Wishna, 2000). Corporate cultures that treat people with respect retain employees. One industry that is notoriously plagued with high turnover is the restaurant industry. Turnover for the restaurant industry, as a whole, is around 100 percent annually, according to the National Restaurant Association. Organizational culture is the most often-cited reason for turnover in the restaurant industry, including strained relationships with the boss or co-workers, unfair treatment, and harassment. "It's not rocket science why people leave us," says HR senior vice president for Carlson Restaurants Worldwide (parent company of TGI Friday's). "The newest generation of workers has different needs than those of us who are managers had when we were entry-level workers. We've got to be prepared for making changes around that." Every time an organization wants to change, it does so within the context of its culture (Wishna, 2000).

Selecting Employees to Fit the Culture

Organizations can take advantage of the interview and selection process to ensure they hire employees who match their organizational culture. Candidates most likely to fit into the organizational cultural can be identified by using specific tools to assess whether the employee meets job requirements, possesses the skills necessary to do the job, and to determine whether the employee has desired specific attributes (such as judgment ability). After more than 10 years of analyzing the employee behavior, Southwest Airlines' HR department developed specific needs and requirements for each job and for shared attributes, such as common sense, judgment, and decision-making skills. In 1 year, Southwest hired more than 5,000 new employees from 70,000 candidates they interviewed from an initial pool of 160,000 applicants. The organization feels that their hiring process, with specific emphasis on hiring for both a job fit and cultural fit, has resulted in a 9 percent turnover rate for entry-level positions and 6 percent turnover rate for higher level management—a turnover rate that is the lowest in the industry (Stein, 2000).

Employee Involvement

Organizations can develop a culture that is responsive to changing times and values employee input. By valuing employee input and listening to employee concerns, organizations can make improvements in culture and, thereby, employee retention. Building supply retailer Home Depot prides itself on having a culture that is built from the inside out and values employee input even from the most junior associates. By placing floor employees' input on par with management teams' input, the organization keeps a better pulse of customer needs. Home Depot also demonstrates confidence in employees by using the term "associate" to suggest an equity-based culture. These practices have resulted in a turnover rate that is 20 percent below the average turnover rate for the retail industry (Stein, 2000).

Positive Communication

Employee retention is influenced by organizational communication. Organizations that want to improve retention place a great deal of emphasis on ensuring that communication is positive and keep employees informed of all organizational issues and changes. Communication forums include the use of town hall meetings, open-door policies, and tolerance for vigorous discussions in which everyone need not agree. The overriding goal of positive communication is to ensure that people are heard, ideas are shared, and differences are tolerated.

OmniCom, a New York City–based advertising and marketing services organization with more than 43,000 employees, is a huge company with a commitment that supports internal communication and cooperation. Its ad agencies have developed popular ad campaigns for Budweiser, Pepsi, Visa, and Anheuser-Busch. Despite having ad agencies that can often compete for the same client, OmniCom has kept internal communication open and positive by creating a culture that supports cooperation *and* competition. The company holds "jazz" sessions that bring together CEOs from their various business units to network and exchange ideas. They feed off each other's ideas, enabling all the embedded knowledge in the room to cascade into different business units. Additionally, the organization has created a 12-member management team to ensure that the environment remains frictionless. OmniCom's turnover rate of 18 percent is nearly 50 percent below the industry average (Stein, 2000).

Welcoming Programs

Welcoming programs focus on making the first impression as positive as possible. When new employees arrive, they find the e-mail, phone, and other systems they need already up and running. An orientation session teaches them how to navigate the company. Each new employee is assigned a sponsor to make sure that the initial experience in the organization is as positive as possible. Sponsors, who are not bosses, are assigned to help guide the employee through the first few weeks of employment and assist the individual in understanding the corporation's culture. In this age of mergers and acquisitions, no one does a better job of integrating new businesses and acclimatizing new employees than Cisco. Over a 1-year period, Cisco acquired more than 20 companies—and lost only 7 percent of its employees. So how does the company do it? Cisco will not consider acquiring a company unless the culture is similar to its own, according to the HR director. Over 1 year, the organization lost only 7 percent of its employees and feels that making employees feel welcome, from day one, is key to its retention success (Battey, 2000).

Annual Surveys on Culture

Caring about employees' needs is one way to improve retention because it demonstrates an organizational culture committed to employee welfare. Annual surveys can assess an organization's culture in many areas. The most important part of the process is the response of management to the top survey findings of employee concerns. Although no single survey can be used for every organization, some of the topics of assessment reflect categories in this book, including pay, job satisfaction, safety, diversity, and life balance.

Because surveys are often anonymous (i.e., employees are not required to identify themselves on the survey), the organization can receive uncensored, honest feedback directly. Such information is valuable in helping address employee concerns because the information is highly reliable. When organizations depend strictly on obtaining information through managers, there is the possibility of having concerns censured or sanitized because management might unintentionally or intentionally pass on employee feedback that is not in management's best interest. Surveys can assess employee responses on a systematic basis, perhaps even several times over a year, to determine whether improvement has taken place. Surveys can become a means through which management takes the pulse of employees on a variety of issues within specific departments or the entire organization.

Three financial services organizations that use yearly surveys as part of their cultural and retention efforts are Allstate, American Express Traveller's Cheque, and Discover Card Services. These organizations use surveys and respond to employee needs to retain employees. In 1 year, Discover Card Services experienced a significant improvement in employee retention in one operations center through implementing retention improvement strategies that emphasized welcoming programs and positive communication techniques.

Life Balance

Although employees have responsibility to achieve organizational goals, they have lives away from their work. *Life balance* refers to the need of employees to balance personal life and work. When organizations support the employee's nonwork activities, balance is achieved, and employees are more satisfied and loyal.

Need for Life Balance

When work interferes with family time and relationships, there is a higher absenteeism rate and turnover than when the individual is able to balance family needs with the support of organizational programs (Yardley, 1995). Studies show that employees who perceive family support from their supervisors and organizations are more committed to the organization and tend to remain with their employer (Jahn, 1998). One company saved an estimated $70 million per year as a result of low turnover (Schu, 2001), which is attributed to their benefits that include on-site subsidized child care centers, a health care facility, a fitness center, and a swimming pool.

People value organizations that have family-friendly values. In a study of more than 500 employees from different organization, family support programs were important for creating a work environment that helped retention (Allen, 2001). How the employee perceives this support is also a factor that significantly predicts job satisfaction, organizational commitment, and intention to leave (Hubley, 1999). Employees may be unaware they are in need of family support programs, according to a study that evaluated stress and family issues and their impact on the organization. In studies of HR managers, executives, and employees conducted by Development Dimensions International, Bridgeville, Pennsylvania, the top job-related value was the ability to balance work and personal life. Interestingly enough, people did not report that lack of ability to balance work and personal life was a reason for voluntary turnover, but 47 percent of individuals left the organization because of high stress and burnout, which may stem from an inability to manage personal and professional life.

Women with children form a significant portion of the workforce, and attracting them to the job market may require employers to offer more family support programs. The chairman of JC Penney said, "For most of our lifetimes, people have had to adjust their lives to the schedules of employers. Now employers will have to become more flexible." (Bernstein, 2002)

Part-Time Work and Flextime Schedules

One way for organizations to help employees balance family needs and work is by offering part-time work and flextime schedules. Part-time work and flextime benefit both the organization and the employee because these programs reduce absenteeism and turnover and allow people who cannot, or do not want to, work full time an opportunity to be employed. Such individuals may include disabled employees, older employees, students, and mothers and fathers desiring more time with their children. The number of part-time professionals in the United States has expanded. In 1989 there were

3 million part-time employees, in 1997 that figure climbed to 4.5 million and today, there are an estimated 6 million part-time employees. An estimated 70 percent of organizations employ part-time professionals who once were full time. According to a study by Catalyst, 46 percent of respondents who had switched from full-time to part-time work reported an increase in productivity, morale, commitment to the company, and retention.

Flexible work options, such as part-time employment and job sharing, are becoming increasing attractive to employees. Flextime, for example, has become the most popular flexible work arrangement and results in a bonus to employers and employees alike. The solution allows full-time employees to work at convenient times and offers employers a low-cost method of providing personal time off, extending service hours (without overtime pay), and reducing absenteeism and turnover.

CIGNA Corp., which has businesses in health care, insurance, and financial services, has discovered that by letting employees work part time or in a compressed work week with full benefits saves money by reducing turnover, lowering training and recruitment costs. Of CIGNA's 37,000 employees, 12,000 work part time, a third of them in professional and management positions, and any employee working more than 24 hours a week receives full benefits.

Family Support Options

Companies have found they can increase productivity, revenue, or both by as much as 20 percent simply by implementing a work/life balance program (Withers, 2001). Ten firms were profiled in a 2-year study by Work in America Institute (WAI, Scarsdale, N.Y.), a nonprofit research and membership organization. Although turnover/retention was not a factor in the study, they found that companies using life balance programs to address employee's personal needs improved performance in areas of absenteeism, customer service, overtime, stress, flexibility, collaboration, innovation, and creativity. Family support program solutions include the following:

- Flextime or changing an individual daily work schedule to leave time for outside activities. Some organizations allow employees to accrue comp time that can be used when partial days off are needed.
- On-site day care for children allows employees to feel they are never far from their children. A modification of this solution is

sick child day care, either on-site or off-site, and may be necessary to reduce absenteeism.

- Nursing mothers' rooms may be necessary if day care is on-site.
- Sick child leave allows employees to use personal sick leave to take care of ill children.
- Elderly care insurance is a form of insurance that pays for nursing home care or elder day care for dependents of employees in the event that the employee's dependents become unable to care for themselves.
- Maternity and parental leave offers paid-for leave for several weeks following the birth of a baby; progressive organizations allow both men and women equal time off for the birth or adoption of a child.
- Sabbaticals are sometimes offered to allow employees to attend to family issues with guaranteed employment when returning. Disasters, death, accidents, and turmoil can happen to any family, and the support of the organization will transfer into long-term loyalty.
- Exercise areas, such as weight rooms, swimming pools, or merely walking paths, are part of the life balance approach that also mixes with organizational culture.

Before investing in family support programs, organizations should assess the specific needs of their employees. Surveys are a way of pinpointing which programs are desired. Prior to implementation, each benefit should be studied and reviewed to ensure that it is practical and cost-effective. Assessing the specific needs of employees identifies what kinds of benefits to put in the organization's family support programs. Additionally, it helps ensure that the organization creates well-balanced programs.

Balanced Programs

Because culture and employee demographics differ, each organization will differ in its life balance program. JC Penney's solution was to offer more family support programs, including flexible hours, part-time work, on-site day care, and sick child backup care.

Striving to improve a dismal turnover rate and boost employees' job satisfaction, Cross Country Staffing, a medical staffing company in Boca Raton, Florida, embarked on a series of improvements that culminated in its being named one of the best 100 companies for working mothers by *Working Women* magazine. By listening to the needs of its 80-percent female corporate staff, many of whom were working mothers, Cross Country implemented family support programs that helped reduce a turnover rate that was up to 80 percent at its high point and helped the business to grow. The family support programs included allowing employees to share jobs, telecommute, and have flexible schedules. All the programs were successful: "The turnover rate is in the low double digits and the company rarely loses employees to voluntary attrition," according to the president of Cross Country. "I found that people were more focused on work, that they redoubled their efforts and made sure they worked well."(Corzo, 2000)

SAS Institute has an attractive program combining family support programs, benefits, and life balance in order to retain employees in the highly competitive information technology industry. Its headquarters boast four subsidized child care facilities, a health care facility, a 55,000-square-foot fitness center complete with swimming pool, dry cleaning pickup and delivery, massage, and a hair salon. Employees at other offices enjoy subsidized day care and health club memberships. Break centers offer free pastries, six different kinds of crackers, fruit baskets, soda, coffee, tea, juice, and chocolate. Although seemingly extravagant, each benefit is studied for cost-effectiveness before it is adopted. This company saved more than $70 million a year as the result of low turnover as estimated by researcher Jeffrey Pfeiffer (Schu, 2001). SAS received a *Workforce Optimas Award* for general excellence in 2000 and has experienced steady growth. The CEO commented, "You can pay that money to employees in the form of benefits, or you can pay headhunters and corporate trainers to fund the revolving door of people coming in and out. To me it is a no-brainer."

DIVERSITY

At present, diversity programs are based not just on issues of race and gender. Today's organizations must include all types of employees, including the elderly (now joining the workforce in increasing numbers) and those who are physically and mentally challenged. All employees want to experience a workplace that has tolerance for each person, regardless of their differences. Diversity can have many meanings—almost as many as the number of employees that are in any given company.

Diversity can be defined as the sum of all the ways individual employees are different. For example, one employee may have a higher knowledge base in a specific skill set than another, or one individual might have greater talents in communication than another. The employee's identity is sometimes based on being a member of a diverse group. Identity diversity refers to how an employee describes himself or herself and how others may view that same employee. Employee identity may be based on differences in gender, religion, age, race, sexual orientation, physical challenges, and ethnicity.

Need for a Diverse Work Environment

A tolerance and acceptance of a diverse work environment is important because employees from all backgrounds and cultures are needed for organizations to be successful. A lack of tolerance and acceptance of diversity not only negatively impacts the employees who are considered as being different, but it negatively affects those who see inequitable treatment. Employees will not long remain in an organization in which they feel preferential treatment is given to one group of employees. Fairness and acceptance of people from every background and culture expands the organization's labor pool. As the labor pool shrinks in the years to come, being able to provide a work environment in which all kinds of employees can thrive (regardless of age, gender, or ethnicity) will be a competitive edge for organizations. Additionally, being an employer of choice when it comes to diversity issues helps organizations avoid nonproductive time addressing diversity complaints.

Diversity Policies

Organizations should establish policies and practices regarding their encouragement of diverse workforces. These policies respond to the various identities of employees within the organization and usually make statements regarding the equitable treatment of all employees. These policies may be a part of the organization's mission statement or specific goals. Regardless of where the policies are housed, the intent should be to encourage and promote diversity throughout the entire organization. An employee handbook is often used to state an organization's diversity policy. For example, Allstate insurance company gives each employee a booklet, *The Allstate Partnership*, that identifies what the employee and Allstate can expect from one another. Within this handbook are three explicit statements related to diversity. Employees are expected to exhibit no bias in interactions, promote an environment that is inclusive and free from bias, and foster dignity and respect (Wah, 1999).

Diversity Programs

Diversity programs are implemented by some organizations to both retain employees and assist them in experiencing growth and development. Some programs include creation of performance models, which require equitable treatment of all employees. Development plans, training, job assignments, and career advancement can all be used to improve how all employees, including those members of diverse groups, are treated. Allstate developed such an employee program and builds diversity into its performance model. Coupled with Allstate's performance model is an individualized development plan for each employee. Each employee is given an individualized development plan to support career development. Career development and succession planning are the additional elements of Allstate's diversity strategy. Diverse employees are given training and opportunities to help them advance in their careers. In succession planning, Allstate looks for both outside candidates and employees to fill key assignments. If a hiring manager cannot find enough diverse employees to apply for a specific position, development plans will be put into place so that diverse candidates are available at a future time. Both classroom training and job assignments are used to prepare candidates for succession planning. This requires long-range planning and a financial commitment to the diversity program, but Allstate is committed to making such an investment in diversity and retention (Wah, 1999).

In focus group settings or in one-on-one discussions, employees are asked about their own work experiences. These discussions can focus on both positive and negative experiences without prompting employees to feel that management is concentrating on just the poor treatment of diverse employees. It is important to determine if the outcome experienced by the diverse group is the same as the outcome experienced by the majority in the organization. When the assessment has been made, a program can be developed to address issues.

Leadership Practices

Accepting and encouraging diversity in the workplace is also shown through organizational practices and top executive leadership. Through role modeling, the leader establishes acceptable practices, which other employees can see and emulate. As part of the leader's behavior, managers need to be willing to investigate complaints and negative employee experiences. The willingness of leaders to investigate reports of bias and prejudice demonstrates the organization's value for that employee and the talent that the individual brings to the company.

Targeting Specific Populations

One way to recruit a diverse workforce is to respond to the needs of diverse employees. If an organization wants to retain more female employees, flexible work arrangements might be implemented to allow for mothers to be home to take care of their children. Ernst and Young implemented a cultural program to attract more women.

Over the past 5 years, it has doubled the number of minorities in its organization with nearly half of its workforce being women (15,000 of 33,000). Because of these efforts, Ernst and Young has a great reputation for being sensitive to the issues that some women in the workforce experience. "But, it has taken a few years and a range of initiatives to achieve it," says national director at Ernst and Young's Office for Retention. "Through initiatives like mentoring, networking, and flexible work arrangements, we have successfully retained women." (*globalhr*, 2001).

Recruiting diverse employees is a part of many organizations' employee strategies, including Ford Motor Company. Ford recruits prospective employees at universities and gives special attention to disability groups within the local community. "To reach diverse communities, we're doing things like targeting universities with a higher percentage of women and minority groups, as well as getting involved with disability groups and local communities," says the European diversity director at Ford. "By making these links, we're expanding the pool that we can fish in for our future talent." (*globalhr*, 2001).

FINAL THOUGHTS

This chapter furthered the discussion of employee needs and solutions begun in the previous chapter. It presented the essentials necessary for an acceptable work environment. It explored issues such as leadership, job satisfaction, workplace design, safety, security, culture, life balance, and diversity. The chapter examined a variety of solutions that would ensure employees have the supportive and safe surroundings they need to be productive on the job.

REFERENCES

Abrashoff, M.D. "Retention Through Redemption." *Harvard Business Review,* February 2001:137–141.

Allen, T.D. "Family-Supportive Work Environments: The Role of Organizational Perceptions." *Journal of Vocational Behavior,* June 2001; 58(3):414–435.

"American Society of Safety Engineers' Economic Downturn Survey Finds Employer Increase in Realizing Value of Workplace Safety." *US Newswire,* January 24, 2002.

Ashford, S.J., Lee, C., and Bobko, P. "Content, Causes, and Consequences of Job Insecurity: A Theory-Based Measure and Substantive Test." *Academy of Management Journal,* 1989; 32:803–829.

Battey, J. "Retaining Your Most Valuable Assets." *InfoWorld,* July 24, 2000; 22(30):46.

Benjamin, M. "Jobs Built to Last." *US News and World Report*: *Career Guide 2002,* February 15, 2002.

Bernstein, A. "America's Future: The Human Factor." *Business Week,* August 27, 2001:118–122.

Bernstein, A. "Too Many Workers Not For Long," *Business Week,* May 20, 2002.

Berta, D. "Job Satisfaction the Key to Low Turnover." *Nation's Restaurant News,* June 18, 2001; 35(25):18.

Breuer, N.L. "Shelf Life." *Workforce,* August 2000:29–31.

Buckingham, M., and Coffman, C. *First, Break all the Rules.* New York: Simon and Schuster, 1999.

Corzo, C. "Boca Raton, Fla.–Based Medical Staffing Firm Puts Brakes on High Turnover Rate." The *Miami Herald,* Sept. 11, 2000.

Crawford, E. "A Safe Place." *Des Moines Business Record,* February 26, 2001; 17(9):10.

Davenport, Tom, *Human Capital: What It Is and Why People Invest in It.* San Francisco, California: Jossey-Bass Publishers, 1999.

Dobbs, K. "Train Your Managers." *Training,* August 2000:62–66.

Erickson, P.B. "Oklahoma Program Promotes Worker Safety." *The Daily Oklahoman,* September 23, 2001.

Foust, D., Northington, D., Conlin, M., and Wallace, C. "Wooing the Worker." *Business Week,* May 22, 2000; 3682:44.

"From the Editor's Desk." *Harvard Management Update,* May 2000; 5(5):11.

Girion, L. "Office Design." *Los Angeles Times,* May 13, 2001.

Hall, J. "Does Your Safety Program Go Far Enough?" *Air Conditioning Heating and Refrigeration News*, June 11, 2001; 213(6):31.

Harris, J. "What Do You Know?" *Business Wire News, Hawaii Business*, July 2001; 47(1):61.

Henry, L., and Henry, J. "Leading with Soul: Retaining Employees." *The Physician Executive*, January/February 2002:50–53.

Hensdill, C. "Employee Recruitment and Retention Tactics." *Hotels*, March 2000; 34(3):28.

Hubley, J. "Organizational Justice and the Perceived Fairness of Work-Family Programs and Policy." *Dissertation Abstracts International: Section B: The Sciences and Engineering*, October 1999; 60(4-B):1896.

Jahn, E.W. "The Impact of Perceived Organizational and Supervisory Family Support on Affective and Continuance Commitment: A Longitudinal and Multi-Level Analysis." *Dissertation Abstracts International: Section A: Humanities and Social Sciences*, July 1998; 59(1-A):0237.

Joyner, J. "Corporate Culture Defines Success." *Computing Canada*, May 18, 2001; 27(11):26.

Kaye, B., and Jordan-Evans, S. *Love 'Em or Lose 'Em: Getting Good People to Stay*. San Francisco, California: Berrett-Koehler Publishers, 1999.

Mathieu, J., and Zajac, D. "A Review and Meta-Analysis of the Antecedents, Correlates, and Consequences of Organizational Commitment." *Psychological Bulletin*, 1990; 108:171–194.

Moss, B. "Chain of Loyalty." *SDM: Security Distributing and Marketing*, December 2000; 30(15):79.

Nagy, M.S. "Using a Single-Item Approach to Measure Facet Job Satisfaction." *Journal of Occupational and Organizational Psychology*, March 2002; 75(1):77.

Oss, M.E. "Job Security vs. Employability Security." *Behavioral Health Management*, March/April 2001; 21(2):6.

Richter, C. "Workplace Design: A Laboratory for Inventiveness." *Journal for Quality and Participation*, Summer 2001; 24(2):52.

Schu, J. "Even in Hard Times, SAS Keeps Its Culture in Tact." *Workforce*, October 2001; 80(10):21.

Shaw, J.D., Delery, J.E., Jenkins, G.D., Jr., and Gupta, N. "An Organization Level Analysis of Voluntary and Involuntary Turnover." *Academy of Management Journal*, 1998; 41(5):511–525.

Smith, P.C., Balzer, W., Josephson, H.I., Lovell, S.E., Paul, K.B., Reilly, B.A., Reilly, C.E., and Whalen, M.A. *Users' Manual for the Job Descriptive Index (JDI) and the Job in General (JIG) Scales*. Bowling Green, Ohio: Bowling Green State University, 1989.

Stein, N. "Winning the War to Keep Top Talent." *Fortune Magazine*, May 2000; 132–137.

Tamosaitia, W., and Schwenker, M. "Recruiting and Retaining Technical Personnel at a Contractor-Operated Government Site." *Engineering Management Journal*, March 2002; 14(1):29.

"Tapping into Diversity." *globalhr*, May 2001; 21–25.

Wah, L. "Diversity at Allstate." *Management Review*, July/August 1999; 88(7):24.

"Why Employees Stay—or Go, *Facilities and Design Management*, October 2000; 19(10):46.

Wishna, V. "Leaving for Good." *Restaurant Business*, May 1, 2000; 99(9):64.

Withers, P. "Finders Keepers." *CMA Management*, October 2001; 75(7):24.

Yardley, J.K. "The Relationships of Work-Family Conflict with Work Outcomes: A Test of a Model." *Dissertation Abstracts International: Section B: the Sciences and Engineering*, May 1995; 5(11-B):5113.

FURTHER READING

Ashby, F.C., and Pell, A.D. *Embracing Excellence: Become an Employer of Choice to Attract and Keep the Best Talent*. Paramus, N.J.: Prentice Hall Press, 2001.

Gonthier, G. *Rude Awakenings: Overcoming the Civility Crisis in the Workplace*. Chicago: Dearborn Trade Publishing, 2002.

Griffeth, R.W., and Hom, P.W. *Retaining Valued Employees*. Thousand Oaks, Calif: Sage Publishing, 2001.

Gubman, E.L. *The Talent Solution: Aligning Strategy and People to Achieve Extraordinary Results*. New York: McGraw Hill, 1998.

Harris, J. *Getting Employees to Fall in Love with Your Company*. New York: American Management Association, 1996.

Harris, J., and Brannick, J. *Finding and Keeping Great Employees*. New York: American Management Association, 1999.

Jensen, B. *Work 2.0: Rewriting the Contract*. Cambridge, Mass.: Perseus Publishing, 2002.

Johnson, M. *Winning the People Wars: Talent and the Battle for Human Capital*. Paramus, N.J.: Prentice Hall, 2000.

Levin, R., and Rosse, J. *Talent Flow: A Strategic Approach to Keeping Good Employees, Helping Them Grow, and Letting Them Go*. San Francisco, Calif.: Jossey-Bass, 2001.

Michaels, E., and Axelrod, B. "The War for Talent." *Harvard Business School Publishing*, October 2001.

Solution Set: Creating Equitable Pay and Performance Processes

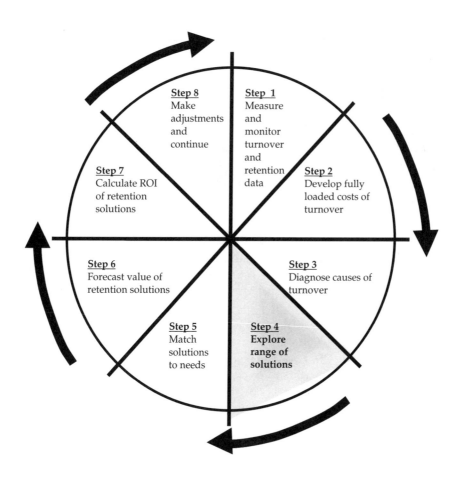

The circular diagram shows eight steps:

Step 8 Make adjustments and continue

Step 1 Measure and monitor turnover and retention data

Step 2 Develop fully loaded costs of turnover

Step 3 Diagnose causes of turnover

Step 4 Explore range of solutions

Step 5 Match solutions to needs

Step 6 Forecast value of retention solutions

Step 7 Calculate ROI of retention solutions

This chapter explores the critical issue of employee pay and recognition. It identifies what employees seek in terms of pay and benefits, as well as their need for recognition and rewards. It also presents the essentials necessary to successfully manage job performance. Table 8-1 presents the four categories associated with equitable pay and performance processes. It outlines employee needs in each category and lists possible solutions.

PAY

Most employees feel that they are worth more than they are actually paid. There is a natural disparity between what people think they should be paid and what organizations spend in compensation. When the difference becomes too great and another opportunity occurs, turnover can result. *Pay* is defined as the wages, salary, or compensation given to an employee in exchange for services the employee performs for the organization.

Need for Adequate Pay

Pay is more than "dollars and cents;" it also acknowledges the worth and value of the human contribution. What people are paid has been shown to have a clear, reliable impact on turnover in numerous studies. Pay has been identified by some as the "most critical

Table 8-1
Employee Needs and Organizational Solutions for Equitable Pay and Performance Processes

Category	Need	Solution
Pay	To be paid fairly and equitably	Use a pay system that is fair, equitable, and competitive.
Benefits	To have competitive benefits to meet individual needs	Offer economically feasible employee benefit programs tailored to individual needs.
Rewards and Recognition	To be rewarded and recognized for contribution	Implement a rewards and recognition program tailored to individual needs.
Job Performance	To know performance expectations for success and growth	Implement a performance management process.

outcome of organizational membership for employees" (Gupta and Shaw, 2001). The first and obvious solution to the need for pay is to compensate employees with the highest possible wages. However, even in an organization that is the leader in compensation for its industry, pay dissatisfaction can result in turnover. The value that people assign to pay helps determines, in large part, their satisfaction with pay (Lum et al., 1998). The more people value pay and the more highly they are paid, the more satisfied they will be and the more likely they will be to remain with the organization.

Distributive and Procedural Justice

Employees have two major needs with regard to pay. The first is for pay to be distributed equitably within the organization. This is called *distributive justice*. If employees feel that the organization has a fair distribution of pay, the employees' intent to leave is lower than those who feel pay is unfairly distributed (Liang, 2000).

Second, employees need to understand the process through which pay is administered. If problems with the administration and delivery of pay occur, employees need to be able to address organizational procedures. This is called *procedural justice*. Pay procedures address the employee's perceptions about pay inequality and the extent to which employees understand how performance affects salary. If necessary, employees should be able to appeal their concerns about unfair pay practices. If employees feel that they have not been paid fairly, an appeal mechanism allows for disputes to be settled. Pay disputes can be resolved through the appeal mechanism.

Guidelines for Selecting Pay Strategies

Organizations go to great lengths to determine the appropriate pay rate. They compare pay schedules to industry standards and local companies. Pay consultants often are engaged to analyze pay structures. In many instances, pay is augmented with bonuses, monetary rewards, and monetary incentives to maintain pay parity with the industry or other companies in the area. The goal is to provide the best pay value for its employees and for the organization. The following guidelines can be used to select the appropriate pay solution for the organization.

1. *Include market research when selecting a pay solution.* Evaluate the compensation of similar companies and industries when

creating the pay structure. Include geographic considerations in assessing pay policies and schedules.

2. *Keep pay on par with other changes in the organization.* Most organizations do not think of pay as keeping pace with other changes in the workplace, but pay is a dynamic, evolving process. When the organization is being revamped and restructured, pay solutions are often stagnant. When change occurs in the organization, the organization should assess whether a change in pay strategy is necessary.

3. *Align pay and business strategies.* Assessing the pay needs of an organization requires alignment. Establish a clear link between organizational performance and the pay structure of the organization. Pay is first and foremost an issue about business strategy.

4. *Solicit employee input.* Employees should have input to and understand the type of pay structure in the organization. The organization should listen to employee input and solicit feedback on pay strategies.

5. *Assess customer feedback.* Customers, both internal and external, should affect pay. These customers, and their opinion about their customer service, should be integrated into the pay solution. Good customer service should be rewarded and included as part of the organization's pay strategy.

6. *Communicate that pay increases are not automatic.* Communicate that entitlement pay (automatic yearly raises or standard bonuses) is no longer part of the pay strategy. Pay raises and bonuses should come from performance. This is especially applicable for government organizations.

7. *Create guidelines for pay.* Identify when the organization should consider pay increases and when the organization should not. The guidelines will be valuable, equitable standards to help make key judgments about pay.

Typical Pay Solutions

The following five pay strategies represent some of the most common pay solutions used in organizations today.

1. *Pay schedules.* Identify an established schedule for pay in the various levels of the organization and are published so that everyone in the organization has knowledge of pay structure. Usually pay schedules are based on the job classification and

the number of years worked in the organization. Schedules are used by the federal governmental agencies, state and local governments, government contractors, and military.

2. *Pay for skills or knowledge.* Reward people for their skills or knowledge (instead of a specific job type). This takes into account the individual's competencies, which include skills, knowledge, capabilities, and behaviors that help the individual achieve superior performance.

3. *Broadbanding.* Taken from radio terminology, this concept groups employees who perform certain functions into a specific classification (i.e., all management is banded together, all administrative staff is banded together, and all technical workers are banded together). Banding allows workers to be rewarded for performance without requiring them to advance in a managerial position. A highly technically skilled employee could advance in pay through a competency-based pay structure. (Nau, 1999)

4. *Variable or commission pay.* Variable pay allows employees, especially managers, to share in organizational profits by aligning compensation with achievement. Commission pay is purely by unit; a car salesman earns pay on the number of cars he sells. Some people are highly motivated by commissions and variable pay; others do not want the risk.

5. *Retention bonuses.* Some organizations provide bonuses to reward employees for staying with the organization. When such pay is given, the employee is usually asked to sign a contract that guarantees that she or he will remain with the organization for a specific length of time.

Pay Increases

The key to increasing pay is to achieve a balance between what employees need (in order to remain with the organization) and what the organization can afford to pay. The Institute of Management and Administration, Inc, located in New York City, publishes a monthly report on pay. A recent issue discussed the relationship between pay increases and employee retention. Although specific turnover improvements are not specifically identified (probably due to confidentiality issues), the experience of one organization provided a real-world example of how pay increases solved the problem of keeping good employees. One West Coast bank with 9,975 employees who faced with a shortage of qualified candidates. Their response to the poor labor market was to increase pay to avoid the loss of its critical employees (*Pay for Performance Report*, 2002). The salary increases worked, and the employees who were considering leaving the organization remained.

Another organization that needed to raise pay to respond to its employee retention issue was reluctant to do so but did adjust compensation. A nonprofit organization with 580 employees faced a retention issue that required higher compensation for its employees. The manager of employment and compensation stated, "It is difficult to keep up with the increasing compensation in the marketplace and, therefore, retain staff. . . . We sometimes adjust compensation—where warranted—to remain competitive." (*Pay for Performance Report*, 2002)

Retention Bonuses

Selective pay programs that give employees money to remain with the organization are successfully used to retain employees. Archives Management Inc., a records storage company in Watertown, Connecticut, uses pays to help with its recurring retention problem. Jobs within the organization are often somewhat boring and repetitive. The organization uses a "Pay-to-Stay Bonus" that amounts to $100 for every 6 months of continuous employment in the most repetitive jobs. The owner states, "To the extent that you can defer departures and deferment costs only $100, you're ahead of the game because turnover is expensive."

Many companies resort to bonuses as a means for improving employee loyalty. Right Management Consultants examined 829 Canadian and U.S. companies that were experiencing cutbacks, acquisitions, and other difficult situations. Half of these companies enticed essential employees using financial incentives. The bonuses typically ranged from 26 percent of base pay for supervisory and technical staff to 47 percent for executives. The bonuses were in cash in more than 90 percent of cases. In return, 59 percent of the companies required employees to sign agreements to remain with the organization for a specific time period. Generous retention bonuses can be a powerful method for achieving retention. The Right Management Consultants found that of the companies offering the retention bonuses, they were able to retain 90 percent of supervisory and technical employees (Kiger, 2000).

In another pay-related retention program, Archives Management loans or gives up to $25,000 to employees who are first-time homebuyers. This money is paid in the form of a grant. If the grant comes through, the company lends workers the money for a down payment at 2 percent interest and does not require principal payments for 5 years. If the employee is still working at Archives Management after 5 years, the loan is forgiven. Archives Management uses this program as part of its retention strategy (Barker, 2000). The company feels that paying for home loans for its valued employees is an important and successful retention strategy that saves the organization money in the long term.

BENEFITS

A typical benefit solution has several components, including medical insurance, dental insurance, vacation time, and sick time. Other benefits might include flextime, part-time work, daytime care for sick children (taking place in a medical facility), job sharing (in which one job is shared by two employees), elder care insurance (nursing care coverage for elderly relatives with deteriorating health), and use of physical fitness facilities.

Need for Adequate Benefits

In some instances, the individual has a greater need for benefits than pay. Like pay, benefits are costly to the organization. Many organizations value and understand the basic need employees have for benefits and may spend an additional 25 to 50 percent of the employee's salary on benefit packages. However, providing a benefit package addresses only half of this need—the other half is communicating what the benefits do for employees and their families.

According to a survey by the Society for Human Resource Management, health care benefits were the top organizational tactic used for employee retention, with 94 percent of respondents saying they use benefits. This placed it slightly ahead of new hire orientation (90 percent), an open communication policy (89 percent), and pay raises (87 percent) (Josefak, 1999).

Communicating Benefits

Benefits should be understood by the employee to be appreciated. Communicating the sometimes complex enrollment process and the ways in which employees can maximize the use of these benefits is a key need for employees. A study conducted in 2000 by Conning and Company and Eastbridge Consulting Group found that work-site insurance enrollment procedures are often inadequate in educating and counseling employees about benefits choices (Hutchins, 2002). Employees often become frustrated with the benefits package itself if they do not understand proper usage. Information should be presented to employees individually and in groups to ensure they understand their benefits (*National Petroleum News*, 2000). Because some of these benefits are complicated, explanation should be provided both in writing and verbally. Periodic sessions should be held with employees (usually yearly) to confirm that the benefits they have selected fit their needs in the best possible way. Organizations should use written materials, question-and-answer session meetings, and one-on-one follow-up discussions to explain benefits and ways to properly use them.

Flexible Benefit Packages

An effective benefit solution allows individuals to select the specific type of benefit package that fits their unique needs. Such an option requires a highly customized process in distributing benefits. Because of this, more organizations are turning to the cafeteria approach, which allows employees to select from a variety of possible programs in creating their own, unique benefit package. Creating a cafeteria approach solution is accomplished by placing points of value on both the salary and components of the benefit package itself. The president of Baltimore-based RewardsPlus states, "As employees become more familiar with customized service over the Internet, they'll expect and appreciate the availability of customized benefits. Employees are going to select what makes sense for them, not just take what the employer is giving to everyone." (Laabs, 2000)

Benefit Surveys

Ensuring that the benefit program addresses the kinds of needs employees have can be determined by an employee satisfaction survey. Employee surveys assess the satisfaction of individuals in the organization with a wide variety of issues. Satisfaction with benefits often is a part of the survey content. Another feasible method to address the kinds of benefit needs employees have might be to administer a benefit survey that specifically identifies what employees most need (*Employee Benefit News*, 2001).

Benefits should match employee needs; some employees may want retirement plans, whereas others want more money; still others need adult care benefits for aging parents, and others want on-site day care. Flexible companies address the need for benefits by allowing employees to select from a variety of choices and benefit plans. For example, organizations may allow employees to decline certain parts of the benefit plan or increase benefits if they contribute. Many employees may choose to decline medical coverage when their spouse's employment already provides excellent medical coverage. Other organizations allow employees to buy and sell a limited number of vacation days, providing employees with different abilities to trade cash for time off and vice versa.

REWARDS AND RECOGNITION

Employees want to be recognized for a job well done. Rewards and recognition respond to this need by validating performance and motivating employees toward continuous improvement. Rewarding and recognizing people for performance not only affects the person being recognized, but others in the organization as well. Through a rewards program, the entire organization can experience the commitment to excellence.

When the reward system is credible, rewards are meaningful; however, if the reward system is broken, the opposite effect will occur. Employees may feel that their performance is unrecognized and not valued, or that others in the organization are rewarded for the wrong behaviors. Unrecognized and nonvalued performance can contribute to turnover. Recognition for a job well done fills the employees' need to receive positive, honest feedback for their efforts.

Need for Rewards and Recognition

Recognition should be part of the organization's culture because it contributes to both employee satisfaction and retention. Organizations can avoid employee turnover by rewarding top performers. Rewards are one of the keys to avoiding turnover, especially if they are immediate, appropriate, and personal. A Harvard University study concluded that organizations can avoid the disruption caused by employee turnover by avoiding hiring mistakes and selecting and retaining top performers. One of the keys to avoiding turnover is to make rewards count. Rewards are to be immediate, appropriate, and personal. Organizations may want to evaluate whether getting a bonus at the end of the year is more or less rewarding than getting smaller, more frequent payouts. Additionally, a personal note may mean more than a generic company award. Employees should be asked for input on their most desirable form of recognition. Use what employees say when it comes time to reward for performance (St. Amour, 2000).

Designing a Rewards and Recognition Solution

In designing a rewards and recognition program, the following guidelines should be considered.

1. Rewards should be *visible* to all members of the organization.
2. Rewards should be based on well-defined, credible standards that have been developed using observable achievements.
3. Rewards should have meaning and value for the recipient.
4. Rewards can be based on an event (achieving a designated goal) or based on a time frame (performing well over a specific time period).
5. Rewards that are spontaneous (sometimes called on-the-spot awards) are also highly motivating and should also use a set criteria and standard to maintain credibility and meaning.
6. Rewards should be achievable and not out of reach by employees.
7. Nonmonetary rewards, if used, should be valued by the individual. For example, an avid camper might be given a 10-day pass to a campsite, or, if an individual enjoys physical activity, that employee might be given a spa membership. The nonmonetary rewards are best received when they are thoughtfully prepared and of highest quality. Professionalism in presenting the reward is also interpreted as worthwhile recognition.
8. Rewards should be appropriate to the level of accomplishment received. A cash award of $50 would be inappropriate for someone who just recommended a process that saved the organization a million dollars. Determining the amount of money given is a delicate matter of organizational debate in which organizational history, financial parameters, and desired results are all factors.

Recognition for a job well done can be just as valued and appreciated as monetary awards.

Formal recognition program can be used with success. First Data Resources, a data processing services company that employees more than 6,000 individuals in Omaha, Nebraska, uses a formal recognition program (Adams, Mahaffey, and Rick, 2002). Rewards are given on a monthly, quarterly, and yearly basis, and range from Nebraska football tickets, gift certificates, pens, plaques, mugs, and other items. One of the most popular awards at First Data is called the "Fat Cat Award" that consists of:

- $500 gift check
- Professional portrait of the employee
- Appreciation letter from the CEO and senior management
- E-mails, phone calls, and notes from peers

In addition to nonmonetary rewards, employees can be rewarded using money in numerous ways. Cash is a welcome motivator and reward for improving performance, whether at formal meetings or on the spot. Variable bonuses linked to performance are another popular reward strategy. Profit sharing and pay-for-skills are monetary bonus plans that both motivate individuals and improve goal achievement.

Small acts of recognition are valuable for employee daily motivation. Sometimes a personal note may mean more than a generic company award. In one survey, employees cited the following as meaningful rewards (Moss, 2000):

- Employee of the month awards
- Years of service awards
- Bonus pay (above and beyond overtime) for weekend work
- Invitations for technicians to technical shows and other industry events

Meaningful and Motivational Rewards

What gives meaning to rewards and recognition? What makes them effective? First, rewards and recognition should be based on a clear set of standards, with performance verifiable or observable. The standards for the reward should also be achievable. If the reward is based on an unachievable result, such as a production goal that is beyond employees' power, then those employees will not be motivated. Meaningful rewards and recognition that are achievable have the greatest impact.

The information technology industry has been a victim of turnover in alarming rates, hovering around 22 percent a year by some estimates. However, the information technology department of optics manufacturer Corning has a turnover rate that is only 3 percent. One of the ways they achieve such excellent retention rates is through their rewards and recognition program. Here are just a few of the things that Corning does (Reimers, 2001):

1. Offers monthly department and team outings
2. Provides schedules that allow all new employees a flexible period during which they can find a place to live
3. Gives away a 2-hour "early" out from work every Friday
4. Supplies free dinners for new employees from Monday through Friday (good during the first few months that they are in the organization)

An example of meaningful rewards and recognition is demonstrated in another organization, BroadJump. This organization provides automated customer interface software to handle new customer service requests. Its rewards and recognition program tailors the award to the needs of the recipient. For example, an employee who was about to get married won an award that was created just for her stressful life—a day at the spa. Another group of employees developing special software for a product launch won a free weekend in Las Vegas, a trip that all the group members valued and wanted. BroadJump made the effort to customize these awards for each specific employee (Reimers, 2001).

What makes rewards and recognition motivational? Motivation comes, in part, from the value that employees have for the reward or recognition. Highly valued rewards and recognition motivate people to achieve and receive. Rewards themselves may be intrinsically motivational; some employees become highly motivated after a well-presented, highly attended awards event. Being recognized as both an employee and an individual is one component that makes recognition successful. Individuals want to feel that they are not just recognized as an employee, but that they are also being recognized as a partner in achieving organizational success (Shim, 2001).

Retaining Top Performers

Keeping the best employees may mean that the company has to concentrate more on rewarding top performers rather than average and poor performers. A study, which focused on rewards and recognition and its relationship to turnover, evaluated a group of employees who were in the top half of performance but who voluntarily terminated employment. Interestingly, these individuals were not rewarded or recognized. The top performers demonstrated a higher need for recognition than employees who performed in the lower half of the performance ranking structure (Allen and Griffeth, 1999). A similar study echoed the finding that high performers who did not receive rewards were more likely to leave the company than poor performers. Managers implementing a rewards and recognition solution should account for this principle when designing their recognition solution.

PERFORMANCE MANAGEMENT

Performance management is the vehicle by which organizations help individuals track and improve their work behaviors and, thereby, achieve their performance goals. Individual goals, in turn, help the organization achieve its business strategy. Employees need to receive feedback on job performance. Without feedback, employees are working in a vacuum. Job performance refers to how well an individual is meeting the organization's expectations. How the organization interprets the employee's performance becomes the basis for creating performance reviews.

Need for Performance Management

Turnover researchers have studied the importance of individual job performance and turnover for more than 30 years (Allen and Griffeth, 1999). Recently a study conducted in an Australian international banking organization of nearly 4,000 staff in 611 branches and business outlets showed that job performance affects voluntary turnover (Iverson and Deery, 2000).

Performance problems may lead to turnover through several ways. Employees who do not perform well might feel the need to move to another organization to avoid the consequences of a poor performance review. Employees who perform poorly and are not rated or rewarded equally with high-performing peers are often "shocked" (through receiving a poor performance review) into seeking employment elsewhere. Employees who feel that their performance is not appreciated or undervalued might decide to leave an organization. High-performing employees who are not given positive feedback might leave the organization because they are not being recognized and because their high skill level may make them more employable outside the organization (Jackofsky, Ferris, and Breckenridge, 1986).

Communicating the Performance Review

A key component of the performance management need is the communication exchange between the leader and the employee. Open, honest feedback facilitates necessary adjustments in work performance. Through feedback, competency gaps can be identified and reduced and progression comparisons for team goals are possible. As a result, performance management keeps good employees performing well by reinforcing their positive contribution to the company.

Communication is the cornerstone of any performance management solution because it clarifies what is desired and helps identify the necessary steps to accomplish goal achievement. When successful, the job review process helps employees improve by positively communicating how to make improvements to achieve goals.

Critical to this process are the resources that the organization can offer to help the employee improve skill levels. Skill levels can be addressed during a performance review and, if necessary, employee training identified. In this way, communication during the job performance review is the positive means to help both the employee and the organization achieve desired goals.

Ideally, goals are communicated to all employees throughout the entire organization in a well-designed performance review process. Such a process integrates individual goals with the organization's strategic goals. From an individual's perspective, having a performance management program communicates an answer to the following questions:

- How am I doing?
- Am I on track?
- What am I doing well?
- What can I do better?
- How will the organization help me improve?

Aligning Performance Goals with Strategic Objectives

Each organization should identify its strategic goals before designing a performance management system. These objectives are linked to the performance goals of the various divisions, departments, teams, and individuals within the organization. This link enables employees to see their contribution to organizational success. An organization that is highly profit oriented will have different performance management solutions than a company that emphasizes service over monetary results.

For example, a branch of the military will have markedly different performance management than a Fortune 500 organization. The U.S. military has as a key performance objective to protect and defend the country against all acts of terrorism. In contrast, a Fortune 500 organization might have as a key performance objective the goal of achieving a specific profit margin and market share. Both performance objectives are, however, equally important and both reflect the organization's strategic goals. These goals are, in turn, broken down and communicated to divisions, departments, and employees within the organization.

Performance management has helped create a culture of achievement for Britain's largest information technology services company, Logica (Hoggarth, 2002). With revenues of more than $1 billion annually, the performance review system that the organization uses has had an enormous impact on the company's speed of progress, making it one of Britain's most successful software firms. The group marketing director of Logica in charge of one third of the organization's 11,000 employees attributes the success of the organization to several key initiatives. First, there is a huge emphasis on communication. The leadership at Logica uses communication to take employees where they need to go to be successful. The organization also gives employees clear objectives. The performance management system (PMS) involves an annual appraisal in which employees meet with their managers to review achievements and set new goals. These goals are based on the corporate strategy. In each case, the staff is graded on their financial, technical, and interpersonal skills, their ability to win and keep clients, their own career development, and their contribution to the overall business strategy. Additionally, the organization has implemented a "Star Consultant Program" that assigns specific individuals to mentor and help groups of employees. These Star Consultants ensure that people are "looked after" and that appraisals are done. The result has been a highly profitable organization with an enviable employee retention rate of between 10 percent and 15 percent (Wheatley, 2001).

Goals should be identified at both the collective and the individual levels. A well-designed performance management solution supports varying objectives among organizations and within depart-ments. For example, a CEO in one organization might have a goal to increase market share by 20 percent. At the individual level, the way to support this goal might be to help design and develop new marketing materials to improve market share. These two goals are aligned and support one another. Through alignment, the individual is fully engaged and understands how what he or she does con-tributes to organizational success.

Key Components of Successful Performance Management

In addition to aligning performance with the organization's objectives, there are nine other major components to a successful program.

1. *Performance is aligned with the key performance-driven areas.* Goals should be aligned with consideration of the customers, vendors, internal customers, external customers, and so on. This alignment supports performance in a positive way and helps to make goal achievement possible.
2. *Performance goals are behavioral, results-oriented, and achiev-able.* Organizations identify specific behaviors that demonstrate goal achievement. Ensuring that these behaviors are achievable is key because unless employees have a sense that they can succeed, they will not make the effort. At the risk of repetition, the behav-iors must be tied to results that are meaningful to the team and the organization, and not based on personal whim.
3. *Performance is tracked and measured.* The gaps between what is expected in terms of performance and what is achieved should be clear, measurable, and identifiable. Performance accomplishments should be recorded to understand where and how the individual or team can make improvements.
4. *Performance measures are mutually agreed on and discussed by both the employee and leadership.* This conversation must take place at the beginning of the performance cycle, not at the end. Measures should be discussed as an outgrowth of the overall organizational goal. If things change, these changes must be for-mally acknowledged. Measures that are not discussed, but are dic-tated, have less buy-in from employees and are not as successful as are those that are agreed on.
5. *Performance is discussed on a regular basis.* Performance improvement requires that performance issues have a specific time

frame. Whether it is weekly, monthly, or quarterly, most employees need feedback to understand how they are meeting or not meeting requirements.

6. *Performance is appropriately rewarded with raises, incentives, rewards, recognition, etc.* There must be positive reinforcement for good performance. This reinforcement can be in terms of rewards of money, verbal praise, written awards, or special rewards. Positive behaviors may not continue without recognition and reinforcement. The end of a performance evaluation is a good time to reinforce positive behavior.

7. *Performance is linked to key competencies.* The specific areas that are needed for outstanding performance should be identified as competencies. The competencies can include skills, knowledge, ability, and talent an individual possesses to do a job.

8. *Poor performance is discussed in a positive way.* When employees understand that the work environment is a place where improvement is positively encouraged, they will be able to learn more rapidly in a safe job environment. Employees will understand that mistakes are tolerated and improvements are encouraged. This environment creates an atmosphere in which growth is possible because fear is minimized. Managers should explain poor performance in a clear and positive way so that employees who do not meet performance objectives understand the consequences. Such an environment supports and fosters productivity and improves retention.

9. *Performance opportunities are provided for all individuals to improve their skills through coaching, development, and training.* Providing the requisite training and coaching is essential for maximum performance. In addition, leaders need training in how to mentor and coach employees for maximum benefit to individuals, leaders, and the company.

One organization that views the need for performance reviews as integral to its success and employee retention is Delta Hotels. The organization has an employee retention rate of 89 percent, which is one of the best rates in the hospitality industry. Employees are given regular feedback on their job performance, and this feedback is backed by a guarantee. Any Delta employee who does not receive such feedback may claim an extra week's salary each year. The senior vice president of people and quality for the Toronto-based chain of 39 hotels says, "This guarantee shows that we're willing to commit." Delta pays an extra week's salary to about 30 people a year. This is tracked and becomes a part of the benchmarking improvement process for the hotel (*Toronto Star*, 2001).

Performance management is an excellent vehicle for organizations to use in aligning individual and organizational goals. The performance management solution also helps employees understand how their performance supports organizational objectives. The nine key components of the performance management solution help companies design and develop solutions that help improve turnover.

Final Thoughts

Receiving adequate and equitable pay is one of the critical reasons employees choose to remain in an organization. However, pay is more than "dollars and cents." It acknowledges the employee's worth and the value of his or her contribution. This chapter presented guidelines to use in selecting appropriate pay solutions and some typical pay strategies, such as pay for skill and knowledge and retention bonuses.

In some instances, employee have a greater need for benefits than pay, and this chapter discussed typical benefit solutions, such as medical insurance, day care for children, and elder care insurance. Providing a benefit program that addresses the kinds of needs employees have will help promote employee satisfaction and increase retention.

In addition to pay and benefits, employees want to be recognized for a job well done. This chapter offered guidelines for designing a rewards and recognition program that will contribute to both employee satisfaction and retention.

Finally, the chapter addressed the often-difficult topic of performance management. It showed how the performance review can be used to align individual and organizational goals. It presented nine key components of the performance management solution to enable organizations design and develop solutions to improve turnover.

References

Adams, B., Mahaffey, G., and Norm, R. First Data Resources, Omaha, Nebraska. Interviewed by author 2002.

Allen, D.G., and Griffeth, R.W. "Job Performance and Turnover: A Review and Integrative Multi-Route Model." *Human Resource Management Review*, Winter 1999; 9(4):525.

Barker, E. "The Company They Keep." *Inc.*, May 2000; 22(5):84.

Brown, B.L. "Part-Time Work and Other Flexible Options." Columbus, Ohio: Eric Clearing House on Adult, Career, and Vocational Education. January 1, 1998, Digest No. 192:5.

"Delta Hotels Knows How to Keep Workers." *Toronto Star*, August 29, 2001.

Employee Benefit News, August 1, 2001; 15(10).

Gupta, N., and Shaw, J. "Pay Fairness and Employee Outcomes: Exacerbation and Attenuation Effects of Financial Need." *Journal of Occupational and Organizational Psychology*, 2001; 74(3):22.

Hoggarth, R. Logica. Interviewed by author. October 8, 2002.

Hutchins, J. "How to Make the Right Voluntary Benefit Choices." *Workforce*, March 2002; 81(3):42.

Iverson, R.D., and Deery, S.J. "Job Performance and Voluntary Turnover: An Examination of Linearity, Curvilinearity, and the Moderators of Time, Unemployment Rate, and Perceived Ease of Movement Using Event History Analysis," *Academy of Management Proceedings*, 2000; 1.

Jackofsky, E.F., Ferris, K.R., and Breckenridge, B.G. "Evidence for a Curvilinear Relationship between Job Performance and Turnover." *Journal of Management*, 1986; 12(1):105–111.

Josefak, L. "Keeping Employee Turnover to a Minimum." *Personnel Management*, June 18, 1999; 47(25):22.

Kiger, P.J. "Retention on the Brink." *Workforce*, November 2000; 79(11):58.

Laabs, J. "Will To-Die-for Benefits Help Retention?", *Workforce*, July 2000; 62–65.

Liang, K.-G. *Dissertation Abstracts International: Section B: The Sciences and Engineering*, June 2000; 60(11-B):5818.

Lief, L. "An End to the Dead-End Job?" *US News and World Report*, October 27, 1997; 123(16):86–87.

Lum, L., Kervin, J., Clark, K., Reid, F., and Sirola, W. "Explaining Nursing Turnover Intent; Job Satisfaction, Pay Satisfaction or Organizational Commitment." *Journal of Organizational Behavior*, May 1998; 19(3):305–320.

Moss, B. "Chain of Loyalty." *SDM: Security Distributing and Marketing*, December 2000; 30(15):79.

McShulskis, E. "Part-Time Plans Have a Positive Impact." *HR Magazine*, January 1998; 43(1):26.

Nau, S. "Adopting Fairer Compensation." *American City and County*, January 1999; 114(1).

"Part Time Professionals Push Positive Image." *CQ Researcher*, October 24, 1997; 7(40):944.

Pay for Performance Report. New York: Institute of Management and Administration, Inc., 2002.

"Recruit and Retain." *National Petroleum News*, November 2000; 92(12):48.

Reimers, B.D., "Keep Talent from Taking Flight." *Network Computing*, August 6, 2001; 12(16):42.

Shim, G. "Fast Food Group Uses Alternative Methods to Retain Workers." *Omaha World-Herald*, September 24, 2001.

St. Amour, D. "Ten Ways to Retain High Performance Employees." *Canadian Manager*, Summer 2000; 25(2):21.

Wheatley, C. "British Software Services Firm Logica Plots Course for Good Year," *Sunday Business*, October 23, 2001.

FURTHER READING

Beam, B.T., Jr , and McFadden, J.J. *Employee Benefits*, 6th ed., Chicago: Dearborn Trade Publishing, November 2000.

Dibble, S. *Keeping Your Valuable Employees*. New York: John Wiley & Sons, 1999.

Gudman, E.L. *The Talent Solution: Aligning Strategy and People to Achieve Extraordinary Results*. New York: McGraw-Hill, 1998.

Harrington, J.H., and Lomax, K.C. *Performance Improvement Methods: Fighting the War on Waste*. New York: McGraw-Hill, August 1999.

Harris, J., and Brannick, J. *Finding & Keeping Great Employees*. New York: American Management Association, 1999.

Sears, D. *Successful Talent Strategies: Achieving Superior Business Results through Market-Focused Staffing*. New York: American Management Association, 2003.

Tropman, J.E. *The Compensation Solution: How to Develop an Employee-Driven Rewards System*. San Francisco, Calif.: Jossey-Bass, 2001.

CHAPTER 9

Solution Set: Building Motivation and Commitment

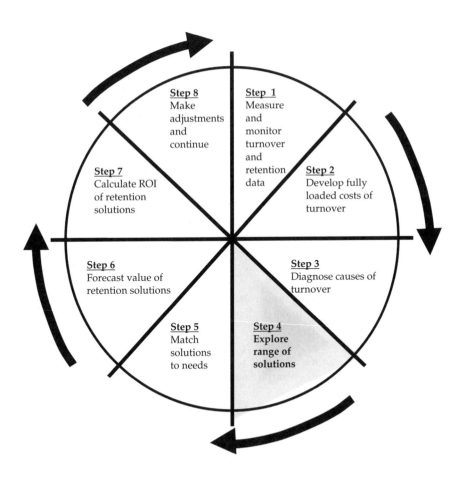

The previous three chapters identified typical workplace needs of employees and provided solutions for those needs. This chapter concludes that discussion by addressing the final set of solutions. It explores the issues aimed at building commitment and growth. Table 9-1 presents six employee needs that relate to these issues and the organization's solutions for meeting these needs.

QUALITY OF LEADERSHIP

Excellent leadership motivates employees to stay in an organization. Effective leaders have good interpersonal skills and are able to guide, coach, and mentor employees. Because each organization is unique, the challenge is to identify and develop leaders who meet the organization's specific production needs while addressing more general needs of employees. The challenge for any organization is to

Table 9-1
Needs and Solutions for Building Motivation and Commitment

Category	Need	Solution
Quality of leadership	To have a leader who is respectful and one who inspires employees	Provide leadership mentoring, development training, and development.
Empowerment	To be involved in job decisions and allowed to take actions on job issues	Implement an empowerment program.
Teamwork	To be part of a supportive, productive team	Create team-building programs; build effective, productive teams.
Ethics and trust	To work in a trusting and ethical environment	Implement an ethics program; treat people fairly, openly, and honestly.
Organizational commitment	To be attached to the company, the team, and to other employees	Create team-building programs that improve employee commitment at all organizational levels.
Professional growth and career advancement	To develop have a variety of skills and competencies To have the opportunity to grow and prosper with the organization	Offer a variety of training and development programs to improve skills. Implement a career management system.

develop and maintain leadership and, thereby, keep qualified employees. Solutions may include some or all of the following: developing leadership competencies, creating leadership development plans, training, hiring consultants, role modeling, coaching, and participating in reading discussion groups.

Need for Effective Leadership

"People don't quit companies, they quit bosses." (Kaye and Jordan-Evans, 1999) Good leaders affect every aspect of the retention solution. For this reason, leadership cannot be overemphasized. Some experts argue that the most important measure of leadership is whether the leader can retain employees. Good leaders are a key to employee retention. One study based on more than 80,000 interviews conducted by a respected polling organization concluded that the front-line manager is the key to attracting and retaining talented employees. By focusing on leadership, organizations improve employee retention (Buckingham and Coffman, 1999).

Leadership Competencies

As a starting point, organizations should identify the competencies desired for their leaders. Effective leadership training and development can then focus on these key competencies. The desired competencies for individual leaders should be directly linked to the organization and support the organization's goals. Once these competencies are identified, plans and training to improve specific skill levels can be developed.

Competencies are also identified, in some writing, as talents. The Gallup Organization has studied leadership across hundreds of roles. As a result of surveys from managers, they identified 40 common competencies or talents, which are listed below (Buckingham and Coffman, 1999). This list is organized into three main categories: striving, thinking and relating.

Striving Talents
- Achievement: One's internal drive
- Kinesthetic: Expending physical energy
- Stamina: Capacity for physical endurance
- Competition: Gauging success comparatively
- Desire: Claiming significance through independence
- Competence: Expertise for mastery

- Belief: Orienting life around values
- Mission: Putting beliefs into action
- Service: Being of service to others
- Ethics: Understanding right and wrong, which guides actions
- Vision: Future orientation

Thinking Talents
- Focus: Setting goals and using them to guide actions
- Discipline: Imposing structure onto life and work
- Arranger: Possessing an ability to orchestrate
- Work orientation: Mentally rehearsing and reviewing work
- Gestalt: Order and accuracy
- Responsibility: Assuming personal accountability for work
- Concept: Developing a framework for making sense of things
- Performance orientation: Being objective and measuring performance
- Strategic thinking: Play out alternative scenarios
- Business thinking: Evaluating financial application of strategic thinking
- Problem solving: Thinking things through with incomplete data
- Formulation: Finding coherent patterns within incoherent data
- Numerical: An affinity for numbers
- Creativity: Break existing configurations in favor of more effective appealing ones

Relating Talents
- Woo: Gaining the approval of others
- Empathy: Identifying the feelings of others
- Relator: Building bonds that last
- Multi-relator: Building an extensive network of acquaintances
- Interpersonal: Purposefully capitalizing on relationships
- Individualized perception: Awareness of and attentiveness to individual differences
- Developer: Need to invest in others and derive satisfaction from doing so
- Simulator: Creating enthusiasm
- Team: Building feelings of mutual support
- Positivity: Looking on the bright side
- Persuasion: Convincing others logically
- Command: Taking charge
- Activator: Impatience to move others to action
- Courage: Using emotion to overcome resistance

Leadership Development Plans

Leadership development plans identify the competencies and training courses that individuals can use to improve their leadership skills. These plans are unique for each individual and should be tailored to match each individual's needs, schedule, and learning style. Usually a discussion is conducted in which the leader and her or his manager list the specific improvement goals and a time frame in which the goals are to be achieved. In some cases, 360-degree feedback can be used as part of the leadership plan to identify whether improvement has taken place. The feedback asks the leader's peers, subordinates, and superiors about how they see the leadership behavior from their perspective. The results are compiled and provided to the individual being evaluated as feedback. In this way a real-world assessment of the progress can be made on the leadership development plan. Based on the feedback, the plan can be refined and updated, concentrating on new leadership competencies or focusing on existing ones. The use of leadership plans is an excellent way for organizations to track, measure, and assess leadership improvement.

Formal Training

Leadership training can be conducted in a classroom setting or online. Whatever the method, training should be designed and developed in accordance with the organization's desired competencies.

Despite recent layoffs, Charles Schwab & Co., Inc., the nation's largest discount stockbroker, has struggled with employee turnover. Their response to their turnover needs has been to concentrate on training. The most significant aspect of their leadership improvement process is the training Schwab is providing to its management team. Schwab's director of human resources (HR) policies stated, "Everything we learn about retention always leads us back to managers." Dozens of leaders have attended leadership training as a result of input from employees. If an employee criticizes a manager's interpersonal skills, that manager must receive leadership training and be mentored by a senior colleague.

Training for new managers focuses on the basics skills that organizations need for their leaders. One organization that requires new managers to participant in skill-based leadership training is Macy's. Their new manager training, "Lights, Camera, Action: A New Store Executive's Guide to Stardom," explores the initial leadership skills

Macy's wants to develop, including how to run meetings, complete performance evaluations, and interview employees.

Providing external leadership training is another way to address employee leadership needs. Some organizations simply do not have the internal resources to provide training and must rely on external providers. Other organizations prefer to use external consultants because, for some employees, receiving leadership training is more valued when it is presented by external "experts." One organization using outside consultation to address its leadership needs is American Science and Engineering (ASE) of Massachusetts. The organization produces x-ray technology that can detect drugs, explosives, and other illegal substances for the United States and international governments. Its turnover rate in 1 year was 40 percent. "Retention is a major issue for us," states the HR vice president. ASE engaged a consulting firm to assist with leadership training that emphasized the impact managers have on retaining employees. The success of the leadership initiative has been difficult to assess because of changing economic markets, but, according to the HR vice president, "people who are leaving are doing so for different reasons than ineffective supervisory behavior, so it must be making an impact."

Role Modeling and Coaching

Role modeling is one solution that helps leaders improve skills through mentoring and being mentored. The person receiving the coaching watches an admired leader, observes that leader's behaviors, and tries to emulate similar behavior. Discussions with the role model help to reinforce the coaching experience and often are used in combination with role modeling. The availability of someone with whom to discuss leadership problems and issues is a way to make improvements. A coach to listen, give advice, and champion the leader's efforts helps improve skill levels.

Navy Commander D. Michael Abrashoff transformed his leadership approach by following the role model William J. Perry, Secretary of Defense from 1994 to 1997. Secretary Perry's personal interactions typified excellent communicative leadership skills. Whether he was speaking with someone in the Pentagon, the President of the United States, or a sailor on a ship, that person was given his full attention. Because he listened, people wanted to give their best effort for Secretary Perry.

Abrashoff had been mentored and coached by Secretary Perry until he was given command of the U.S. Navy's Destroyer *USS*

Benfold at a time when all the ship's 310 sailors were deeply demoralized. He inherited a significant retention problem—morale was so low that when the previous commander left, the men cheered. Commander Abrashoff admitted that listening was not easy for him, but he decided to follow Perry's model. He created a program called "Get-to-Know-You" with sessions in which the commander met with each person individually. It worked. "At one time, sailors couldn't leave the USS Benfold fast enough. Today, the vessel is the pride of the Pacific fleet, and sailors from other ships are clamoring to join its crew." (Abrashoff, 2001)

In another example, the manager of staffing for Hyatt's Chicago-based hotels created a mentoring program for newly selected employees. The goal is to improve employee retention through interaction among new employees and those who are more experienced. During the first 10 months of employment, management pairs new entry-level employees with more-senior employees to assist them in adjusting to their new job and workplace surroundings. Leaders also pay special attention to new employees and spend time discussing issues with them and addressing employee concerns.

Reading and Discussion Programs

Initial leadership training can be combined with reading and discussion programs in which desired leadership principles are reinforced. In this solution, employees are assigned leadership books to read using a format of monthly discussion groups. These groups talk about the leadership books and then relate the books to real-world leadership issues within their particular experience. In this way, the books become more practical and peers can help each other while utilizing an expert's advice found within a specific leadership book. There is a plethora of leadership books and materials. Table 9-2 identifies the 10 most popular books on leadership from amazon.com.

EMPOWERMENT

Empowerment is the process of transferring authority and responsibility to individuals at lower levels in the organizational hierarchy (Wellins et al., 1991). It provides employees a way to exercise authority and control in the sphere of their job. Empowerment can occur either from the top down throughout the entire organization or on an individual case-by-case basis. It is important to communicate the degree or scope of empowerment desired. Leaders should be certain

Table 9-2
Top Ten Best-Selling Leadership Books on amazon.com

Title	Author	Publisher
1. *Good to Great: Why Some Companies Make the Leap and Others Don't*	Jim Collins	Harper Collins Publishers
2. *Fish! A Remarkable Way to Boost Morale and Improve Results*	Stephen C. Lundin, Harry Paul, John Christensen	Hyperion Press
3. *Leadership 101: What Every Leader Needs to Know*	John C. Maxwell	
4. *The Five Dysfunctions of a Team: A Leadership Fable*	Patrick M. Lencioni	John Wiley & Sons
5. *Primal Leadership: Realizing the Power of Emotional Intelligence*	Daniel Goleman, Richard Boyatzis, Annie McKee	Harvard Business School Publishing
6. *The Heart of Change: Real Life Stories of How People Change Their Organizations*	John P. Kotter, Dan S. Cohen	
7. *Supreme Command: Soldiers, Statesmen, and Leadership in Wartime*	Eliot A. Cohen	
8. *Fish! Tales: Real-Life Stories to Help You Transform Your Workplace and Your Life*	Stephen C. Lundin (Editor), Phillip Strand, John Christensen, Harry Paul	Hyperion
9. *Leading Change*	John P. Kotter	
10. *The 21 Irrefutable Laws of Leadership*	John C. Maxwell, Zig Ziglar	

that everyone in the organization understands the empowerment structure within the organization (Lawler and Bowen, 1992).

Need for Empowerment

When employees are empowered in their job task, they will take more responsibility for what they produce. The advantages of maintaining a viable empowerment solution include higher-quality products and services, less absenteeism, better decision making, timely problem solving, and lower turnover (Dennison, 1984). Turnover was higher in companies that used less empowerment compared to companies that used a rule-oriented management style, according to research done at Purdue University. In a study of 30 steel mini-mills, employee turnover was related to how people are managed and the level of empowerment. Organizations where employees are allowed involvement in making management decisions experience higher labor efficiency and lower waste and scrap rates. When employees are able to be involved in decision making and experience greater levels of empowerment, turnover is reduced (Arthur, 1994).

Empowerment Solutions

Empowerment varies from company to company, department to department, and situation to situation. The level of empowerment is affected by the individuals involved and the type of work. For example, if there is only one employee in an organization, it is relatively simple to expand authority and responsibility as the employee becomes more knowledgeable and experienced. However, large organizations have a more difficult time empowering employees because of the multiple organizational levels that traditionally exist.

General Electric Capital Fleet Services (GECFS) used empowerment as a means to reorganize, but not without some upheaval. Just 4 years after its organization, the company changed from the traditional hierarchical organization. GECFS asked employees to be informal leaders within their scope of responsibility. All employees became leaders in a nontraditional sense of the word. The hierarchical system was replaced with a cross-functional career development path, which enabled employees to gain a wider variety of skills. The company implemented a team-driven organization and encouraged employees to develop a sense of pride in being leaders in innovative change. While there was some difficulty from managers and supervisors who felt displaced, employees were told that they were empowered to make decisions and work with new team members to make decisions (Dibbs, 1993).

Because of the problems mentioned earlier, GECFS was restructured again in 1991 with apparent success. Elimination of hierarchical layers improved communication, organizational speed, and the organization's overall capability, according to CEO Jack Welch.

This change in empowerment also fostered excitement in employees about a greater opportunity for growth, development, and autonomy. In May 1992, about a year after the second restructuring, a consistent improvement began to emerge from the customer services surveys. The improvement from customer satisfaction steadily improved for more than 13 quarters. Although employee turnover increased immediately after these restructuring activities, it leveled out to less than one third the rate of its prestructuring levels. The new empowerment model used at GECFS was credited, in part, as being a key driver for the success the organization experienced throughout the 1990s (Dibbs, 1993).

Companies with viable empowerment solutions experience less turnover. Employees perceive that they are empowered when their actions affect the quality of their work. Additionally, people feel empowered when they sense that they have a choice about how to do their job, as well as to make decisions or perform actions that are within their authority. The key components of the empowerment solution are its levels, structure, time frame, and review process.

Potential Problems

Empowerment can have some negative influences if it is not carefully managed. The reorganization of GECFS had some downsides; there was concern about the delayering of hierarchy because it eliminated the traditional promotion model of going up the corporate ladder. Additionally, employees were concerned about how people outside the organization would accept the new titles of people inside the company. Finally, there was also some confusion about the roles and responsibilities of managers who became co-workers with employees. The perceived problems at GECFS might have been averted with proper communication. Employees need to know what is negotiable about the scope of empowerment, and this decision must come from the organization. The necessary components for effectively establishing empowerment include the level of empowerment, the structure, the time frame, and the review process.

Factors of Empowerment

Empowerment can have significant benefits to the organization when it is properly configured and implemented. The following factors create an effective empowerment solution:

The *levels of empowerment* relate to the various work situations and the corresponding freedom of individuals to make decisions and take action without seeking management approval. Empowerment can create the belief among employees that they are entitled to more authority than is approved or is reasonable. However, if these expectations are not fulfilled, employees may experience a lack of satisfaction from the empowerment exercise, even if their expectations are unrealistic. To avoid such issues, communication about the empowerment levels is absolutely necessary.

The *structure of empowerment* defines the hierarchy for who can give empowerment authority within the organization. The organization's empowerment structure should negotiate and resolve issues of empowerment, especially when empowerment will help or hurt productivity. Only through involvement from employees can realistic empowerment occur. The organization can establish an office to monitor performance and support the empowerment changes.

The *time frame of empowerment* is necessary to give everyone the same expectation for the length of time for the empowerment structure. Employees may need weeks or months to be trained in key areas to assume the responsibility they desire.

The *review process of empowerment* evaluates the successes and opportunities for improvement of the empowerment solution by providing valuable feedback. Without a review process, there may be the unfulfilled expectations that make the process unproductive.

TEAMWORK

A *team* is a group of employees working together on a common goal. Teams are created for many purposes with the understanding that productivity and effectiveness improve as a result of processing work within organized groups of employees. Employee bonding is improved through team creation. Often employees on one team work on several processes that cut across the organization. These are called *cross-functional teams*.

Need for Teamwork

Employees have a need to be part of a supportive, productive team. A 2001 Australian study assessed teams in 17 private and public sector industries, with a range of organization sizes. The survey on a variety of workplace issues found organizations with team structures have higher labor productivity, a flatter management structure, and reduced employee turnover (Glassop, 2002).

Occasionally teamwork can succeed where other means of retention fail. Mid-level administrators in a large public doctoral research university had high satisfaction levels, but turnover rates were also high. A survey found that teamwork had a positive impact on morale and a substantial indirect effect on intent to leave (Edwards, 2001). By creating closely knit teams to carry out projects, organizations can increase the likelihood that teams will remain intact. Employees can become teammates and remain with the organization (Cappelli, 2000).

Teambuilding

Teams are built with a central purpose in mind, whether it is to produce a new product, improve an existing method, or eliminate the stagnant atmosphere that organizations sometimes create. Being a member of a group helps improve identity with the organization. The purpose for team creation may be as general as promoting correlation within the organization or as specific as planning a workshop. When the goal of the team is clear and identifiable, the progress toward the goal can be measured and a feeling of achievement is realized. A sense of belonging and improved productivity result from teamwork.

WorldNow, an Internet company that provides solutions for television stations has a exemplary record of retention; their turnover rate is 3 percent and they have lost only one nonadministrative employee in their 2-year existence. Teambuilding, with benefits and recognition, keeps employees loyal. The company sponsored an off-site teambuilding activity to promote interpersonal relationships, followed by periodic teambuilding events, and even offered perks such as daily free lunch and one-on-one breakfast with the CEO. The company is divided into eight working groups, each with its own employee recognition budget. Despite growth from 35 employees to 110 in just 2 years, there is a constant effort to impress on managers the importance of connecting with their staff (Alonzo, 2000).

Support for teams requires a commitment of resources, such as office space, computers, equipment, budget, and assigned employees. More important is the support from leadership that entails the team structure, clear roles and responsibilities, and unambiguous expectations of the team and team leader. "There is no substitute for a manager who can provide parameters and guidance," according to Bandow (2001). Managers can also help remove barriers and keep the team on track.

Team Chartering

The team organization should be formalized in a team charter. The charter should be a written document that clarifies the purpose, makeup, and responsibilities of a team. It should be circulated both for approval and for communication with the organization. A charter should include the following:

- Purpose—identifying the end product of the team
- Goals—stating clear and achievable goals
- Authority—defining levels of power and responsibility
- Roles—establishing the power of the team leader and team members
- Division—creating the division of work
- Process—defining how problems may be raised, addressed, and solved; identifying how the team will respond to requests for information, products, and services

Microsoft uses the concept of team chartering for its "super teams" that comprise a system of educating teams in self-improvement. The team leader works with a facilitator and then the team identifies factors, such as needed individuals, required resources, desired results, team responsibilities, and delineation of the factors that the team is empowered to control. When all team members understand their responsibilities, the charter is formalized by creating a contract that teams can revisit to ensure that they remain on track. The super teams and the use of mentoring have resulted in reduced turnover, according to Microsoft (Glover, 2002).

Lending Teams: Leasing Employees

A program called LEND (Lending Employees for National Development) was created in southern California among several defense contracting organizations (Lockheed, Boeing, and Northrop). If one of the organizations lost a contract (from the government), it would hire out a team of experienced employees to the organization that won the contract. The team members remained employees of the first organization, allowing the organization to retain its investment in key employees. This allowed the organization to retain its ability to bid on future contracts, and it broadened the experience of the employees it leased to the other organization. Employees liked the program because it permitted them to keep their jobs while gaining valuable new experience (Cappelli, 2000).

Fostering Interpersonal Relationships

Developing trust among team members is essential to good team productivity. Teams work best when they are able to develop interpersonal relationships that help them to rely on each other. Personal understanding can occur during creative activities, such as luncheons, dinners, outdoor recreational activities, contests, motivational meetings, and brainstorming sessions. The possibilities are inexhaustible for creating social experiences, communication, and commitment to team members. Other options for team building include creation of team T-shirts, mugs, or caps that emphasize team identity. Competition between teams can also improve cohesion, whether the game is product related or simply intramural softball. Activities foster a sense of belonging and improve teamwork.

One example of teambuilding can be seen at Ingage Solutions, a Phoenix-based division of AG Communication Systems, which has kept the turnover of software engineers to 7 percent by developing programs that create a social community in the workplace. The organization promotes golf leagues, investment clubs, and softball squads to create social ties that bind workers to each other through fostering relationships with team members. If an employee decides to leave the organization, it also means leaving the social network of company-sponsored activities. Studies have shown that being a member of a team increases commitment to the employee's place of work. Commitment and loyalty to team members is an important way to promote employee retention. By encouraging the development of social ties among employees, organizations can often significantly reduce turnover (Cappelli, 2000).

Teambuilding through Recognition

Recognition is highly positive for teams if it is meaningful and motivational. Awards and recognitions for team members and teams as a whole can foster the dedication to the team. Harrah's Hotel and Casino rewards teamwork by giving a special chairman's award for those who go above and beyond normal job expectations. The hotel and casino has more than 800 employees and strives to retain its employees through programs including team rewards, recognition, feedback tools, and compensation.

ETHICS AND TRUST

Trust

There are two forms of trust, which are related but distinct. The first is trust in the supervisor, which is defined by the Academy of Management Review as the willingness of a subordinate to be vulnerable to the actions of his or her supervisor whose behavior and actions he or she cannot control (Rosseau, Sitkin, Burt, and Camerer, 1998). The second type is the trust the employee has in the organization to act in ways that are beneficial, or at least not detrimental, to him or her (Tan and Tan, 2000). Every interaction with employees and colleagues presents an opportunity to build or destroy trust. To achieve trust, leaders must exude personal integrity so employees can trust them for information, skills, and empowerment (Hill and Ingala, 2001).

Need for Trust

A recent survey asked 655 employees to evaluate 12 different factors that might influence their willingness and intentions to stay with their current employers. The factor of trust correlated most closely with retention. In other words, organizations with high retention have employees who perceive they can trust their managers, team members, and the organization to keep promises, follow through on commitments, and provide accurate information when asked (*HR Focus*, 2001).

Developing Supervisory Trust

Employees need supervisors who demonstrate ability, benevolence, and integrity. The leader needs to possess the ability to perform competently in the work setting (Heathfield, 2002). Organizations should hire and promote people who are capable of forming positive and trusting relationships with subordinates, as well as being competent at necessary skills. Developing the skill levels of supervisors to improve their relationships with employees is good for the organization, leaders, and employees.

To develop trust, organizations should require and expect supervisors to act with integrity and to keep commitments in a timely manner. Protecting the interests of all employees in the work group is accomplished by responding to the needs of employees. Organizations should reward leaders and employees who tell the truth, even when it might be easier for leaders to exaggerate accomplishments to meet organizational goals. Leaders who treat employees fairly, openly, and honestly build trust. Additionally, trust can be created and sustained in employees through teambuilding activities (Heathfield, 2002). Whether trust is built by the leader or through teambuilding activities, it is an important part of employee retention.

When employees trust the supervisor, they may generalize such trust to the whole organization because they think the supervisor is representing the organization (Konovsky and Pugh, 1994). Although supervisor trust and organization trust are distinct, they are related because employees interpret actions of managers as representing the organization itself. Employees make judgments regarding whether to trust the organization by making inferences from interactions with the supervisor. When the employee decides to trust the supervisor and the supervisor, in turn, trusts the employee, there is a spillover effect to the entire organization. Therefore it is important that the organization understands this relationship between trust in supervisors and trust in the organization (Tan and Tan, 2000).

Developing Organizational Trust

Organizations should ensure that their policies and practices have distributive and procedural justice (see Chapter 8) because both help create trust. They should also demonstrate integrity if they want to sustain employee trust.

The question that helps determine whether distributive justice is part of the organizational framework is, "Does the organization treat all employees equally?" Equitable treatment means that all members of the organization adhere to the same set of standards, ensuring that no group receives preferential treatment. However, distributive justice does not mean, for example, that all employees must work the same shift. Organizational requirements may require different shifts. But, it does mean, for example, that the timing of pay increases are consistently distributed to all employees throughout the organization.

The organization should also ensure that benefits are equally distributed. Some managerial benefits, such as profit sharing, are awarded distinctly to leaders for meeting specific goals. However, increasing numbers of organizations use profit sharing as a way to motivate and reward all employees for meeting performance objectives. Profit sharing that is available for the entire employee population is an excellent example of distributive justice.

The question that helps determine whether procedural justice is part of the organizational framework is, "Is there a system employees can use to express complaints?" If a grievance occurs and an employee wants to bring it to the attention of management, is there a process to follow? The process may be as simple as an open-door policy in which employees can express concerns to their supervisors or go to the next higher level of management to discuss complaints. In some cases, an open-door policy is not enough. Organizations should have the capability to listen to employee grievances outside the normal chain of command or standard organizational structure. A committee should be established to listen to employee grievances. This committee may be composed of HR professionals and representatives from the line. Standard operating procedures or by-laws can govern how the committee operates and what kinds of grievances it will address. Some complaints may not be appropriate for the grievance committee, such as employee performance issues that are best handled in a one-on-one coaching and mentoring environment with the employee's immediate supervisor. A grievance committee enables employees to experience a process whereby their concerns and complaints are addressed in an open manner. The grievance committee should be composed of employees who are empowered to act on behalf of the organization. Publication of the grievance process helps ensure that employees are aware of the organization's desire to address procedural issues.

Aligent, a leader in fiberoptic products, succeeded in fostering relationships—while laying employees off. Employees stayed loyal to the organization even while losing their jobs. "This was a matter of saving employees; it sounds hokey, but it's like a family," according to one Aligent employee. How did they do this? Aligent took drastic steps to avoid downsizing, but eventually the cutbacks were inevitable. The organization was honest and straightforward with employees from the beginning of the economic downturn. Town meetings and written communication explained what was taking place and how employees could help. All over the organization, employees engaged in cost-cutting behavior, saving the organization

50 percent in travel expenses and 70 percent in computer purchases. Even across-the-board salary cuts, which saved $280 million in annual savings, were not enough. When the downsizing effort began, Aligent implemented a layoff program that was two parts communication and one part execution. The CEO delivered the initial message with managers explaining the need to cut staff while thanking them for their cost-cutting efforts. Being brutally honest with employees about what management was doing helped create trust and integrity. This integrity is critical to retain the hearts and minds of employees, along with maintaining productivity, according to a general manager of one of Aligent's divisions. The economy, a lack of new orders (because Aligent's customer base was failing), and a result of September 11, 2001, forced the organization to lay off 27 percent of its workforce. In 1 year, Aligent laid off 8,000 employees, but because of its ability to foster relationships, Aligent succeeded in turning a divisive experience into one in which former employees supported and spoke well of Aligent (Roth, 2002).

Integrity

Organizational integrity consists of communication and follow-through. Communication should be timely and accurate. Organizations need to share critical information as soon as possible with employees. If leaders fail to release information to employees or wait to share information, employees may perceive that they are being kept in the dark and that leaders either do not care or do not trust employees with information. Management should take care to provide information that is accurate. Even if the news is bad and involves potential layoffs, employees need to hear the truth.

The organization should also follow through on what is says it will do. For example, if the organization states that it is going to implement a new pay structure within a certain timeframe, it should do so. If it is unable to meet the time frame, communication should be forthcoming as to why the organization cannot meet its promise. Keeping promises is critical for organizations to establish integrity.

Trust and Organizational Ethics

Trust is the basis for the ethical behavior within the organization. Employees need to feel that they can trust and believe in the integrity of their employers. An example of betrayed trust was seen in the scandal surrounding Enron. The entire life savings of many Enron employees vanished when the company misused the funds of employee 401(k) retirement accounts. Employees who had trusted the organization to behave ethically were devastated, both emotionally and financially, through the unethical behavior of Enron's corporate officials. Only by demonstrating truthfulness and ethical behavior can the organization develop trust within its employees and provide the basis for an ethical program.

Ethics

Ethics are based on organizational values. Trust is integral to all ethical behavior. Organizational values are reflected in the organization's culture. Standards of ethics help the organization and its employees understand that workers will be valued and fairly treated. Ethical standards also usually state that customers, suppliers, vendors, and the general public will be treated honestly and fairly.

Need for Ethics

Employees need to be able to trust their organization and depend on it to act with integrity. A survey at a college of education in a Midwestern metropolitan university found that both faculty and students perceived the ethical climate to be an important factor in the retention of students in the undergraduate academic program (Schulte, 2001). An organization's ethical climate directly influences employee job satisfaction and the employee's commitment to the organization (Schwepker, 2001). According to a November 1999 survey by the Ethics Resource Center (ERC), a Washington, D.C.–based nonprofit educational organization, there is a direct correlation between employee satisfaction and employers' ethical practices. High ethical standards and satisfied employees mean lower turnover (*HR Briefing*, 2001).

Ethics Program

The ethical climate of the organization and the ethical preferences of employees are related to increased feelings of job satisfaction and decreased intentions to turnover (Sims and Keon, 1997). In a study of Australian professional accountants, conflict between what the profession demanded and what the organization demanded resulted in an increased likelihood of resignation (Fawcett, 1988). The enforcement of a formal code of ethics, as well as lower levels of organizational and professional work conflict (conflict between the organization and the professional demands of the job itself), are related to lower intentions to turnover for a variety of employees (Sims, 2000). These findings support the creation of an ethics programs to help address such conflicts, and, in turn, lower turnover.

The director of organizational programs for the Society for Human Resource Management (SHRM) and a specialist in workplace ethics cites six key aspects to an ethics program:

- Make ethical behavior a priority and communicate the ethical position.
- Get buy-in for an ethics program and solicit help for maintaining the program.
- Appoint an HR manager (or executive management leader) to assume the role of chief ethics officer.
- Create an ethics task force that creates a statement of ethics pledging the organization's commitment to ethical behavior. Such a statement serves as a guide for employees.
- Ensure that management models high ethical standards.
- Offer ethics training sessions using real-world scenarios, and provide support programs and an ethics hotline for employees who find themselves conflicted about appropriate conduct on the job (HR Briefing, 2001).

Professional Codes of Ethics

Many professional groups have codes of ethics that govern their behavior and professional conduct. Employees can subscribe to these codes, and organizations can support employees by encouraging them to follow the ethical codes of their particular industry. To support ethical codes, organizations can help pay for any fees associated with membership to professional organizations that have ethical codes. The codes can be imperatives that are written as statements of personal responsibility and describe issues professionals are likely to face. A code of ethics may outline fundamental ethical considerations and address specific considerations of professional conduct.

Sometimes ethical programs are directed at leaders. For example, the Association of Computing and Public Policy has a code of ethics and professional conduct. It contains general moral imperatives, identification of specific professional responsibilities, organizational leadership imperatives, and compliance recommendations to adhere to the code.

When organizations openly support codes of ethics, employees are able to see that their organization supports integrity. There are numerous examples of industries and professions adopting codes of ethics, including home inspectors, realtors, electrical engineers, computer programmers, journalists, ecologists, sociologists, civil engineers, reporters, fundraisers, archivists, internet professionals, photographers, auditors, travel agents, lawyers, and health care professionals (Internet research search engine, Google.com searching Code of Ethics).

Leadership and Ethical Behavior

The integrity, trust, and ethical behavior of an organization should start at the top and should be integrated throughout the organization. Leaders are responsible for building the foundation of trust and ethical behavior. They should be role models for trustworthiness, honesty, and ethical behavior. Leaders' actions reflect both positively and negatively on the organization. Unfortunately, on occasion leaders are found to "fudge" or exaggerate numbers to achieve goals, and this behavior is tolerated in the name of organizational success. Such a tolerance is wrong and sends a mixed message to employees who are often aware of the dishonesty in the leader's reporting actions. Instead, leadership should be encouraged to demonstrate the highest standards of the organization's ethics. The actions of Mayor Giuliani following the September 11 disaster reflected positively on the entire New York City municipality. Conversely, the unethical conduct of Jeffrey Skilling, the former CEO of Enron, and Martha Stewart reflected negatively on their organizations.

COMMITMENT

Organizational commitment is a willingness to exert considerable effort on behalf of the organization and the desire to maintain membership (Mowday, Porter, and Steers, 1982). Management consultants encourage managers to "establish strong emotional links between employees and organizations" that will produce extraordinary effort and superior performance (Bartlett and Ghosal, 1994). Employees who are truly committed to a common goal will not only perform well, but will also stay with the organization longer (Boshoff, Christo, Mels, and Gerhard, 2000).

Individuals who demonstrate organizational commitment have a strong belief in, and acceptance of, the organization's goals and values. They are often willing to work hard on behalf of the organization. Not surprisingly, employees who have high organizational commitment want to remain members of the company for which they work (Walsch, 2001).

Need for Commitment

Organizational commitment has been shown to be consistently related to turnover; the less committed an employee is, the more likely that employee is to leave the organization (Blau and Boal, 1989; Miner, 1992; Wright and Bonett, 1991). High levels of commitment often correlate with high levels of productivity and performance; employees who are committed do seem to perform and produce better than noncommitted individuals (Walsch, 2001). Measuring organizational commitment helps the organization understand how motivated people do the job, and, in turn, remain with the organization.

Commitment was an accurate predictor of turnover, according to two studies conducted in China. The first study was of 205 middle-level managers and technical workers, and the second study was of 245 university graduates in Hong Kong, including school teachers, accountants, social workers, marketing and sales executives, engineers, reporters, programmers, HR executives, and middle-level administrators in banking. Researchers recommended that organizations build commitment through long-term, positive relationships with employees. Two major recommendations were identified. First, developing trust emphasizes open and fair procedures for communicating with employees and helps to fairly allocate rewards. Second, provide supervisor training in how to treat employees fairly and professionally (Wong, Hui, Wong, and Law, 2001).

Forms of Commitment

There are three main forms of commitment:

- *Commitment to the company.* This is the degree to which employees align with company and team goals, values, philosophy, and practices.
- *Commitment to the profession.* This is the degree to which people dedicate themselves and identify with a specific kind of

work. An example is a nurse or a mechanic who works in their specific profession regardless of the company for which they worked.

- *Commitment to others.* Commitment to others in the organization is the third part of this solution. Friendships at work are often the most important relationships in an employee's life. People spend so much time at work, they can often feel as though fellow employees are members of their families.

Each form of commitment is distinct from the other. This means that employees can be committed to the company without being committed to the job. It also can mean that employees might be committed to others, but not to the company. Experiencing commitment in one area does not necessarily mean that it is transferred to another. However, improving one form of commitment may have a positive impact on the others. For example, employees who have personal relationships will be hesitant to leave the organization and, therefore, organizational commitment is indirectly affected. Similarly, research has found that employees who experience high levels of job satisfaction also experience commitment within the workplace (Williams and Hazer, 1986).

Influences of Commitment

Commitment is closely related to motivation and job satisfaction, but it is also influenced by other factors. Job tasks—the things that people do at work—influence commitment. Other factors include the employees' relationship with their leaders, the level of employee pay, fairness, absenteeism, employee attitudes, job satisfaction, communication, rewards, and family support programs. All these factors influence employee turnover and absenteeism (Eby and Freeman, 1999).

What can the organization do to facilitate commitment from its employees? The solution is as broad as the commitment need itself. All three forms of commitment are addressed in the recommended solution. Although the forms of commitment may be distinct, the solutions can, at times, overlap.

Commitment Solutions

The Loyalty Institute at Aon Consulting has investigated workforce commitment since 1997. Their commitment index has now been directly administered to almost 10,000 North American participants and 50,000 more employees through participating organizations. The goal of this consulting group has been to explore practices that increase employee commitment, pride, productivity, and retention. Data analysis revealed that commitment is not the result of one "silver bullet" solution, but derived from needs.

1. Safety and security—the employee feels safe in the work environment.
2. Rewards—compensation and benefits are received.
3. Affiliation—there is a sense of belonging to a work team and/or the entire organization.
4. Growth—positive individual change is experienced.
5. Work/life harmony—employees achieve a sense of fulfillment in balancing work and life responsibilities.

The five needs related to employee commitment are hierarchical; that is, safety and security should be addressed first. Leaders and HR managers should make the effort to meet employee expectations in all of these five needs to improve their retention levels. Interaction between leaders and employees creates the environment to motivate and retain employees (Stum, 2001).

Job Offers

A job offer is an initial commitment from the organization to the employee in which it commits to provide pay, benefits, a work environment, and placement in a specific job. By accepting the offer, the employee makes a commitment to the organization to work in a specific position. The job offer can be made in a way that creates and builds commitment by explaining the job and the support the employee will receive to ensure success. Identifying the necessary tools, training, and leadership that will be given to the employee should also be a part of the job offer discussion. Explaining how employee support will be given will build trust and create an atmosphere where employees can be committed.

Research conducted in five large organizations in Great Britain showed that employees who had their prejoining expectations met in certain key areas remained with their employer. The five organizations recruited large numbers of new college graduates and found that employees believe there is a psychological contract made during the job offer. In other words, employees have perceptions of promises and commitments that shape their reactions to actual work experiences. Discussion at the time of the job offer is therefore critical in identifying realistic promises and commitments that the organization should keep.

Organizations must understand that new employees believe they have been promised certain behavior by the organization. In the job offer, certain statements and inferences are made. If these promises and commitments are kept, employees tend to remain with the organization. If not, they do not stay (Sturges and Guest, 2001). Realistic job previews that honestly describe the position and the organization are valuable tools that organizations can use to ensure employees' reasonable expectations (Phillips, 1998).

Organizing Work around a Project

When employees are organized to do their work around a specific project, they have greater commitment to quality. When the project goes well, employees get the credit, which increases their prestige. Organizing teams around projects is one way to establish commitment to a team, a quality job, and the organization. Team members develop a strong sense of commitment to the other members of the team because they do not want to let them down. The higher the standards are for performance, the greater the commitment is to quality and to the other team members. The automobile industry is one example where organizing employees around a project has improved employee commitment and made improvements in quality and overall employee performance (Cappelli, 2000).

Identifying Expectations and Benefits

Even in temporary or short-term employment, commitment can be created through helping employees understand what is expected of them and what they will gain as a result of good performance. In a temporary job, employees understand that they will eventually have to leave. However, if organizations explain expectations and help employees achieve the benefits of completing their temporary work tenure, commitment is created. Employees with positive experiences remain committed long after they leave the organization. Examples of this include McKinsey and Company, which is famous for the level of commitment it enjoys from its former consultants, even after layoffs. Another example of employee commitment was studied at Wharton's School where members of the first-year class were asked to explain how they were managed in their previous job. Nearly without exception, those employees who worked in temporary jobs, such as for an investment bank as a junior analyst, are always positive about their former employers. The reason for their strong commitment to former employers was due to receiving a clear idea of organizational expectations, what was gained through their efforts, and a knowledge of their fixed departure date (Cappelli, 2000).

Commitment Study in Health Care Workers

Some authors suggest that to improve commitment, managers must actively market the company's values, mission, and vision to employees just as they market its products and services to customers (Boshoff, Christo, Mels, and Gerhard, 2000). Health care workers say that they are committed to the team and to patients, but not as committed to the organization for which they work, according to a study by the Loyalty Institute. Health care providers do not differentiate themselves as good places to work. A senior consultant for Aon explains: "The cost of turnover is up to two times an employee's salary and benefits. The battle for the workforce share is getting tougher so [health care providers] need to do better at differentiating their organizations." In the study, the six top-suggested solutions for improving commitment in the health care profession were to improve communication, improve wages, provide retirement planning, support employee interests outside of work, provide a work/life family balance, and allocate resources to meet or exceed patients' needs. This conclusion reiterates the solutions of this section. "Organizations that want to build a dedicated workforce must build a sense of spirit and pride that unifies individual, team and organizational goals." (Merisalo, 2001)

PROFESSIONAL GROWTH

Professional growth consists of skill improvement, which is usually accomplished through receiving technical and leadership training. Growth may consist of taking educational courses, receiving internal training programs, experiencing a new assignment that requires use of new skills, or becoming certified or licensed in a new function. Professional growth is a benefit to both the employee and the organization, which often needs qualified employees to fill positions at different levels.

Need for Professional Growth

Today's employees want to be able to grow in their careers by improving skill set and experience in desired positions. Employees also want to advance in the organization, although this may not be through traditional promotion. Growth may mean employees work in areas that lead to new challenges, such as a special project or being a part of a special team. Unless leaders address fundamental questions about individual career development, employees are always likely to move to another organization (Story, 2002).

Training

Internal educational programs link individual objectives with organizational objectives and are dynamic according to the needs of the organization. QUALCOMM, a manufacturer of digital wireless communication products headquartered in San Diego, California, with $2,679 million in annual sales, has positively affected turnover. The organization has created a program in which each of QUAL-COMM's 6,500 employees have an individual development plan (IDP) that is aligned with the organization's goal. The plans provide consistency with the employer's objectives, which leads to a high rate of promotion. Many of QUALCOMM'S additional training programs are linked to business initiatives; for example, the "Rapid Cycle Time" program enabled the company to deliver products to market faster than its competitors. This organization's demonstrated commitment to training has positively affected employee retention with turnover less than 6 percent (Galvin, 2001).

Leadership Training

Leaders need training to grow professionally; leadership training in the principles of business and management helps employees understand how their leadership style can be improved for the benefit of the organization. Training can be internal to the organization or received externally through professional consulting, seminars, conferences, and college courses. The objective of leadership training is to prepare present employees for future management positions within the organization. The Federated Department Stores is the owner of world-famous retailers Bloomingdale's, Macy's, and Burdines. The organization has 450 stores and uses leadership training to help improve employee retention. In 1999, Federated launched its

Leadership Institute with more than 400 store managers and executives attending one of 22 four-day sessions. Many of Federated's senior executives and the CEO took part in the leadership training sessions.

In 2000, the Gallup Organization conducted surveys asking employees to rate their work environment. Stores that ranked in the top 50 percent as having the most positive culture also achieved six times the amount of earnings than did the bottom 50 percent. Workgroups that scored in the top 25 percent also experienced 33 percent lower turnover than those in the bottom 25 percent. In 2000, Federated's Leadership Institute received the American Retail Excellence Best Practices recognition from the National Retail Federation. One store's operating vice president has commented on the organization's leadership effort, "We want people to know that when they join Federated, they will be getting the very best leadership training around, from the time they enter the company until the time they are senior executives." (Schettler, 2002)

Higher Education Programs

One way for employees to experience professional growth is through receiving additional education through high schools, colleges, and universities. Such programs are aimed at providing a means through which employees can improve knowledge and skills outside the organization. The educational programs are usually subsidized by the organization so that they are free or greatly discounted to the employees. Sometimes the organization can host college or technology courses on site, providing easy access to its employees. Usually this education is directly or indirectly related to the employee's profession. For example, many public school districts pay for public school teachers' higher education courses to help them become recertified for their state teaching license. Likewise, a trucking company may pay for the training for its employees to obtain their commercial driver's licenses. Office businesses may pay for employees to learn new computer software applications to improve their knowledge and productivity.

Educational assistance programs are an excellent means for helping retain good employees. United Technologies Corp. of Hartford, Connecticut, offers to pay for postsecondary degrees (job-related or not). The employer picks up the entire cost of tuition, fees, and books, and provides 3 paid hours a week for employees to study.

This generous educational assistance program helped retain employees and inspired their loyalty (Bruinius, 2002).

Other organizations today offer advanced degree programs to draw talented employees and retain them. More than 85 percent of corporations surveyed by the International Foundation of Employee Benefit Plans now offer some sort of education reimbursement program, and the amount that these organizations are spending on the programs is growing every year (Bruinius, 2002).

Licenses and Certificates

Combining training with real-world experience and a higher education program can result in a license or certificate, which provides an excellent way for employees to achieve professional growth. One organization that has created such a program in which its management team can achieve improved professional growth is JD Wetherspoon. A chain of English taverns, or pubs, known as JD Wetherspoon in Great Britain has introduced a professional qualification program for its managers to improve the career path of its staff and improve retention. Wetherspoon has 13,000 employees and has been working on retention for 5 years because of its high turnover problem. The chain, which will be adding another 90 pubs to its present 570, is now establishing formal education that will be required for all management. According to Wetherspoon's personnel and training director, "It's part of an ongoing drive to help staff build a career path in the pub industry. We want to send out the message that you can join the trade, get good training, a professional qualification and move up the career ladder." The course is being developed in cooperation with Leeds Metropolitan University and is called the "Professional Diploma in Licensed Retail." It will last 2 years and consist of workplace training and a series of examinations. Wetherspoon has reduced front-line staff turnover through improved pay and training from 180 percent in 1997 to around 48 percent. The turnover among management has dropped from 25 percent to 12 percent (*Personnel Today*, 2002).

Developmental Assignments and Projects

Interesting work assignments can lead to professional growth and career advancement. Such on-the-job training can offer new challenges, such as special projects or working on a process improvement team. A developmental assignment should be suited to the abilities of the employee. For example, a relatively new employee was assigned to compile and organize a technical training manual for shift supervisors. Teamed with a boss who outlined specifics, the employee was left to gain experience in the organization and meet presenters from different departments. The employee was able to research different aspects of the company and demonstrate initiative in bringing the project together. The result was personal growth and hands-on orientation with others in the organization.

When properly designed, developmental assignments can train employees for more responsibilities. Such assignments provide an environment of growth and development by requiring the employee to use new skills that were not required in the regular job situation. New projects and assignments enable learning and provide a way through which employees can increase skills on the job through doing new tasks. Critical to employee success is the guidance and assistance of leadership. With mentoring, employees can undertake new assignments that benefit their own knowledge and skill level and the organization's goals. Employees who experience professional growth are more inclined to remain with the organization.

FINAL THOUGHTS

This chapter and the three that preceded it focused on the needs of employees in the workplace and appropriate solution sets to meet these needs. This chapter specifically addressed the issues of commitment and growth. Solutions in these areas involve implementation of empowerment and teambuilding programs, building trust, displaying ethical behavior, offering opportunities through training, and employee development for job growth and career advancement. By satisfying these key needs, organizations can strengthen employee commitment and loyalty and reduce turnover.

REFERENCES

Abrashoff, M.D. "Retention through Redemption." *Harvard Business Review*, February 2001; 137–141.

Alonzo, V. "Passing the Test of Turnover." *Incentive*, November 2000; 174(11):14.

Arthur, J.B. "Effects of Human Resource Systems on Manufacturing Performance and Turnover." *Academy of Management Journal*, 1994; 37(3):670–687.

Bandow, D. "Time to Create Sound Teamwork." *Journal for Quality and Participation*, Summer 2001; 24(2):41.

Bartlett, A., and Ghosal, S. "Changing the Role of Top Management: Beyond Strategy to Purpose." *Harvard Business Review*, November/December 1994; 79–88.

Blau, G.J., and Boal, K.B. "Using Job Involvement and Organizational Commitment Interactively to Predict Turnover." *Journal of Management*, 1989; 15(1):115–127.

Boshoff, C., and Mels, G. "The Impact of Multiple Commitments on Intentions to Resign: An Empirical Assessment." *British Journal of Management*, September 2000; 11(3):255–272.

Bruinius, H. "Free Degrees, Loyal Employees." *Christian Science Monitor*, May 14, 2002; 94(119):11.

Buckingham, M., and Coffman, C. *First Break All the Rules*. New York: Simon and Schuster, 1999.

Cappelli, P. "A Market-Driven Approach to Retaining Talent." *Harvard Business Review*, January/February 2000; 79(1):103.

Collins, W.W. "Spotlight on Roofing: A Rewarding Job with a Promising Career Path." *Tech Directions*, December 1998; 58(5):32.

Dennison, D.R. "Bringing Corporate Culture to the Bottom Line." *Organizational Dynamics*, 1984; 13(2):5–22.

Dibbs, J. "Organizing for Empowerment." *Business Quarterly*, Autumn 1993; 58(1):97.

Edwards, R.L.R. "The Morale and Satisfaction of Midlevel Administrators: Differentiating the Constructs and their Impact on Intent to Leave." *Dissertation Abstracts International Section A: Humanities and Social Sciences*, August 2001; 62(2-A):482.

Eby, L.T., and Freeman, D.M. "Motivational Bases of Affective Organizational Commitment: A Partial Test." *Journal of Occupational and Organizational Psychology*, December 1999; 72(4):463.

"Ethics Plans Pay off in Staff Retention and Profits." *HR Briefing* (Aspen), June 15, 2001:7.

Emerging Workforce Study. Fort Lauderdale, Fla.: Interim Services, 1999.

Fawcett, T. "O.P.C. Organizational Professional Conflict." *Australian Accountant*, 1988; 58(7):93–96.

Galvin, T. "Birds of a Feather." *Training*, March 2001; 38(3):58.

Glassop, L.I. "The Organizational Benefits of Teams." *Human Relations*, February 2002; 55(2):225–249.

Glover, C. "Good for the Soul." *People Management*, July 11, 2002; 8(14):28.

Heathfield, S. "Trust Rules! The Most Important Secret." Human Resources, About Inc. 2002, Internet article, http://humanre-sources.about.com/library/weekly/aa041401a.htm

Hill, K., and Ingala, J. "Trust Me or Not?" *Nursing Management*, November 2001; 32(11):41.

Internet research search engine, Google.com http://www.google.com (search: Code of Ethics, October 2002).

Kaye, B., and Jordan Evans, S. Love 'Em or Lose 'Em. San Francisco, Calif.: Berrett-Koehler Publishers, 1999.

Konovsky, M.A., and Pugh, S.D. "Citizenship Behavior and Social Exchange." *Academy of Management Journal*, 1994; 44:265–285.

Lawler and Bowen. "The Empowerment of Service Workers: What, Why, How and When." *Sloan Management Review*, Spring 1992:31–39.

Merisalo, Laura J. "Cultivating Commitment Is Key to Curb Turnover." *Newsletter for Health Care Registration Professionals*, May 2001; 10(8):3–6.

Miner, J.B. *Industrial Organizational Psychology*. New York: McGraw-Hill, 1992.

Mowday, R.T., Porter, L.W., and Steers, R.M. *Employee-Organizational Linkages: The Psychology of Commitment, Absenteeism and Turnover*. New York: Academic Press, 1982.

Phillips, J. "Effects of Realistic Job Previews on Multiple Organizational Outcomes: A Meta Analysis." *Academy of Management Journal*, 1998; 41(6):673–690.

"Pub Group Sets Course to Push Staff Retention," *Personnel Today*, April 16, 2002:3.

Rosseau, D.M., Sitkin, S.B., Burt, R.S., and Camerer, C. "Not So Different After All: A Cross-Discipline View of Trust." *Academy of Management Review*, 1998; 23:393–404.

Roth, D. "How to Cut Pay, Lay Off 8,000 People and Still Have Workers Who Love You." *Fortune*. February 4, 2002; 145(3): 62–68.

Schettler, J. "Federated Department Stores, Inc." *Training*, March 2002; 30(3):65.

Schulte, L.E. "Undergraduate Faculty and Student Perceptions of the Ethical Climate and Its Importance in Retention." *College Student Journal*, December 2001; 35(4):565.

Schwepker, C.H., Jr. "Ethical Climate Relationship to Job Satisfaction, Organizational Commitment, and Turnover Intention in the Sales Force," *Journal of Business Research*, October 2001; 54(1):39–52.

Sims, R.L., and Keon, T.L. "Ethical Work Climate as a Factor in the Development of Person-Organization Fit." *Journal of Business Ethics*, 1997; 16:1095–1105.

Sims, R.L. "The Relationship between Employee Attitudes and Conflicting Expectations for Lying Behavior." *Journal of Psychology*,
November 2000; 134(6):619.

Story, M. "Winning the Battle for Talent," *New Zealand Management*, March 2002; 49(2):39.

Stum, D. "Maslow Revisited: Building the Employee Commitment
Pyramid." *Strategy and Leadership*, MCB University Press, April
29, 2001:4–9.

Sturges, J., and Guest, D. "Don't Leave Me This Way! A Qualita-
tive Study of Influences on the Organizational Commitment and
Turnover Intentions of Graduates Early in their Careers." *British
Journal of Guidance and Counselling*, 2001; 29(4):447–462.

"Survey Says that Trust Is the Basis for Employee Retention." *HR
Focus*, February 2001; 78(2):8.

Tan, H.H., and Tan, C.S.F. "Toward the Differentiation of Trust
in Supervisor and Trust in Organization." *Genetic, Social and
General Psychology Monographs*, 2000; 126(2):241–260.

Walsch, M.W. "Luring the Best in an Unsettled Time: Money Isn't
Everything." *New York Times*, January 30, 2001; 150(516):
G-1.

Wellins, Richard S., *et al. Empowered Teams: Creating Self-Directed
Work Groups that Improve Quality, Productivity, and Participation*. San Francisco: Jossey-Bass, January 1991.

Williams, L.J., and Hazer, J.T. "Antecedents and Consequences of
Satisfaction and Commitment in Turnover Models: A Reanalysis."
Journal of Applied Psychology, May 1986; 71(2):219.

Wong, C.-S., Hui, C., Wong, Y.-t., Law, K.S. "The Significant Role
of Chinese Employees' Organizational Commitment: Implications
for Managing Employees in Chinese Societies." *Journal of World
Business*, Fall 2001; 36(3):326.

Wright, T.A., and Bonnet, D.G. "Growth Coping, Work Satisfaction
and Turnover: A Longitudinal Study." *Journal of Business and
Psychology*, 1991; 6(1):133–145.

Further Reading

Ashby, F.C., and Pell, A.A. *Embracing Excellence: Become an
Employer of Choice to Attract and Keep the Best Talent*. Paramus,
N.J.: Prentice Hall Press, 2001.

Bolman, L.G., and Deal, T.E. *Leading with Soul: An Uncommon
Journey of Spirit*. New York: John Wiley & Sons, 2001.

Branham, L. *Keeping the People Who Keep You in Business: 24
Ways to Hang on to Your Most Valuable Talent*. New York:
American Management Association, 2001.

Cloke, K., and Goldsmith, J. *The End of Management and the Rise of Organizational Democracy.* Hoboken, N.J.: John Wiley & Sons, 2002.

Cohen, D.S. *The Talent Edge: A Behavioral Approach to Hiring, Developing, Keeping Top Performers.* New York: John Wiley & Sons, 2001.

Galford, R.M., and Drapeau, A.S. *The Trust Leader.* Nokomis, Ill.: Free Press, 2002.

Kaye, B., and Jordan-Evans, S. *Love 'Em or Lose 'Em: Getting Good People to Stay.* San Francisco, Calif.: Berrett-Koehler Publishers, 1999.

Maxwell, J.C. *The 17 Indisputable Laws of Teamwork: Embrace Them and Empower Your Team.* Nashville, Tenn.: Thomas Nelson Publisher, 2001.

McKeown, J.L. *Retaining Top Employees.* New York: McGraw-Hill, 2002.

Thomas, K.W. *Intrinsic Motivation at Work: Building Energy and Commitment.* San Francisco, Calif.: Berrett-Koehler Publishing, 2003.

CHAPTER 10

Match Solutions
to Needs

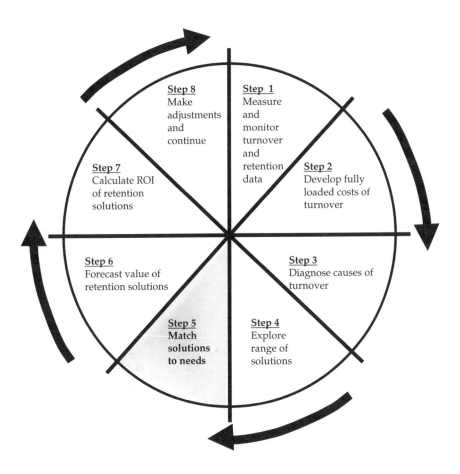

Step 1
Measure and monitor turnover and retention data

Step 2
Develop fully loaded costs of turnover

Step 3
Diagnose causes of turnover

Step 4
Explore range of solutions

Step 5
Match solutions to needs

Step 6
Forecast value of retention solutions

Step 7
Calculate ROI of retention solutions

Step 8
Make adjustments and continue

INTRODUCTION

With a range of potential solutions in hand and much evidence of the causes of turnover, the next task for the retention team is to match the solution to a particular need or cause of turnover. At times this step is obvious. In other situations, it is neither obvious nor easy. Too often, solutions are implemented without being properly matched to the cause, or too many solutions are applied in an attempt to chase every cause of turnover rather than focusing on the relative priority of the various causes of turnover. This chapter presents the methods and techniques used to combine data on the causes, determine the strengths of the causes, and present the conclusion to various groups so that a proper match of solution to need can be accomplished. Instead of attempting to take on a wide variety of solutions, only the solutions with maximum payoffs are attempted. The problems of avoiding mismatches are explored in addition to techniques to ensure the match is appropriate and effective.

COMBINING DATA FROM DIFFERENT SOURCES

Chapter 5 explored the various approaches to determine the causes of turnover. Multiple methods are often used and, consequently, the immediate task is to combine the data in some meaningful way so that the most significant causes of turnover can be addressed. For example, in many settings, the annual feedback survey process may reveal certain issues that should be addressed. Exit interviews often uncover concerns or red flags. Focus groups explore in more detail the specific reason why employees are leaving. Given these three sets of data, the challenge is to combine the data in a meaningful way. The approach depends on the consistency of the data from various sources.

Ideally, all data sources should consistently reflect the same causes of turnover. The task is to combine the data in a way to show the relative priority. In some situations, it is a matter of adding the strength of the data, if the input measure is on the same scale (e.g., a 5-point scale). In reality, this may not always occur because some sources are more credible than others, some input is more reliable than others, and some input scales are different. The difficulty lies in addressing the inconsistencies.

Four basic approaches can be used to deal with inconsistent and conflicting data from the different sources. The first approach is to let the relative strengths and weaknesses support or cancel each other. In essence, this is a mathematical approach. For example, if one report shows the need for flexible working hours as the No. 1 reason for causing turnover, but another source has this problem listed as No. 5, then the data are averaged in some convenient way. The problem is still there—somewhere between No. 1 and No. 5 in strength.

The second approach is to examine the relative strength of the data. For example, if the nominal group technique concluded by a wide margin that the No. 1 cause of turnover was unfair treatment by supervisors, this cause should not be ignored even if it did not show up in another data collection source. Strength of the ranking must be a consideration for keeping it on the list of causes.

This leads to the third approach—considering the credibility of the data collection method. Several questions need to be asked. Was the data collected anonymously? Did respondents have an opportunity or a reason to be biased? Was there a motive for respondents to provide data that are either inaccurate or purposely distorted? The critical issue is the objectivity of the data and the credibility of the source. Anonymous data will be more credible if the respondents clearly perceive that the data collection process *is* anonymous. Other methods, such as the nominal group technique, have a way of refining the input, digging deeper into the issue, and using the synergy of the focus group to help understand complex issues of why people make decisions to leave an organization. If conducted properly, the nominal group technique is more credible when the groups sufficiently represent a cross section of the target population. The important step in this process is to rank the data sources in terms of their credibility.

The final approach is to use expert input from a group of individuals who best understand the retention process in the organization. Group members should include human resource (HR) specialists and team leaders from the area where the turnover is occurring. Individuals should not have ownership of the solution; however, they should have knowledge about the retention issue. Using a consensus-making process, the group should reach a conclusion as to the actual causes of turnover, given the conflicting data sources. More information on the consensus method is presented later in the chapter.

DETERMINING THE SIGNIFICANCE OF THE CAUSE

The next step is to judge the relative strength of the cause after all the data sources have been combined. In essence, the task is to determine how much turnover is being caused by a particular issue or could be prevented by a particular issue. Determining the relative strength of the cause is the beginning point to develop the potential payoff for addressing a particular cause. Four techniques are appropriate when tackling this issue.

The first technique is to **examine relative rankings of the data**. For example, on the annual feedback survey, the highest-rated issue is probably driving the highest percentage of turnover. After examining the data, a rule is developed to allocate the percent of turnover. For example, the top 10 issues could account for 80 percent of the turnover. If the turnover rate is 30 percent, 24 percent (80% × 30%) is caused by the top 10 reasons. The 24 percent is then allocated by the relative strength of the rankings. In another example, using data from the nominal group technique, each ranking could be translated into turnover, assuming that all the points assigned represent the entire turnover. Table 10-1 shows the calculation for the No. 1, No. 2, and No. 3 causes of turnover, taken directly from the nominal group progress data.

In this example, a 35 percent turnover in an 820-employee group translates into 287 turnovers annually. The No. 1 cause of turnover, inadequate pay, accounts for 21.8 percent of that figure, or 63 turnovers. Thus, if the perception of inadequate pay were removed, there would be 63 fewer turnover statistics in the group during the year.

Table 10-1
Allocation of Turnover to Cause

Priority	Turnover Cause	Points	% of Total	% of Turnover
No. 1	Inadequate pay	252	21.8	7.6
2	Feedback and recognition	193	16.7	5.8
3	Ability and opportunity	102	8.8	3.1

Sample Calculation:

Total points from the nominal group process—all causes	1,155
Total points for No. 1 cause	252
Percent of total (252 ÷ 1,155)	21.8%
Total turnover rate	35%
Turnover rate allocated to No. 1 cause (22% × 35%)	7.6%

The second technique is to **ask participants to provide input**. As data are collected (by survey, focus group, or interviews), participants indicate the percentage of actual turnover that is caused by this particular issue. This figure is an estimate, but it can be adjusted for error, applying techniques described later. Using a pie chart, the participants are asked to allocate the turnover "pie" by different causes of turnover. The estimate should total 100 percent (i.e., all turnovers during a specified time period, such as a month or year, are considered a complete pie). Given the estimates of allocating the pie, participants indicate their level of comfort with each allocation. As they consider each piece of the pie, participants indicate their level of confidence with the allocation to a particular cause. Figure 10-1 shows the pie chart from a group.

The level of confidence may be the same for each allocation. However, participants may be more comfortable with some allocations than others. This step provides an opportunity to reflect on the certainty of the estimation. The two percentages are then multiplied, discounting the allocation by the level of confidence. This is an error adjustment described in Chapters 11 and 12. For example, if participants indicated that 30 percent of turnover is caused by unfair treatment from supervisors and they are 80 percent confident, then at least 24 percent (30% × 80%) of the actual turnover is connected to this particular issue.

A third technique is to **use the experiences of others**. When other organizations have experienced similar problems—and many of them have, it may be appropriate to capture the experience of others.

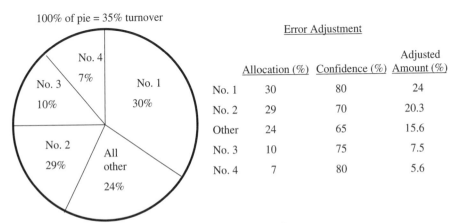

	Error Adjustment		
	Allocation (%)	Confidence (%)	Adjusted Amount (%)
No. 1	30	80	24
No. 2	29	70	20.3
Other	24	65	15.6
No. 3	10	75	7.5
No. 4	7	80	5.6

Figure 10-1. Allocation of turnover.

For example, if other organizations have found that supervisor problems usually account for the majority of the issues, this may mean that the solutions aimed at correcting the problem will have a higher priority. Any experience gained through reports from previous projects should be used to reach a conclusion about the relative strength to the cause.

Finally, the **use of expert input** may be appropriate. As in the issue described in the previous section, a group of experts could meet to make this decision. The experts are those who understand the issue most (i.e., they understand the causes of turnover and have an understanding of the relative strength of those issues). The HR staff and part of the management team directly involved in the target areas where the turnover is excessive is appropriate for this input.

REACHING A CONSENSUS

When reaching a **consensus** on the issues of turnover, it is important to include those individuals familiar with the causes and the solutions. Although no formal procedure is recommended a consensus is reached in an atmosphere where individuals are free to offer suggestions, critique, and disagree with others. Consensus is reached when individuals understand the underlying assumptions and can clarify any misstatements or misperceptions. Consensus is not reached when individuals mistrust or purposely mislead others, restrict their comments, ideas, or suggestions, lose their tempers during the process, or will not agree on any point.

PRESENTING DATA FOR DECISION MAKING

The next step in the process is to present the data, showing the relative priority of the causes. A simplified approach should be used to illustrate the relative strength of the cause of turnover. Three very simple methods are used, although others could be appropriate.

Pie Charts

A pie chart is one of the most common ways to present the top causes of turnover. Three to five pieces work well to illustrate a balanced chart. The largest piece of the pie would reflect the No. 1 reason for turnover; the second largest would be No. 2, etc. Figure 10-2 is an example of a pie chart.

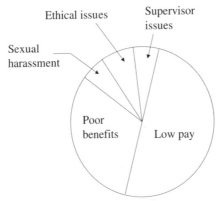

Figure 10-2. Causes of turnover.

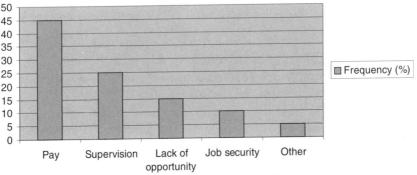

Figure 10-3. The Pareto chart.

Pareto Principle

The Pareto Principle is a method used to display information so that the most critical issues are easily recognized. Priorities are determined and the percentage of impact of a particular problem revealed. Figure 10-3 shows the Pareto chart on the causes of turnover in a particular situation.

In this example, four primary causes are identified and the others are combined into one category. Pay is the most critical and immediate issue, accounting for 43 percent of the total turnover. The quality of supervision is next, accounting for 22 percent of the turnover problem, and lack of opportunity is next with 11 percent. These charts quickly show the key problem areas and the causes that must be addressed. Pareto charts can be used in three potential scenarios.

1. The original turnover problem can be presented in terms of regions, job categories, race, and ethnic backgrounds, or any combination totaling 100 percent. The chart will reflect where the turnover has occurred most often.
2. The chart can also be used to display the actual causes of turnover, as was illustrated in Figure 10-2. Detailing the causes in chart form quickly reveals the area where attention is needed.
3. Finally, the Pareto charts can be used to reflect the actual costs of turnover and illustrate which categories represent the most critical turnover costs. This can give impact to a presentation when showing a fully loaded cost profile.

Trend Charts

A basic method for presenting turnover is the use of trend lines or line charts. These charts present graphical plotted data and show changes over a designated period of time. The most likely use of this approach is to track turnover to show the effect of other events that have occurred during the time frame that might influence the turnover (seasonal or otherwise). Also, a plot of the turnover by regions or job groups indicates how the turnover varies in different categories. Finally, the causes of turnover could be displayed over time. For example, the particular response to exit interview questions could be plotted to show the monthly reasons for leaving. The most common measure could be charted to show how turnover causes are changing and to measure reaction to a particular solution designed to decrease it.

MATCHING SOLUTIONS TO NEEDS

Perhaps the most difficult part of this stage in the model is matching the solutions to needs. The specific solution to address a cause must be identified. It is as much an art as it is a science to ensure that the solution addresses all the needs or causes. Several principles should be followed during this process.

Guiding Principles

A cause is not automatically translated into a solution

Not every cause has an obvious solution based on the cause of turnover. For example, if supervisors are not providing positive feedback or creating a supportive work environment, it does not necessarily mean that they need training. (Too often the training solution is implemented when other causes are the dominant issue.) The challenge is to ensure that the cause includes enough detail to identify the solution. In other words, if supervisors are not providing positive feedback or creating a supportive environment, is it because they do not know how to do it (a training issue), because there has been no requirement (a policy issue), or because there has been no role modeling for that type of behavior (a coaching issue)? The training solution is only a solution when the knowledge and skills are not adequate.

Some solutions are obvious

Some causes point directly to a solution. If the employees need more flexibility in scheduling their work hours, flexible scheduling is the obvious solution. If employees need the flexibility to work at home, telecommuting is an appropriate solution. Although there are important design issues, the solutions become obvious in these situations.

Solutions can come in different sizes

Solutions have a full range of options that represent the magnitude of the investment and complexity of the solution. For example, if employees have expressed a need for better child care, the solution could range from identifying recommended child care facilities to operating an on-site center completely funded by the organization. It is helpful to understand what would be considered an acceptable solution to prevent turnover compared with the issue not being addressed at all.

The design of the solution is critical

Because solutions can be varied, the actual design is often just as important as providing a solution. For example, if employees indicate that they want their salary connected directly to their perform-ance, dozens of solutions can accommodate this need. Some designs can be counterproductive and, perhaps, create more problems, whereas others can be very motivating and uplifting. Targets and standards can be established too loosely or too tightly, depending on the design parameters. The design should be considered in relation-ship to the cause of turnover to ensure that concerns are addressed. This principle requires more effort on the analysis to identify what would actually correct this problem.

Some solutions take a long time

Whereas some issues may require only a short-term fix, such as flexible working schedules, others take longer to rectify. For example, if employees are leaving because of the public image of the organization (e.g., bad press, recent negative events, tarnished image), it could take a long time to repair the situation. Repair must start from the top of the organization. This principle must be rec-ognized early. It may take a long time to build trust and credibility with all of the employees.

Solutions should be tackled for the highest-priority items first

This is an obvious principle, but it requires further discussion. The issues causing the most turnover are also those demanding the most attention, perhaps even the most investment. The next section describes this issue in more detail.

Collectively, these principles will help the retention team develop the appropriate mix of solutions and design an effective solution to resolve major issues, if not all of them. The results of these steps are easily presented as a matrix diagram.

Using a Matrix Diagram

A matrix diagram organizes a large group of information so that elements are logically connected and presented in a graphic form. It also shows the importance of each connecting point in a relation-ship. It is used to establish and present the relationships that exist among these variables. The matrix diagram can be L shaped, where there is one column across the top and one down the side of the page, or it can be T shaped, in which two columns containing two types of data are compared with a third.

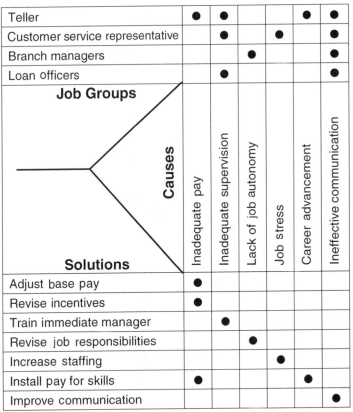

Teller	●	●			●	●
Customer service representative		●		●		●
Branch managers			●			●
Loan officers		●				●

Figure 10-4. Matrix diagram: a plan to reduce turnover in four job groups.

Figure 10-4 shows a T-shaped matrix diagram that presents a plan to reduce turnover in four job groups. The job groups with the most turnover in this large banking organization are listed at the top of the matrix. Six causes of turnover are identified along the middle of the diagram, with each matched to a job group. Listed at the bottom are the solutions that are matched to the particular causes. For example, "Install Pay for Skills" is aimed primarily at the branch teller group and focuses on both the concern about inadequate pay and the lack of career advancement. As an alternative, words can be used in place of a dot to indicate the relative priority, strength, or importance of a particular cause, solution, or job group. Overall, matrix diagrams provide an excellent way of summarizing information about turnover causes and relating them to job groups, regions, or other breakdowns. In addition, as shown in Figure 10-4, it can also be used to relate to solutions.

Selecting Solutions for Maximum Payoff

As solutions are matched to a particular cause, the next step is to ensure that the focus is only on the solutions representing maximum payoff. Two major issues can affect the payoff of the solution: the cost of the solution and the monetary benefit from the implementation of the solution. As more fully described in the next two chapters, the return-on-investment (ROI) formula is a ratio of net benefits to costs. To achieve the maximum payoff, costs should be considered—the smaller the cost, the greater the potential payoff. From the benefits side, the greater the benefits, the greater the potential payoff. Several issues must be considered.

Short-term versus long-term costs

Some solutions, such as building a day care center, will be very expensive to implement on a short-term basis. This solution will have high initial cost for the organization and may not be feasible. Other solutions, such as implementing an incentive plan, may have very little up-front cost, but a tremendous long-term expense—one that may exceed the actual payoff. Compensation plans are usually perceived as long-term solutions and are changed with caution. The short-term versus long-term cost implication needs to be considered.

Forecasting ROI

Chapter 11 illustrates a method for developing the ROI forecast for a solution. An ROI forecast can be developed in conjunction with this step, showing the expected monetary benefits compared to the projected cost of the solution. The solutions with the highest forecasted ROI value become the best prospects for implementation.

The time needed for implementation

Some solutions can be implemented quickly, whereas others require more time. This may mean that long-term solutions should be implemented in conjunction with short-term fixes. In other words, the organization recognizes that both "quick fixes" and long-term changes are in store. A combined action shows employees that the organization is taking steps now and also building for the future, subsequently enhancing commitment and loyalty.

AVOIDING PROBLEMS

Avoid Mismatches

As solutions are considered, the impact of a mismatch must be taken into consideration. If a solution proves to be inappropriate, what will be the consequences? Some mismatches can result in tremendous morale issues. For example, having to discontinue an employee incentive plan can have huge job satisfaction consequences. Mismatches can cause three major problems:

1. The funds are wasted because money is spent on a solution that did not correct the problem and drained the organization's resources.
2. Some solutions have a negative impact if they are inappropriate. For example, if training is implemented as a solution when there is no deficiency in knowledge and skills, the impact can be adverse. The participants being trained (e.g., supervisors or managers) may resent the training because they have been coerced into participating in a program that has no value for them or develops skills that they already possess.
3. When time, effort, and money are spent on a solution that is mismatched, an opportunity to implement the correct solution has been missed. This may be more devastating because an unmet need still exists—the cause is still there. Going unchecked, it is still causing damage to the organization while resources have been wasted on other solutions.

The message: avoid mismatches at all costs.

Tackling Multiple Solutions

How many solutions should be tackled? Is it possible to tackle several solutions at the same time? There is no clear answer to these questions. To a certain extent, the answer depends on the relative priority of the causes. Clearly, tackling too many solutions is a problem. Too many activities undertaken at the same time can handicap the organization and reduce the potential effectiveness of each of the solutions. The primary output is confusion and waste.

The important issue is to examine the top priorities to determine which are feasible, given the current resources, the time it takes for implementation, and the level of involvement needed from others. This may translate into tackling three or four (a maximum of five) solutions. Beyond that, it may be too much of a problem. Avoid the quick fix, especially if it is not a quick-fix issue. Most turnover problems do not fit into this category. They are issues that have evolved over time (either internally or externally) and, in most cases, will take time to correct, at least on a logical, rational, and economical basis.

An important consideration is the level of involvement and support needed. Most employees must be involved in the solution in some way, requiring time away from routine duties or precious time to keep track of what is being developed. The level of support from the management team is also critical. Middle-level managers need to be supportive of solutions and their implementation. How much they can (or are willing to) support is an important issue.

Finally, the available resources is a very important issue. For most organizations, the costs of the solutions can be very substantial. Trying to tackle too many solutions may drain resources and even have an impact on the earnings of the organization, potentially creating yet another serious problem.

Verifying the Match

It is important to verify early that an appropriate match exists between the need and the solution. It is often helpful to return to the source of input (focus groups, employees, etc.) and ask for opinions on a particular solution to determine whether it meets the need. Obviously, this approach is not applicable for every solution because employees may become biased with their input—always wanting more of whatever is being provided. However, their input may provide insight into progress made or confirm if the solution is on target or off base. When input is obtained from interviews or focus groups, it may be easier to return to the previous groups to see if this solution is addressing the cause of turnover. The important issue is to uncover the mismatch early.

It may be helpful to examine data from groups immediately following the implementation of the solution. Early feedback can often check the pulse to ensure the solution is working and, more important, meeting the particular need. Early feedback can lead to adjustments, or in worst-case scenarios, abandonment of the solution altogether. This situation represents another opportunity to involve a group of experts to examine data and determine how closely the solution matches the need.

In concert with collecting early feedback about the success of the solution, it is helpful to disseminate the early results through the entire group quickly. This approach allows the target group to know that the solution has been implemented and the results are positive (or developing, or need improvement). It also provides an opportunity to collect feedback to determine if adjustments are needed. Employees need to see that action is being taken, progress is developing, and, more important, that the organization is responsive.

FINAL THOUGHTS

This brief chapter has tackled the critical issue of matching the solution to the actual cause of turnover. Although some may consider this step an obvious one, it can be one of the most critical steps because of the risks of mismatching. Mismatches can be disastrous. If the cause is not fully understood, the solution is not appropriate. If the solution is addressing the cause in an ineffective way, the results will be less than optimum. In addition, taking on too many solutions can create significant problems in the organization, diminishing the overall effort of retention management. It is important to ensure that causes are understood, the relative priority of the various causes are clearly developed, solutions are matched to those causes, and only the high-priority, high-payoff solutions are addressed quickly to manage retention effectively.

FURTHER READING

Gubman E. L. *The Talent Solution: Aligning Strategy and People to Achieve Extraordinary Results*. New York: McGraw-Hill, 1998.
Sears, David *Successful Talent Strategies: Achieving Superior Business Results through Market-Focused Staffing*. New York: AMACOM, 2003.

Forecast the Value
of Retention Solutions

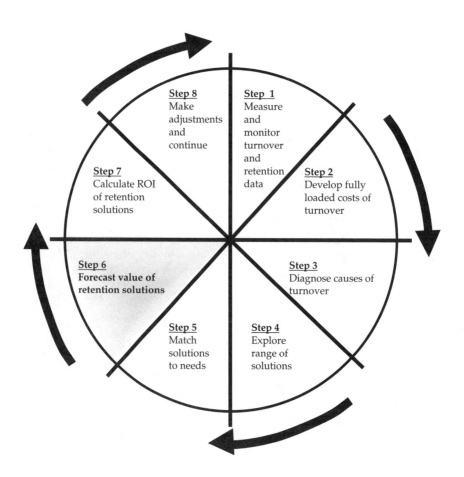

Confusion exists regarding when it is appropriate to develop the return on investment (ROI) for a retention solution. The traditional approach is to base ROI calculations strictly on business results obtained from the retention solution. In this scenario, business performance measures are easily converted to monetary values, which are necessary for an ROI calculation. Sometimes these measures are not available, and it is usually assumed that an ROI calculation is not possible. This chapter shows that ROI calculations are possible at several different stages—even before the retention solution is implemented.

WHY FORECAST ROI?

Although ROI calculation based on postimplementation data is the most accurate way to assess and develop an ROI calculation for a retention solution, it is often important to know the forecast *before* the solution is implemented or the final results are tabulated. Forecasting the impact of a solution, even before the project is pursued, is an important issue when the reasons for the need for a forecasted ROI are examined. Five reasons usually surface. These reasons are discussed below.

Reduction of Uncertainty

It is helpful to reduce uncertainty in a new retention solution whenever possible. In a perfect world, the sponsor (client, senior management) would like to know the expected payoff before any action is taken. Realistically, knowing the exact payoff may not be possible and, from a practical standpoint, may not be feasible. However, the desire still exists to remove the uncertainty from the situation and act on the best data available. This can push the project to a forecasted ROI before any resources are expended. Some senior managers will not proceed without a preproject forecast for a retention solution. They need some measure of expected success before allocating any resources to the solution.

Expense of Pursuing Retention Solutions without Supportive Data

In some cases, even a pilot retention solution is not practical until some analysis has been conducted to examine the potential ROI. For example, if the solution involves a significant amount of work or costs, a senior manager may not want to expend the resources, even for a pilot solution, unless some assurance is provided for a positive ROI. This is particularly true for solutions involving changes in compensation. The preproject ROI becomes an important issue in these situations, prompting some clients to stand firm until an ROI forecast is produced.

Comparison with Postimplementation Data

Whenever there is a plan to collect data on the success of the application and implementation, impact, and ROI of the retention solution, it is helpful to compare actual results to preproject expectations. In an ideal world, a forecasted ROI should have a defined relationship with the actual ROI—or at least one should lead to the other with some adjustments. One important reason for forecasting ROI is to determine how well the forecast holds up under the scrutiny of postproject analysis.

Save Costs

Several cost-saving issues may prompt the ROI forecast. First, the forecast itself is often a very inexpensive process because it involves estimations and several assumptions. Second, if the forecast itself becomes a reliable predictor of the postproject results, then the forecasted ROI might substitute for the actual ROI, at least with some adjustments. This could save the costs of the postproject analysis. Finally, the forecasted ROI data might be used for comparisons in other areas, at least as a beginning point for other types of solutions. Thus the forecasted ROI might have some transfer potential to other retention solutions.

Compliance with Policy or Regulation

More organizations are developing policy statements, and in the case of government agencies, enacting legislation, even passing laws to require a forecasted ROI before major projects are undertaken. For example, in one organization, any project exceeding $300,000 must have a forecasted ROI before it can be approved. In one foreign government, a company can receive partial refunds on the cost of a project if the ROI forecast is positive and likely to enhance the performance of the organization. This formal policy and legal structure is a growing reason for developing the ROI forecast.

Collectively, these five reasons are causing more organizations to examine ROI forecasts (or at least during a project) so that the retention solution coordinator will have some estimate of the expected payoff.

THE TRADEOFFS OF FORECASTING

The ROI can be developed at different times and at different levels. Unfortunately, the ease, convenience, and low cost involved in capturing a forecasted ROI create tradeoffs in accuracy and credibility. As shown in Figure 11-1, there are five distinct time intervals during the implementation of a retention solution when the ROI can actually be developed. The relationship with credibility, accuracy, cost, and difficulty is also shown in this figure.

The time intervals for developing ROI are as follows:

1. **A preproject forecast** can be developed using estimates of the impact of the retention solution. This approach lacks credibility and accuracy, but it is also the least expensive and least difficult ROI to calculate. The value in developing the ROI on a preproject basis (observed earlier) is discussed in more detail in the next section.

2. **Reaction and satisfaction data** can be extended to develop an anticipated impact, including the ROI. Team members collect data after they have been exposed to the solution through briefings, explanations, or training sessions. In this case, team members actually anticipate the chain of impact as a retention solution is applied, implemented, and turnover measures are influenced. While the accuracy and credibility increase from the preproject basis, this approach still lacks the credibility and accuracy desired in most situations.

3. **Learning data** in some retention solutions can be used to forecast the actual ROI. Data are collected after team members learn how to use the solution, usually following a training program. This approach is applicable only when learning data show a relationship between acquiring certain skills or knowledge and subsequent business performance. When this correlation is available (usually developed to validate a test), test data can be used to forecast subsequent performance. The performance can then be converted to monetary impact and the

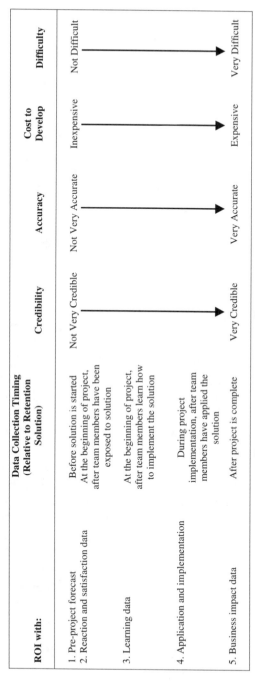

Figure 11-1. Data collection timing.

ROI can be developed. This approach has less potential as an evaluation tool due to the lack of situations in which a predictive validation can be developed. Because of the limited use of this forecasting situation, additional detail is not offered in this chapter.

4. In some limited situations, when frequency of skills and actual use of skills and knowledge are critical, the **application and implementation** of those skills or knowledge can be converted to a monetary value using estimations. This is particularly helpful in situations where competencies are being developed as a major part of the solution and values are placed on improving competencies. Because of the limited use of this application and the preference to use business data (i.e., turnover), this approach is not explored further in this chapter.

5. Finally, the ROI can be developed from **business impact data,** usually turnover, converted directly to monetary values and compared to the cost of the solution. This postproject evaluation is the basis for most of the ROI calculations in this book and is the principal approach used in the next chapter. It is the preferred approach because of the pressures outlined above; it is important to examine ROI calculations at other times and at levels other than using business data.

This chapter discusses, in detail, preproject evaluation and the ROI calculations based on reaction data. The ROI calculations developed from learning and application data are not discussed but are examined in other publications (see Phillips, Stone, and Phillips, 2001).

PRE-PROJECT ROI FORECASTING

Perhaps one of the most useful steps in convincing a client that a retention solution expense is beneficial is to forecast the ROI for the solution. The process is similar to the postproject analysis, except that the extent of the impact must be estimated along with the forecasted cost of the solution.

Basic Model

Figure 11-2 shows the basic model for capturing the necessary data for a preproject forecast. This model is a modification of the postproject consulting ROI process model presented in the next chapter,

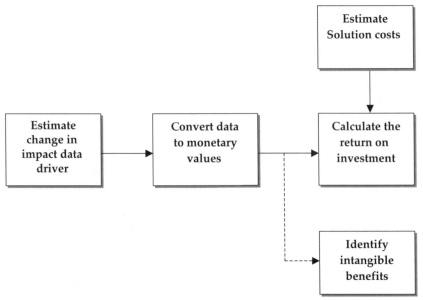

Figure 11-2. Basic model for capturing data for preproject forecast.

except that data are projected instead of being collected during the various time frames. In place of the data collection is an estimation of the change in impact data expected to be influenced by the solution. Isolating the effects of the retention solution becomes a non-issue, as the estimate of output takes the isolation factor into consideration. For example, when an individual is asked to indicate how much of the particular improvement can be driven by a solution, the influence of other factors is already taken into consideration. Only the solution factor is an issue because the other factors have been isolated in the estimation process.

The method to convert data to monetary values is exactly the same because the data items examined in a preanalysis and postanalysis should be the same. Estimating the project's cost should be an easy step because costs can easily be anticipated based on previous solutions using reasonable assumptions about the current solution. The anticipated intangibles are merely speculation in forecasting but can be reliable indicators of which measures may be influenced in addition to those included in the ROI calculation. The formula used to calculate the ROI is the same as in the postanalysis. The amount of monetary value from the data conversion is included as the numerator while the estimated cost of the solution is inserted as the denominator. The projected cost/benefit ratio can be developed along with the ROI value (%). The steps to develop the process are detailed next.

Steps to Develop the ROI

The detailed steps to develop the preproject ROI forecast are presented in simplified form below:

1. Develop the implementation and impact objectives with as many specifics as possible. Developed from the initial needs analysis and assessment, these objectives detail what would actually change as the retention solution is implemented and identify which business measures (usually turnover) would actually be influenced. If these are not known, the entire forecasting process is in jeopardy. There must be some assessment of which measures will change as a result of the solution, and someone must indicate the extent to which this change will materialize.

2. Estimate or forecast the monthly improvement in the business impact data. This is considered to be the amount of change directly related to the solution and is denoted by ΔP.

3. Convert the business impact data to monetary values using one or more of the methods described in Chapter 12. These are the same techniques and use the same processes as a post-project analysis; this value is denoted by V.

4. Develop the estimated annual impact for each business measure. (Although turnover is the principal business measure, other measures may be driven by the retention solution.) In essence, this is the first-year improvement from the retention solution, showing the value for the change in the business impact measures directly related to the solution. In formula form, this is $\Delta I = \Delta P \times V \times 12$.

5. For long-term retention solutions, improvement may be forecast for a period greater than 1 year. In this case, additional years should be factored into the analysis if a solution will have a significant useful life beyond the first year. These values may be discounted to reflect a diminished benefit in subsequent years. The client or owner of the retention solution should provide some indication as to the amount of improvement expected (turnover reduction) in years 2, 3, and later. However, it is helpful to obtain input from as many team members as possible.

6. Estimate the fully loaded costs of the retention solution. Using the cost categories contained in this chapter, the fully loaded cost would be estimated and projected for the retention solution. This is denoted as C. Again, all direct and indirect costs should be included in the calculation.

7. Calculate the forecasted ROI using the total projected benefits and the estimated cost in the standard ROI formula:

$$\text{ROI}\,(\%) = \frac{\Delta I - C}{C} \times 100$$

8. Use sensitivity analysis to develop several potential ROI values with different levels of improvement (ΔP). When more than one measure is changing, that analysis should be developed using a spreadsheet showing different possible scenarios for output and subsequent ROI values.

9. Identify potential intangible benefits by securing input from the individuals most knowledgeable of the project and retention solution. These are only anticipated and are based on assumptions from previous experience with this type of solution.

10. Communicate the ROI projection and anticipated intangibles with much care and caution. The target audience must clearly understand that the forecast is based on several assumptions (clearly defined), and that the values are the best possible estimates. However, there is still much room for error.

These 10 steps make the ROI forecast feasible. The most difficult part of the process is the initial estimate of performance improvement. Several sources of data are available for this purpose and are described next.

Estimating Performance Improvement

A variety of input is available when attempting to estimate the performance improvement that will be influenced by a retention solution. In most retention solutions, the performance improvement involves turnover reductions only. The following important considerations should be explored when estimating performance improvement:

1. Those individuals in the organization with experience in a similar, previous retention solution or similar solutions may

help form the basis of the estimate. Utilizing a breadth of experience can be an important factor as comparisons are rarely, if ever, exact.

2. The retention solution team may have experience with similar solutions in other organizations or in other situations. Here, the experience of the designers, developers, and implementers involved in the solution will be helpful as they reflect on their experiences with other organizations.

3. The input of external experts (usually retention consultants) who have worked in the field or tackled similar retention solutions in other organizations can be extremely valuable. Consultants, suppliers, designers, or others who have earned a reputation as knowledgeable about this type of solution in this type of situation may be helpful.

4. Estimates can be obtained directly from a subject matter expert (SME) in the organization. This is an individual who is very familiar with the internal processes being altered, modified, or improved by the retention solution. Internal SMEs are very knowledgeable and sometimes the most favored source for obtaining conservative estimates.

5. Estimates can be obtained directly from the senior manager or the sponsor of the project. This individual, who is ultimately making the implementation decision, may be capable of providing data or input on the anticipated change in a measure linked to the retention solution. The influential position of this individual makes it a credible source.

6. Individuals who are directly involved in the retention solution, often labeled participants or target audience, may know how much of a measure can be changed or improved with a specific retention solution. These individuals understand the processes, procedures, and performance measurements being influenced. Their close proximity to the situation makes them credible and often the most accurate sources for estimating the amount of change in turnover.

Collectively, these sources provide an appropriate array of possibilities to help estimate the value of an improvement. Preprogram forecasting is the weakest scenario in the ROI forecast and deserves the most attention. The stakeholders in a forecasted ROI project should understand the source of the estimates. More importantly, the sponsor must view the source as credible. Otherwise the forecasted ROI has little utility.

Case Study

It may be helpful to illustrate how a forecasted ROI can be developed using the processes explained here. A manufacturing plant of a large multinational corporation was experiencing a serious turnover problem—a 60 percent annual rate in an industry with an average of 25 percent. An assessment and initial analysis identified several needs. Three solutions were recommended and placed in a priority arrangement. The most critical and expensive solution was comprehensive supervisor and team leader training. However, before pursuing the project and contracting for the training, a forecasted ROI was needed. Following the steps outlined earlier in this chapter, it was determined that several business impact measures would be influenced by the implementation of this training.

With comprehensive supervisor training in place, team leaders and supervisors should improve work unit performance (productivity and quality) and increase job satisfaction, as well as team manager retention. However, the forecasted ROI would be developed on turnover alone.

To determine the extent to which turnover would be reduced, input was collected from four sources:

1. Analysts (who identified the causes of turnover and recommended solutions)
2. Department managers (who are responsible for the supervisors and team leaders)
3. Project sponsors (the plant manager who initiated the project)
4. Finally, the training supplier and facilitators (who designed and delivered the training)

When input is based on estimates, the actual results may differ significantly; however, the project sponsor was interested in a forecast based on very limited analysis but was strengthened with the best expert opinions available. After some discussion of the benchmarking data and examining turnover cost studies for similar types of jobs, it was decided to use a standard value of 75 percent of annual wages as the cost of a turnover statistic.

The forecasted ROI calculation was developed for this plan only. After reviewing the possible scenarios, it was decided that there could be a range of possibilities for reducing turnover. The value should be in the range of 10 to 25 percentage points, reducing turnover from

Table 11-1
Expected ROI Values for Various Scenarios

Potential Turnover Reduction (Annualized Values; %)	New Annual Turnover Values (%)	Expected ROI (%)
10	50	30
15	45	100
20	40	250
25	35	400

60 percent to 35 to 50 percent. Four scenarios were developed using a 10, 15, 20, and 25 percentage point decrease.

The turnover reduction was easily converted to monetary values using standard values. The cost for the proposed training was easily estimated based on input from the training contractor. The total cost of training was developed to include facilities for training session, lost time for learning activities, and coordination. This fully loaded project cost, when compared to the benefits, yielded a range of expected ROI values. Table 11-1 shows a list of the four possible scenarios.

The ROI values range from a low of 30 percent to a high of 400 percent. With these values in hand, the decision to move forward was a relatively easy one, as even the worst-case scenario is positive, and the best case was more than 10 times that amount. Thus the decision was made to move forward with the project. As this example illustrates, the process should be kept simple, using the most credible resources available to quickly arrive at estimates for the process. Although this is an estimate, its advantage is simplicity and low cost, and these factors should be considered when developing the processes.

FORECASTING WITH A PILOT PROGRAM

Although the steps listed above provide a process for estimating the ROI when a pilot or trial implementation is not conducted, a more favorable approach is to develop a small-scale pilot of the retention solution and develop the ROI based on post-implementation data from the pilot. This scenario involves the following steps:

1. As in the previous process, develop implementation and impact objectives.
2. Initiate the retention solution on a very small-scale sample as a pilot project, without all the "bells and whistles". This keeps the cost extremely low without sacrificing the fundamentals of the solution.
3. Conduct the pilot solution and fully implement it with one or more groups of target audiences who can benefit from the retention solution.
4. Develop the ROI using the ROI methodology for postproject analysis. This is the same ROI methodology used in the previous chapters.
5. Finally, decide whether to implement the retention solution throughout the organization based on the results of the pilot implementation.

This approach provides a much more accurate analysis, withholding full implementation until results can be developed from the pilot study. In this scenario, data can be developed using all six types of measures outlined in chapter 12.

Forecasting ROI with Reaction Data

After participants in the retention solution become involved in the solution, usually through training or briefings, a reaction questionnaire is often administered. When a reaction evaluation includes planned application, these important data can be used in ROI forecast calculations. Higher-level evaluation information can be developed with questions focusing on how participants plan to use what they learned. The questions presented in Table 11-2 illustrate how these types of data are collected with a reaction questionnaire. Participants are asked to state specifically how they plan to use the retention solution and the results they expect to achieve with it. They are asked to convert their planned accomplishments into annual monetary values and show the basis for developing the values. Participants can adjust their responses with a confidence factor to make the data more credible and allow them to reflect their uneasiness with the process. With advanced notice, discussion of the questions, explanation of the use of the data, encouragement to provide data, a simple typical example, and ample time to complete the form, a high participation rate can be achieved; 80 to 90 percent is normal.

Table 11-2
Important Questions to Ask on Feedback Questionnaires

Planned Improvements

As a result of this retention solution, what specific actions will you attempt as you apply what you have learned?

1. _____

2. _____

3. _____

Please indicate what specific measures, such as turnover, will change as a result of your actions.

1. _____

2. _____

3. _____

As a result of anticipated changes above, please estimate (in monetary terms) the benefits to your organization over a period of 1 year.
$ _____

What is the basis of this estimate?

_____

_____

_____

What confidence, expressed as a percentage, can you put in your estimate (0% = no confidence; 100% = total certainty) _____%

When tabulating data, the confidence levels are multiplied by the annual monetary values, which produces a more conservative estimate for use in the data analysis. For example, if a participant estimated that the monetary impact of the retention solution would be $50,000 but was only 50 percent confident in the estimation, a $25,000 value would be used in the ROI calculations ($50,000 × 50%).

Several steps are taken to develop a summary of the expected benefits. First, incomplete, unusable, extreme, or unrealistic data are discarded. Next, an adjustment is given for the confidence estimate as previously described. Individual data items are then totaled. Finally, as an optional exercise, the total value is adjusted again by a factor that reflects the subjectivity of the process and the possibility that participants will not achieve the results they anticipate. The implementation team can estimate this adjustment factor. In one organization, the benefits are divided by 2 to develop a number to use in the equation. Finally, the ROI forecast is calculated using the anticipated net benefits from the retention solution divided by the solution costs. In essence, this value becomes the expected return on investment once the confidence adjustment for accuracy and the adjustment for subjectivity have been made.

This process can best be described using an actual case. Integrated Systems, Inc. (ISI) designs and builds large commercial systems for banks and financial service companies. Retention is always a critical issue at ISI and usually commands much management attention. To improve the current level of performance, a retention solution was initiated for software designers, project engineers, and system integrators. The retention solution focused on culture change. After implementing the solution, managers were expected to improve the retention in their departments. At the end of the implementation sessions, managers completed a comprehensive reaction feedback questionnaire, which probed specific action items planned as a result of the retention solution and provided estimated monetary values of the planned actions. In addition, managers explained the basis for estimates and placed a confidence level on their estimates. Table 11-3 presents data provided by the first group of participants. Only 15 of the 20 managers supplied data. Approximately 50 to 80 percent of participants will usually provide data on this series of questions. The total cost of the retention solution, including managers' time, was estimated to be $105,000. Prorated development costs were included in this figure.

The monetary value of the planned improvements was extremely high and reflected the managers' optimism and enthusiasm at the end of a very effective retention solution from which specific actions were planned. As a first step in the analysis, extreme data items were omitted. Data such as "millions," "unlimited," and "significant" were discarded, and each remaining value was multiplied by the confidence value and totaled. This adjustment is one way of reducing high subjective estimates. The resulting tabulations yielded a total improvement of $1,095,900. Because of the subjective nature of the process, the values were adjusted by a factor of 2, an arbitrary number suggested by the retention coordinator and supported by the

Table 11-3
Level 1 Data for ROI Calculations

Participating Managers	Estimated Annual Reduction in Turnover (No.)	Monetary Value of Turnover (100% of Annual Salary)	Confidence Level of Estimate (%)	Adjusted Value
1	2	96,000	60	57,600
2	3	152,000	70	106,400
3	0	0	0	0
4	4	183,000	80	146,400
5	5	212,000	30	63,600
6	0	0	0	0
7	3	139,000	60	83,400
8	1	45,000	50	42,500
9	8	420,000	40	168,000
10	10	525,000	20	105,000
11	0	0	0	0
12	6	275,000	60	165,000
13	3	140,000	70	98,000
14	2	100,000	60	60,000
15	0	0	0	0
TOTAL				$1,095,900

management group. This "adjusted" value was $547,050, rounded up to $548,000. The projected ROI, which was based on the feedback questionnaire at the end of the retention solution but before job application, was as follows:

$$ROI = \frac{\$548,000 - \$105,000}{\$105,000} \times 100 = 422\%$$

The retention coordinator communicated these projected values to the CEO, but cautioned that the data were very subjective, although they had twice been adjusted downward. The coordinator also emphasized that the forecasted results were generated by the managers involved in the culture, who should presumably be aware of what they could accomplish. In addition, the coordinator mentioned that a follow-up was planned to determine the results actually delivered by the group.

A word of caution is in order when using forecasted ROI with reaction data. The calculations are highly subjective and may not reflect the extent to which managers will apply what they have learned to achieve results. A variety of influences in the work environment can enhance or inhibit the attainment of performance goals. High expectations after implementation is no guarantee that those expectations will be met. Disappointments are documented regularly with solutions throughout the world and reported in research findings.

Although the process is subjective and possibly unreliable, it does have some usefulness. First, if evaluation must stop with the launch of the solution, this approach provides more insight into the value of the retention solution than data from typical reaction questionnaires. Unfortunately, there is evidence that a high percentage of evaluations stop at this first level of evaluation. Managers usually find these data more useful than a report stating, "40 percent of participants rated the project above average." Reporting ROI data forecasted from reaction provides a more useful indication of the potential impact of the retention solution than the alternative, which is to report attitudes and feelings about the solution.

Second, these data can form a basis for comparing different projects of the same type. If one retention solution forecasts an ROI of 300 percent and another solution forecasts 30 percent, it would appear that one solution may be more effective than the other. The participants in the first retention solution have more confidence in the planned application of the second solution.

Third, collecting these data focuses increased attention on solution outcomes. Participants involved in the retention solution will have an understanding that specific behavior change is expected, which produces results for the organization. This issue becomes very clear to participants as they anticipate results and convert them to monetary values. Even if this projected improvement is ignored, the exercise is productive because of the important message sent to participants.

Fourth, if a follow-up is planned to pinpoint postimplementation results, the reaction data can be very helpful for comparison. The data collection helps participants plan the implementation of what they have learned. Incidentally, when a follow-up is planned, participants are usually more conservative with their projected estimates.

The calculation of the ROI with reaction data is increasing in use, and some organizations have based many of their ROI calculations at this level. Although they may be very subjective, the calculations do add value, particularly if they are included as part of a comprehensive evaluation system.

PROJECT COSTS FOR FORECASTING CALCULATIONS

In both previous scenarios, the costs for the proposed solution were developed to provide a forecasted ROI. The costs for the retention solution, whether projected or on a postimplementation basis, contain the same type of categories. The costs should be fully loaded to include both direct and indirect costs associated with the solution. In addition, some costs may be prorated if a particular cost for the solution may have residual value after implementation. Table 11-4 shows the typical cost categories that should be captured for retention solutions. These categories represent all significant costs associated with the solution. Additional information on cost categories is contained in chapter 12 and in additional references (Phillips, Stone, and Phillips, 2001).

Table 11-4
Retention Solution Cost Categories

Category	Cost Item	Prorated	Expensed
A	Initial analysis and assessment		✓
B	Development of solutions		✓
C	Acquisition of solutions		✓
D	Implementation and application		✓
	Policy changes		✓
	Salaries/benefits for coordination time		✓
	Salaries/benefits for participant time		✓
	Materials		✓
	Hardware/software	✓	
	Travel/lodging/meals		✓
	Use of facilities		✓
	Capital expenditures	✓	
E	Maintenance and monitoring		✓
F	Administrative support and overhead	✓	
G	Evaluation and reporting		✓

Final Thoughts

This chapter presented the techniques for forecasting ROI at four different time frames using different levels of evaluation data. Two of these techniques, preproject forecasting and forecasting with reaction data, are useful for very simple and inexpensive projects. They may be helpful even in short-term, low-profile solutions. Forecasting using learning data and application data is rare and should be reserved only for large-scale projects involving significant learning events.

Preproject forecasting may be necessary and actually desired even if it is not required. Because business data are the drivers of the retention solution, business impact measures, such as turnover, should be identified up front. Estimating the actual change in these measures is a recommended and highly useful exercise, as it shows the sponsor the perceived value of the solution. This is a simple exercise that should take no more than 1 or 2 days. The result can be extremely valuable when communicating to the sponsor and provides some clear direction and focus for the retention solution coordinator.

In almost every retention solution, reaction data are collected from the participants. A worthwhile extension of reaction data is to include several questions that allow those individuals to project the actual success of the project. This approach is recommended as another simple tool for forecasting the actual ROI. This planned action provides additional insight into the potential worth of the solution and alerts the management team about potential problems or issue that may need attention as the remaining issues are addressed in the solution. The additional questions are very simple and can easily be obtained with 15 to 20 minutes of the participants' time. For it to be successful and usable, participants must be committed to the process. This can usually be achieved by exploring ways to increase the response rate for the various instruments described in this book.

As expected, preproject ROI calculations are the lowest in terms of credibility and accuracy but have the advantage of being inexpensive and relatively easy to develop. ROI calculations using business impact are rich in credibility and accuracy but are very expensive and difficult to develop. Although ROI calculations at this level are preferred, ROI development at other time frames with other levels of data is an important part of a comprehensive and systematic retention evaluation process.

REFERENCES

Phillips, J.J., Stone, R., and Phillips, P.P. *The Human Resources Scorecard: Measuring the Return on Investment.* Woburn, Mass.: Butterworth-Heinemann, 2001.

FURTHER READING

Dean, P.J., and Ripley, D.E., editors. *Performance Improvement Interventions: Performance Technologies in the Workplace,* Volume 3, *Performance Improvement Series: Methods for Organizational Learning.* Washington, D.C.: International Society for Performance Improvement, 1998.

Esque, T.J., and Patterson, P.A. *Getting Results: Case Studies in Performance Improvement,* Volume 1. Washington, D.C.: HRD Press/International Society for Performance Improvement, 1998.

Friedlob, G.T., and Plewa, F.J., Jr. *Understanding Return on Investment.* New York: John Wiley & Sons, 1991.

Hale, J. *The Performance Consultant's Fieldbook: Tools and Techniques for Improving Organizations and People.* San Francisco: Jossey-Bass/Pfeiffer, 1998.

Kaufman, R., Sivasailam T., and MacGillis, P. *The Guidebook for Performance Improvement: Working with Individuals and Organizations.* San Francisco: Jossey-Bass/Pfeiffer, 1997.

Phillips, J.J. *Return on Investment in Training and Performance Improvement Programs.* Woburn, Mass.: Butterworth-Heinemann, 1997.

Price Waterhouse Financial & Cost Management Team. *CFO: Architect of the Corporation's Future.* New York: John Wiley & Sons, 1997.

CHAPTER 12

Calculate the Return on Investment of Retention Solutions

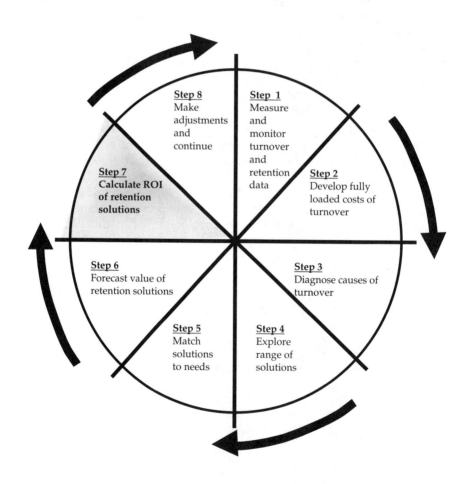

Step 1 Measure and monitor turnover and retention data

Step 2 Develop fully loaded costs of turnover

Step 3 Diagnose causes of turnover

Step 4 Explore range of solutions

Step 5 Match solutions to needs

Step 6 Forecast value of retention solutions

Step 7 Calculate ROI of retention solutions

Step 8 Make adjustments and continue

Measuring the return on investment (ROI) in a retention solution is a topic with much interest. For clients, this process shows the ultimate payoff for retention strategies. For human resources (HR) staff and others involved in retention, it provides important insight into the strengths and weaknesses of solutions.

Understanding the drivers for the ROI process and the inherent weaknesses and advantages of ROI makes it possible to take a rational approach to this important issue. This chapter presents the basic issues and steps needed to develop ROI measurement for retention.

KEY ROI ISSUES

The ROI process is a comprehensive methodology that provides a scorecard of six measures. These measures represent input from various sources during different time frames. The measures include (1) reaction and satisfaction, (2) learning, (3) application and implementation, (4) business impact, (5) ROI, and (6) intangible benefits. In addition, the ROI process uses at least one technique to isolate the effects of the retention solution from other influences. This comprehensive measurement system requires success with many issues and must become a routine part of the strategic accountability approach to turnover reduction (Phillips, Stone and Phillips, 2001).

Why ROI?

ROI is a hot topic for several reasons. Although the viewpoints and explanations may vary, some points are very clear. First, in most organizations, HR budgets have continued to grow year after year with a significant portion focusing on retention. Retention solutions are becoming more expensive with long-term commitments. As expenditures grow, accountability becomes a more critical issue. A growing budget creates a larger target for internal critics, often prompting the development of an ROI process.

Second, total quality management and continuous process improvement have brought increased attention to measurement issues. Today, organizations measure processes and outputs that were not previously measured, monitored, or reported. This focus has placed increased pressure on the HR function to develop measures of retention solution success.

Third, restructuring initiatives and the threat of outsourcing have caused HR to focus more directly on bottom-line issues. Many HR processes have been restructured so that programs are more closely aligned with business needs, and maximum efficiencies are required in the HR cycle. These change processes have brought increased attention to evaluation issues and have resulted in measuring the contribution of specific solutions.

Fourth, the business management mindset of many current HR managers causes them to place more emphasis on economic issues within the HR function. Today's HR manager is more aware of bottom-line issues in the organization and more knowledgeable of operational and financial concerns. This new "enlightened" manager often takes a business approach to retention.

Fifth, a persistent trend of accountability has evolved in organizations all over the globe. Every support function is attempting to show its worth by capturing the value that it adds to the organization. From the accountability perspective, the HR function should be no different from the other functions—it must show its contribution to the organization.

Sixth, top executives are now demanding ROI calculations from departments and functions where they were not previously required. For years, HR managers convinced top executives that HR solutions could not be measured, at least at the monetary contribution level. Yet, many of the executives are now aware that ROI can and is being used in many organizations to measure HR thanks in part to articles in publications aimed at top executives. Subsequently, top executives are demanding the same accountability for retention solutions. In some extremes, HR's being asked to show the ROI or face significant budget cuts.

Concerns with ROI

Although much progress has been made, the ROI methodology is not without problems and drawbacks. The mere presence of the process creates a dilemma for many organizations. When an organization embraces the concept and implements the process, the management team is usually anxiously waiting for results, only to be disappointed when they are not quantifiable. For an ROI process to be useful, it must balance many issues, including feasibility, simplicity, credibility, and soundness. More specifically, three major audiences must be pleased with the ROI process to accept and use it.

Practitioners

For years, HR practitioners have assumed that ROI could not be measured. When examining a typical process, they found long formulas, complicated equations, and complex models that made the ROI process appear to be too confusing. With this perceived complexity, practitioners could visualize the tremendous efforts required for data collection and analysis, and more importantly, the increased cost necessary to make the process work. Because of these concerns, practitioners are seeking an ROI process that is simple and easy to understand so that they can easily implement the steps and strategies. Also, they need a process that will not take an excessive amount of time to implement. Finally, a process is needed that is not too expensive. In summary, from the perspective of the practitioners, the ROI process must be user friendly, time saving, and cost efficient.

Senior managers/sponsors/clients

Managers who must approve HR programs and retention solutions, and cope with the results of solutions, have a strong interest in developing the ROI. They want a process that provides quantifiable results, using a method similar to the ROI formula applied to other types of investments. Senior managers have a never-ending desire for a simple solution as an ROI calculation, reflected as a percentage. As with practitioners, they want a process that is simple and easy to understand. The assumptions made in the calculation and the methodology used in the process must reflect their frame of reference, experience, and level of understanding. They do not want, nor need, a string of formulas, charts, or complicated models. Instead, they want a process that they can explain to others, when necessary. More importantly, they need a process with which they can identify—one that is sound and realistic enough to earn their confidence.

Researchers

Finally, researchers will only support a process that measures up to close scrutiny. They usually insist that models, formulas, assumptions, and theories be sound and based on commonly accepted practices. They also want a process that produces accurate values and consistent outcomes. If estimates are necessary, researchers want a process that provides the most accuracy within the constraints of the situation, recognizing that adjustments are necessary when there is uncertainty in the process.

The challenge is to develop acceptable requirements for an ROI process that will satisfy researchers and, at the same time, please practitioners and senior managers. Sound impossible? Maybe not. The ROI process described here meets the requirements of these three groups (Phillips and Phillips, 2002).

BUILDING THE PROCESS

Building a comprehensive measurement and evaluation process is best represented as a puzzle where the pieces are developed and put in place over time. Figure 12-1 depicts this puzzle and the pieces necessary to build a comprehensive measurement and evaluation process (Phillips, 2003). The first piece of the puzzle is the selection of an evaluation framework, which is a categorization of data. The balanced scorecard process (Kaplan & Norton, 1996) or the four levels of evaluation developed by Kirkpatrick (1975) offer the beginning points for such a framework.

Next, the ROI process model must be developed showing how data are collected, processed, analyzed, and reported to various target audiences. This process model ensures that appropriate techniques and procedures are consistently utilized to address almost any situation. Also, there must be consistency as the process is implemented.

The third piece of the puzzle is the development of operating standards. These standards help ensure the results of the study are stable and not influenced by the individual conducting the study. Replication is critical for the credibility of an evaluation processes. Operating stan-

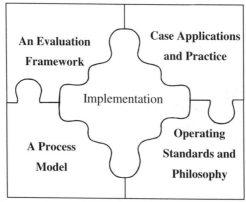

Figure 12-1. ROI: the pieces of the puzzle.

dards and guiding principles allow for replication, so that if more than one individual evaluates a specific solution, the results are the same.

Next, appropriate attention must be given to implementation issues, as the ROI process becomes a routine part of the HR function. Several issues must be addressed involving skills, communication, roles, responsibilities, plans, and strategies.

Finally, there must be successful case applications and practice describing the measurement of a turnover solution within the organization and the value a comprehensive measurement and evaluation process brings to the organization. While it is helpful to refer to case studies developed by other organizations, it is more useful and convincing to have studies developed directly within the organization.

The remainder of this chapter focuses on the individual pieces of the evaluation puzzle: developing a comprehensive ROI process.

An Evaluation Framework

The ROI process described in this chapter adds a fifth level to the four levels of evaluation developed by Kirkpatrick (1975) to measure the success of training. The concept of different levels of evaluation is both helpful and instructive to understanding how the return on investment is developed for retention solutions. Table 12-1 shows the five-level framework used in the ROI process.

Table 12-1
Five Levels of Evaluation

Level	Measurement Focus
1. Reaction and satisfaction	Measures stakeholders' reaction to and satisfaction with the retention solution
2. Learning	Measures changes in knowledge, skills, and attitudes needed to implement the solution
3. Application and implementation	Measures changes in on-the-job behavior and progress with the implementation of the solution
4. Business impact	Measures changes in business impact variables related to the solution
5. Return on investment	Compares monetary benefits of solution to the costs of the solution

Level 1, *Reaction and Satisfaction*, measures satisfaction first with the retention solution then from various stakeholders. This measurement is very important to retention solutions. Almost all organizations evaluate at Level 1, usually with generic questionnaires. Although this level of evaluation is important as a customer-satisfaction measure, a favorable reaction does not ensure that stakeholders have learned new skills or knowledge that may be necessary to reduce turnover.

Level 2, *Learning*, focuses on what stakeholders have learned using tests, skill practices, role plays, simulations, group evaluations, and other assessment tools. Since training for supervisors and team leaders is critical as a retention solution, this measure is important. A learning check is helpful to ensure that stakeholders have absorbed the solution and know how to use it properly. However, a positive measure at this level is no guarantee that what is learned will be applied on the job. The literature is laced with studies showing how learning fails to be transferred to the job (e.g., Broad, 1997).

At Level 3, *Application and Implementation*, a variety of follow-up methods are used to determine the progress with implementation. The frequency and use of skills are sometimes important measures at Level 3. This level also covers a variety of implementation issues, such as new procedures, new policies, new steps, new actions, and new processes. While Level 3 evaluation is important to gauge the success of the implementation of a solution, it still does not guarantee a positive business impact in the organization, with turnover improvement.

The Level 4, *Business Impact*, measure focuses on the actual results achieved from the retention solutions efforts, as stakeholders successfully implement the solution. In addition to turnover, typical Level 4 measures include output, quality, costs, time, job satisfaction, and customer satisfaction. Although the solution may produce a measurable business impact, there is still a concern that it may cost too much.

Level 5, *Return on Investment* (the ultimate level of evaluation), compares the monetary benefits from the solution with the solution costs. Although the ROI can be expressed in several ways, it is usually presented as a percentage or cost/benefit ratio. The evaluation chain is not complete until the Level 5 evaluation is conducted.

Almost all HR organizations conduct evaluations to measure satisfaction, but very few actually conduct evaluations at the ROI level. Perhaps the best explanation for this situation is that ROI evaluation is often characterized as a difficult and expensive process. When business results and ROI are desired, it is also very important to evaluate the other levels. A chain of impact should occur through the levels as the skills and knowledge learned (Level 2) are applied on the job (Level 3) to produce business results (Level 4). If measurements are not taken at each level, it is difficult to conclude that the results achieved were actually caused by the retention solution. Because of this, it is recommended that evaluation be conducted at all levels when a Level 5 ROI evaluation is planned.

THE ROI PROCESS MODEL

The calculations of the ROI for retention solutions begins with the model shown in Figure 12-2, where a potentially complicated process can be simplified with sequential steps (Phillips, 2003). The ROI process model provides a systematic approach to ROI calculations. A step-by-step approach helps keep the process manageable so users can address one issue at a time. Applying the model provides consistency between ROI calculations. Each major step of the model is briefly described below.

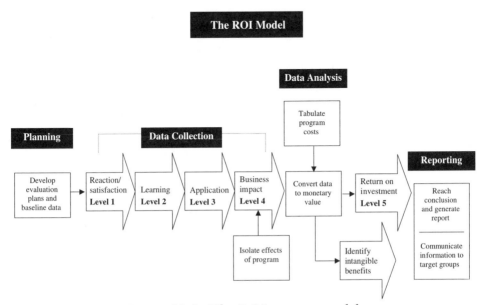

Figure 12-2. The ROI process model.

Evaluation Planning

One of the most important and cost-saving steps in the ROI process is developing evaluation plans. By considering key issues, the time, cost, and frustration involved in evaluation can be significantly reduced. Three specific plans should be considered.

The first step in planning the evaluation is to review the specific objectives for the retention solution using the same multiple-level concept. For example, reaction and satisfaction objectives are established, corresponding with the previous Level 1 evaluation. At this level, specific detail and requirements about the desired level of support and satisfaction for the solution are pinpointed. Learning objectives are established at the next level, particularly if the retention solution involves a significant amount of knowledge and skills enhancement. At this level, which corresponds with the learning evaluation, objectives are based on what each participant should know to make the solution successful.

Application and implementation objectives (Level 3) are established next to detail how the solution is implemented, covering time frames, progress, schedules, activities, and specific steps. These objectives profile precisely what will change as a result of the retention solution. The next level, impact (Level 4), details the specific business measures that should change as a result of the retention solution. Whereas employee turnover is always one of the output measures of retention solution, other important measures may include job satisfaction, customer satisfaction, productivity, quality, and time savings. Finally, at Level 5, the ROI objectives are detailed, indicating the specific return on investment desired. For many retention programs in North America, western Europe, Asia, Australia and New Zealand, 25% is typical; however, the client should specify the acceptable ROI level.

These objectives are directly linked to the evaluation and initial analysis levels. As Figure 12-3 illustrates, the five levels are helpful to see the direct linkages between the initial analysis of the problem and the evaluation. The objectives represent the transition from analysis to measurement and evaluation. It is particularly important to observe the actual direction of the arrow in Figure 12-3. The initial analysis often starts with the feasibility of solving the problem, driving to business needs and a detailed analysis of the job performance needs. Finally, skill and knowledge needs are identified and the preferences for the solution are outlined. Objectives are devel-

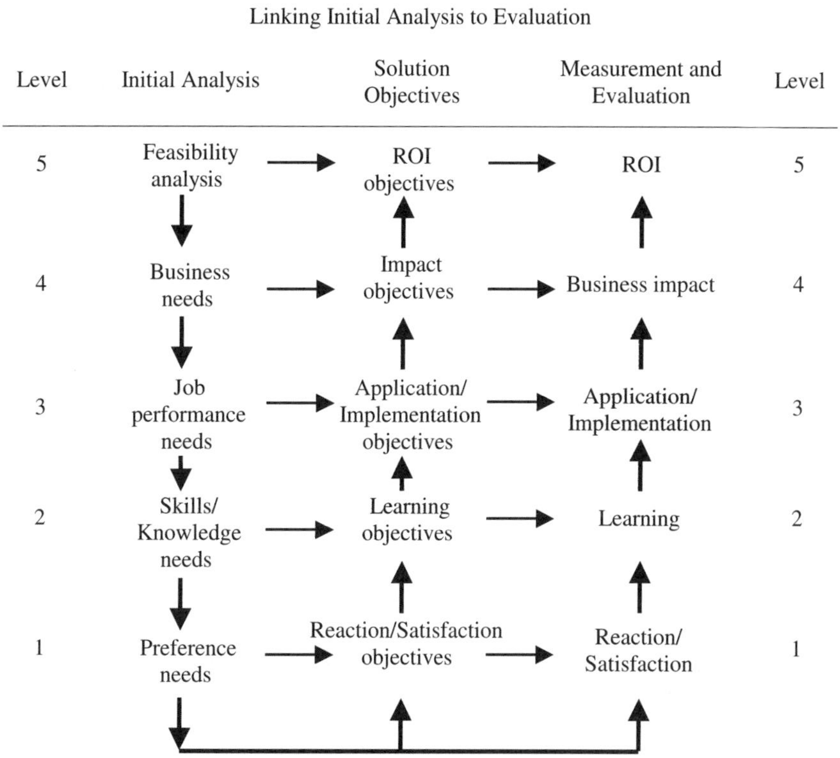

Linking Initial Analysis to Evaluation

Level	Initial Analysis	Solution Objectives	Measurement and Evaluation	Level
5	Feasibility analysis	ROI objectives	ROI	5
4	Business needs	Impact objectives	Business impact	4
3	Job performance needs	Application/ Implementation objectives	Application/ Implementation	3
2	Skills/ Knowledge needs	Learning objectives	Learning	2
1	Preference needs	Reaction/Satisfaction objectives	Reaction/ Satisfaction	1

Figure 12-3. The linkage of objectives, evaluation, and analysis.

oped; the solution is implemented in the opposite direction of the analysis. From the measurement and evaluation perspective, the chain of impact is observed as reaction and satisfaction data are collected, followed by learning, application, and business impact. The ROI value is calculated from the process—benefits compared to costs. Consequently, this parallel alignment of levels and objectives, collected to levels of analysis and measurement and evaluation, provides a very helpful and instructive tool to keep the process aligned and the retention solution on focus.

The data collection plan

After the above elements have been considered and determined, the data collection plan is developed. The plan outlines in detail the steps to be taken to collect data for a comprehensive evaluation, and usually includes the following items:

- Broad areas for objectives of the solution are used.
- Specific measures or data descriptions are indicated when they are necessary to explain the measures linked to the objectives.
- Specific data collection methodologies for each objective are listed.
- Sources of data, such as stakeholders, team leaders, and company records, are identified.
- The time frame to collect the data is noted for each data collection method.
- Responsibility for collecting data is assigned.

Figure 12-4 shows an example of a data collection plan for a retention solution (Phillips and Hill, 2001).

The ROI analysis plan

The ROI analysis plan is a continuation of the data collection plan. This planning document captures information on several key issues necessary to develop the actual ROI calculation. These issues include the following:

- Significant business data items, usually turnover
- The method for isolating the effects of the solution on the business measure
- The method for converting data to monetary values
- The solution cost categories, noting how certain costs should be prorated
- The anticipated intangible benefits
- The communication targets—those to receive the information
- Other issues or events that might influence solution implementation.

Figure 12-5 shows an example of an ROI analysis plan (Phillips and Hill, 2001).

Project plan

A final planning document is the project plan. This document provides a time line of all the major events and milestones that must be completed in the project. It covers the time line from planning to the last communication of results. Almost any project planning software

Solution: Reducing Turnover by Preventing Sexual Harassment

Responsibility: Jack J. Phillips   **Date:** _____

Data Collection Plan

Level	Solution Objectives	Evaluation Method	Data Sources	Timing	Responsibilities
1. Reaction and satisfaction	• Obtain a positive reaction to solution and materials • Obtain input for suggestions for improving solution	• Questionnaire	• Supervisors • Managers	• End of session	• Facilitator
2. Learning	• Knowledge of policy on sexual harassment • Knowledge of inappropriate and illegal behavior • Skills to investigate and discuss sexual harassment	• Pre- and Post-Test • Observation	• Supervisors • Managers	• Beginning of project and end of implementation • During session	• Meeting facilitator
3. Application and implementation	• Administer policy • Conduct meeting with employees • Ensure that the workplace is free of sexual harassment	• Self-assessment questionnaire • Complete and submit meeting record • Employee survey	• Supervisors • Managers • HR records section • 25% sample of all nonsupervisory Employees	• 6 months after solution • 1 month after solution	• Evaluator • HRIS staff • Employee communications
4. Business impact	• Reduce employee turnover • Reduce internal complaints • Reduce external complaints	• Business performance monitoring • Questionnaire	• HR records section • Supervisors	• Monthly for 1 year before and after program	• Evaluator

Figure 12-4. Data collection plan.

Project: Reducing Turnover by Preventing Sexual Harassment

Responsibility: Jack J. Phillips   **Date:** _____

ROI Analysis Plan

Data Items	Methods of Isolating the Effects of the Solution	Methods of Converting Data	Cost Categories	Intangible Benefits	Communication Targets	Other Influences/Issues
Employee voluntary turnover	• Forecasting using percentage of turnover related to sexual harassment	• External studies within industry	• Needs assessment • Development/ acquisition • Coordination/ facilitation time • Materials • Food/refreshments • Facilities • Participant salaries and benefits • Evaluation	• Job satisfaction • Absenteeism • Stress reduction • Public image • Recruiting	• All employees (condensed information) • Senior executives (summary of report with detailed backup) • All supervisors and managers (brief report) • HR/HRD staff (full report)	• Several initiatives to reduce turnover were implemented during this time period • Must not duplicate benefits from both internal and external complaints
Formal internal complaints of sexual harassment	• Trend-line analysis • Participant estimation (as a backup)	• Historical costs with estimation form EEO/AA staff (internal expert)				
External complaints of sexual harassment	• Trend-line analysis • Participant estimation (as a backup)	• Historical costs with estimation form EEO/AA staff (internal expert)				

Figure 12-5. ROI analysis plan.

will fill this need. These three planning documents are necessary to successfully implement and manage the ROI process.

Data Collection

Implementation begins after the planning process. Data collection is central to the ROI process. Both hard and soft data are collected. Data are usually collected during two time frames: during the initial launch of the solution and following implementation.

Retention (Level 1) and learning (Level 2) data are usually collected during initial sessions for the retention solution. For example, if a training program were presented as a solution, Level 1 and 2 data would be collected during that program. Several methods are appropriate for capturing the Level 1 and Level 2 data, as follow:

- Surveys and questionnaires are used to capture reaction and learning data.
- Interviews may be utilized to capture reaction and learning data.
- Focus groups can also capture reaction and, on some occasions, learning data.
- Tests can be constructed to capture learning data. Informal methods are used in many applications, which include self-assessment, facilitator assessment, and team assessment.

A variety of methods are available to collect postimplementation data for an ROI evaluation.

- Follow-up *surveys* are used to determine the degree to which participants have utilized various aspects of the retention solution, Level 3 data. Survey responses are often developed on a sliding scale and usually represent attitudinal data.
- Follow-up *questionnaires* are administered to uncover specific applications and implementation issues, as well as impact data (Level 3 and 4). Participants provide responses to a variety of open-ended and forced-response questions.
- On-the-job *observation* captures actual skill application and use (Level 3 data). Observations are particularly useful in retention solutions involving the team leader and are more effective when the observer is either invisible or transparent.
- Postimplementation *interviews* may determine the extent to which the solution has been implemented. Interviews allow for

probing to uncover specific applications and are appropriate with Level 3 data.

- *Focus groups* are conducted to determine the degree to which behavior change and application has occurred. Focus groups are appropriate with qualitative data (Level 3).
- *Action plans* are developed by major stakeholders and implemented as part of the retention solution. A follow-up of the plans provides evidence of solution success. Level 3 and 4 data may be collected with action plans.
- *Business performance monitoring* is useful where various performance records and operational data (such as turnover data) are examined for improvement. This method is particularly useful for impact data (Level 4).

The important challenge is to select the data collection method or methods appropriate for the setting, stakeholders, and the specific solution, within the time and budget constraints of the organization.

Isolating the Effects of the Solution

An often-overlooked issue in most evaluations is the technique used to isolate the effects of retention solutions. In this step of the ROI process, specific strategies are explored to determine the amount of turnover improvement directly related to the solution. This step is essential because many factors usually influence turnover. The specific techniques utilized at this step will pinpoint the amount of improvement directly related to the solution. The result is increased accuracy and credibility of the ROI calculation. The following techniques have been used by organizations to address this important issue (Phillips, Stone, and Phillips, 2001):

- A *control group* arrangement may be used to isolate the impact. With this technique, one group is involved in the solution while another similar group is not. The difference in the turnover of the two groups is attributed to the program. When properly set up and implemented, the control group arrangement is the most effective way to isolate effects of a retention solution.
- *Trend lines* are used to project the turnover rate based on pre-project data, as if the solution had not been undertaken. The projection is compared to the actual data after the solution is implemented, and the difference represents an estimate of the

impact. Under certain conditions, this strategy can be an accurate way to isolate the impact of retention solutions.

- *Key stakeholders estimate* the amount of improvement related to the retention solution. Here, participants in retention solutions are provided with the total amount of improvement on a preimplementation and postimplementation basis and are asked to indicate the percentage of the improvement that actually relates to the solution. These estimates should be adjusted for the error of the estimates.

- *Supervisors and managers estimate* the impact of retention solutions on turnover. Supervisors are presented with the total amount of turnover improvement and asked to indicate the percentage related to the solution. Senior managers may estimate the impact of retention solutions. In these cases, managers provide an estimate or "adjustment" to reflect the portion of the improvement related to the solution. Although these estimates might be inaccurate, senior management involvement in this process affords some advantages such as ownership of the solution.

- *Experts provide estimates* of the impact of retention solution. Because the estimates are based on previous experience, the experts must be familiar with the type of solution and the specific situation.

- When feasible, *other influencing factors are identified and the impact estimated or calculated,* leaving the remaining unexplained improvement attributed to the solution. In this case, the influence of all other factors is developed and the solution remains the one variable not accounted for in the analysis. The unexplained portion of the turnover reduction is then attributed to the solution.

Collectively, these techniques provide a comprehensive set of tools to isolate the effects of retention solution.

Conversion of Data to Monetary Values

To calculate the ROI, business impact data are converted to monetary values to compare with solution costs. This requires a value to be placed on each unit of data connected with the solution. For most retention solutions, the only output measure is turnover. However, some solutions also drive other measures, such as job satisfaction, productivity, quality, and customer service. Several approaches are available to convert data to monetary values where the specific technique selected usually depends on the type of data and the situation (Phillips, 2003).

- *Output data are converted to profit contribution or cost savings.* With this approach, output increases are converted to monetary value based on their unit of contribution to profit or the unit of cost reduction. These values are standard values, readily available in most organizations.
- The *cost of quality is calculated*, and quality improvements are directly converted to cost savings. These values are standard values, available in many organizations.
- For solutions where employee time is saved in addition to turnover, *wages and benefits are used for the value of time.* Because some solutions focus on improving the time required to complete projects, processes, or daily activities, the value of time becomes an important issue.
- *Historical costs and organizational records* are used when they are available for a specific measure. In this case, organization cost data are used to establish the specific value of an improvement. This approach is used by some organizations to develop the cost of turnover.
- When available, *internal and external experts* may be used to estimate a value for an improvement. In this situation, the credibility of the estimate hinges on the expertise and reputation of the individual. Consultants offering retention practices may be able to provide an estimate.
- *External databases* are sometimes available to estimate the value or cost of data items. Research, government, and industry databases can provide important information for these values. The difficulty lies in finding a specific database related to the situation. For turnover, a significant amount of research is available on the cost of turnover, precluding the development of internal cost value.
- *Participants in a retention solution estimate* the value of the data item. For this approach to be effective, participants must be capable of providing a value for the improvement.
- *Soft measures are linked, mathematically, to other measures* that are easier to measure and convert to value. This approach is particularly helpful when establishing values for measures that are very difficult to convert to monetary values, such

as customer satisfaction, employee satisfaction, stress, and employee complaints.

- *Supervisors and managers* provide estimates when they are willing and capable of assigning values to the improvement. This approach is especially useful when participants are not fully capable of providing the input or in situations where supervisors need to confirm or adjust the participant's estimate.
- *HR staff estimates* may be used to determine a value of an output data item. In these cases, it is essential for the estimates to be provided on an unbiased basis.

This step in the ROI model is very important and is absolutely necessary to determine the monetary benefits from retention solutions. The process is challenging, particularly with soft data, but can be methodically accomplished using one or more of the above techniques.

Tabulating Costs of the Solution

The next step in the process is tabulating the costs of the retention solution. Tabulating the costs involves monitoring or developing all of the related costs of the solution. Among the components that should be included are the following:

- The cost to design and develop the solution, possibly prorated over the expected life cycle of the solution
- The cost of all materials provided to each stakeholder and team leader
- The cost of the facilitator, coordinator, or leader, including preparation times as well as contact time
- The cost of the use of facilities, if applicable
- Travel, lodging, and meal costs for the participants, if applicable
- Salaries plus employee benefits of the participants for the time they are involved in the solution, away from their normal job duties
- Administrative and overhead costs of the HR function allocated in some convenient way to retention solutions

In addition, specific costs related to the diagnostic analysis and needs assessment should be included, if appropriate. The conservative approach is to include all of these costs so that the total is fully loaded.

Calculating ROI

The return on investment is calculated using the benefits and costs. The cost/benefit ratio is the solution benefits divided by solution cost. In formula form it is as follows:

$$BCR = \frac{\text{Solution benefits}}{\text{Solution costs}}$$

The ROI uses the net benefits divided by solution costs. The net benefits are the solution benefits minus the costs. In formula form, the ROI becomes

$$ROI\,(\%) = \frac{\text{Net solution benefits}}{\text{Costs}} \times 100$$

This is the same basic formula used in evaluating other investments where the ROI is traditionally reported as earnings divided by investment. The ROI from some solutions is high because of the huge savings generated when turnover is reduced.

ROI Calculation Example

To illustrate exactly how the calculation is developed, consider the following situation. In a hospital chain, a retention solution was implemented to reduce the number of sexual harassment complaints. The data collection and ROI analysis for this program is presented in Figure 12-4 and 12-5. Table 12-2 shows the calculation of the monetary benefits for this program. Only the calculation is shown. For additional information on this case study, please see the original publication (Phillips and Hill, 2001).

As Table 12-2 shows, most of the monetary benefit was deducted directly from turnover reduction, yielding a total value of $2.8 million. Sexual harassment complaints was another business impact measure directly connected with the program, yielding $360,000. Table 12-3 shows the actual solution costs. These are fully loaded costs that equate to $277,987. The calculations of the ROI for these values are as follows:

$$BCR = \frac{\text{Benefits}}{\text{Costs}} = \frac{\$360,276 + \$2,840,632}{\$277,987} = \frac{\$3,200,908}{\$277,987} = 11.5 : 1$$

Table 12-2
Calculation of Monetary Benefits of Retention Solution

Turnover Reduction

Unit of improvement = One turnover statistic (termination)
Turnover, preprogram = 6,651 × 24.2% = 1,610
Turnover, preprogram, related to hostile environment: 1,610 × 11% = 177
Turnover, postprogram: 6,844 × 19.9% = 1,362
Turnover, postprogram related to hostile environment: 1,362 × 3% = 41
Improvement related to program: 177 − 41 = 136
Cost of one turnover: 75% of annual salary = $27,850 × 0.75 = $20,887
Value of improvement: 136 × $20,887 = $2,840,632

Complaint Reduction

Unit of improvement = One internal complaint
Value of one internal complaint = $24,343
Total improvement: 55 − 35 = 20
Improvement related to program: 20 × 74% = 14.8
Value of improvement = 14.8 × $24,343 = $360,276
Total benefits: $2,840,632 + $360,276 = $3,200,908

Table 12-3
Solution Costs

Cost Category	Total Cost
Assessment (estimated cost of time)	$9,000
Solution development/acquisition	15,000
Coordination/facilitation time	9,600
Travel and lodging for facilitation and coordinators	1,520
Materials (655 @ $12)	7,860
Food/refreshments (655 @ $30)	19,650
Facilities (17 @ $150)	2,550
Participant salaries and benefits ($130,797 × 1.39)	181,807
Evaluation	31,000
	$277,987

$$\text{ROI} = \frac{\text{Net benefits}}{\text{Costs}} = \frac{\$4,300,908 - \$277,987}{\$277,987} = 1,052\%$$

Benefits based entirely on complaint and turnover reduction are used in the costbenefit ratio to yield 11.5:1. Thus for each dollar spent on the program, $11.50 was returned. The ROI calculation, which uses net benefits, shows a return of 1,052%, an impressive and staggering amount. The results were much greater than the evaluation team and senior management expected.

Identifying Intangibles

In addition to tangible monetary benefits, most retention solutions have intangible, nonmonetary benefits. Data items identified that are not converted to monetary values are considered intangible benefits. While many of these items can be converted to monetary values, for various reasons, they often are not. One reason is that the process used for conversion is too subjective and the resulting values lose credibility in the process.

These intangible benefits may include increased job satisfaction, increased organizational commitment, improved teamwork, improved customer service, reduced complaints, and reduced conflicts. For some solutions, these intangible, nonmonetary benefits are extremely valuable, often carrying as much influence as the hard data items.

OPERATING STANDARDS AND PHILOSOPHY

To ensure consistency and replication of studies, operating standards must be developed and applied as the process model is used to develop ROI studies. It is extremely important for the results of a study to stand alone and be consistent, regardless of the individual conducting the study. The operating standards detail how each step and issue of the process is handled. Table 12-4 shows the guiding principles that form the basis for the operating standards.

The guiding principles not only serve as a way to consistently address each step, but also provide a much-needed conservative approach to the analysis. A conservative approach may lower the actual ROI calculation, but it will also build credibility with the target audience for communicating results, especially senior executives. For additional information on calculating return on investment, see other resources (Phillips, 2003).

Table 12-4
Guiding Principles

1. When a higher level evaluation is conducted, data must be collected at lower levels.
2. When an evaluation is planned for a higher level, the previous level of evaluation does not have to be comprehensive.
3. When collecting and analyzing data, use only the most credible source.
4. When analyzing data, choose the most conservative among alternatives.
5. At least one method must be used to isolate the effects of the solution.
6. If no improvement data are available for a population or from a specific source, it is assumed that little or no improvement has occurred.
7. Estimates of improvements should be adjusted for the potential error of the estimate.
8. Extreme data items and unsupported claims should not be used in ROI calculations.
9. Only the first year of benefits (annual) should be used in the ROI analysis of short-term solutions.
10. Costs of the solution should be fully loaded for ROI analysis.

FINAL THOUGHTS

ROI calculations for retention solutions are being developed by many organizations to meet the demands of influential stakeholders. The result is a process that shows the value-added contribution of a retention strategy in a format desired by many senior executives and administrators. This chapter demonstrates that the ROI process represents significant and challenging progress for most organizations. The process must be based on a sound framework, using a process model that provides step-by-step procedures and credible methodologies. Through careful planning, methodical procedures, and logical and practical analysis, ROI calculations can be developed reliably and accurately for any type of retention solution.

REFERENCES

Broad, M.L. (Ed.). *In Action: Transferring Learning to the Workplace.* Alexandria, Va.: American Society for Training and Development, 1997.

Kaplan, R.S., and Norton, D.P. *Balanced Scorecard*. Boston: Harvard Business School Press, 1996.

Kimmerling, G. "Gathering Best Practices." *Training & Development*, September 1993; 47(3):28–36.

Kirkpatrick, D.L. Techniques for Evaluating Training Programs. In D.L. Kirkpatrick (Ed.), *Evaluating Training Programs*. Alexandria, Va.: American Society for Training and Development, 1975:1–17.

Phillips, J.J. (Ed.). *In Action: Implementing Evaluation Systems and Processes*. Alexandria, Va.: American Society for Training and Development, 1998.

Phillips, J.J. (Ed.). *In Action: Measuring Return on Investment*, Vol. 1. Alexandria, Va.: American Society for Training and Development, 1994.

Phillips, J.J. (Ed.). *In Action: Measuring Return on Investment*, Vol. 2. Alexandria, Va.: American Society for Training and Development, 1997.

Phillips, J.J. *Return on Investment in Training and Performance Improvement Programs, 2nd Edition*. Boston, MA: Butterworth-Heinemann, 2003.

Phillips, J.J. *The Consultant's Scorecard*. New York, NY: McGraw Hill, 2000.

Phillips, J.J., and Hill, D. "Preventing Sexual Harassment," *Human Resources Scorecard*. Boston, MA: Butterworth-Heinemann, 2001.

Phillips, J.J., and Phillips, P.P. "Dispelling the ROI Myths." *Corporate University Review*, May/June 1999:32–36.

Phillips, J.J., and Phillips, P.P. "How to Measure the Return on Your HR Investment," *Strategic HR Review*, May/June 2002; 1(4):16–21.

Phillips, J.J., and Phillips, P.P. *In Action: Measuring Return on Investment*, Vol. 3. Alexandria, Va.: American Society for Training and Development, 2000.

Phillips, J.J., Stone, R.D., and Phillips, P.P. *The Human Resources Scorecard: Measuring the Return on Investment*. Boston: Butterworth-Heinemann, 2001.

Phillips, P.P., and Burkett, H. *ROI managing Evaluation shortcuts*, ASTD InfoLine Series. Alexandria, Va.: American Society for Training and Development, 2001.

CHAPTER 13

Make Adjustments and Continue

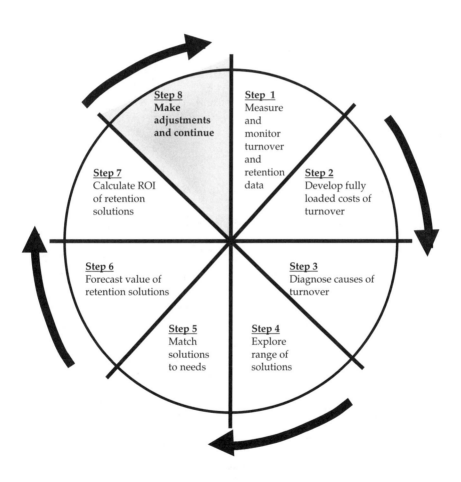

Step 8
Make adjustments and continue

Step 1
Measure and monitor turnover and retention data

Step 2
Develop fully loaded costs of turnover

Step 3
Diagnose causes of turnover

Step 4
Explore range of solutions

Step 5
Match solutions to needs

Step 6
Forecast value of retention solutions

Step 7
Calculate ROI of retention solutions

With data in hand, what is the next step? Should the data be used to modify the retention solution, change the solution, show the contribution of the solution, justify new solutions, gain additional support for managing retention solutions, or build goodwill? How should the data be presented? The worst course of action is to do nothing. Making adjustments is as important as achieving results. This chapter provides useful information to help present data to the various audiences and drive important actions. It discusses how to communicate to, and build relationships with, the senior management team. The chapter concludes with a discussion of how to overcome the resistance to implementing retention solutions and adoption of a long-term view of maintaining workforce stability.

The Importance of Communicating Results

Communicating results is a critical issue when implementing retention solutions. Constant communication throughout the process, and at specific follow-up times, ensures that information is flowing so that adjustments can be made and all stakeholders are aware of the success of the solution. Several issues underscore the importance of communicating results of a retention solution.

Communication Is Necessary to Make Improvements

Because information is collected at different points during the process, the feedback to the various stakeholder groups is the only way for adjustments to be made. Thus the quality and timeliness of communication become critical issues for making necessary improvements. Even after the project is completed, communication is necessary to make sure the target audience fully understands the results achieved and how the results could either be enhanced in future programs or in the current program, if it is still operational.

Communication Is Necessary to Explain Contributions

Communication must be planned and executed to ensure that the audiences understand the contribution of the retention solution using six types of measures. The different target audiences will need a thorough explanation of the results. Communicating business impact and ROI data can quickly become confusing for even the most sophisticated target audiences. A communication strategy, including techniques, media, and the overall process, will determine the extent to which the audiences understand the contribution.

Communication Is a Sensitive Issue

Communication is one of the important issues that can cause major problems. Because the results of an initiative can be closely linked to the political issues in an organization, communication can upset some individuals while pleasing others. At times, the reputation of an individual or group is at stake. Problems can quickly surface if certain individuals do not receive the information or if the information is unfavorable. Not only is it an understanding issue, it is also a fairness, quality, and political correctness issue to make sure communication is presented effectively to all key individuals who need the information.

Various Target Audiences Need Different Information

Because there are so many potential target audiences for data, it is important for the communication to be tailored to their needs. A varied audience will have varied needs. Some groups, such as sponsors and executives, need information on the outcome of the project, measured in reduced turnover and return on investment (ROI). Team leaders and managers need to know if they are implementing the solution properly. Project developers and solutions coordinators need to know if the solution was on track. Employees need to be convinced that the organization is addressing the issue. Table 13-1 lists the questions that should be addressed for each audience.

Table 13-1
Key Questions about Audience Needs

1. Who are the target audiences? Identify specific target audiences that should always receive information and others that will receive information when appropriate.
2. What will be communicated?
3. When will the data be communicated?
4. How will the information be communicated?
5. Where should the communication take place?
6. Who will communicate the information?
7. What specific actions are required or desired?

Collectively, these reasons make communication a critical issue, although it is often overlooked or underestimated in retention solutions. This chapter builds on this important issue and shows a variety of techniques for communicating to various target audiences.

Principles of Communicating Results

The skills required to communicate results effectively are almost as delicate and sophisticated as those needed to obtain results. The style is as important as the substance. Regardless of the message, audience, or medium, a few general principles apply and are explored next.

Timeliness

Usually, results should be communicated as soon as they are known. From a practical standpoint, it may be best to delay the communication until a convenient time, such as the publication of the next newsletter or the next general management meeting. Several issues about timing must be addressed. Is the audience ready for the results when considering other pressing issues? Is the audience expecting results? When is the best time to have the maximum effect on the audience? Are there circumstances that dictate a change in the timing of the communication?

Audience Selection Crucial to Communication Success

When approaching a particular audience, the following questions should be asked about each potential group:

- Are they interested in the initiative?
- Do they really want to receive the information?
- Has someone already made a commitment to them regarding communication?
- Is the timing right for this audience?
- Are they familiar with the retention solution?
- How do they prefer to have results communicated?
- Do they know the human resources (HR) staff members?
- Are they likely to find the results threatening?
- Which medium will be most convincing to this group?

Table 13-2
Common Target Audiences

Reason for Communication	Primary Target Audiences
Secure approval for the retention solution	Client, top executives
Gain support for the retention solution	Immediate managers, team leaders
Secure agreement with the issues	Participants, team leaders
Build credibility for the HR department	Top executives
Enhance reinforcement of the processes	Immediate managers
Drive action for improvement	HR staff members
Prepare participants for the retention solution	Team leaders
Show the complete results of the retention solution	Client team
Underscore the importance of measuring results	Client, HR staff members
Explain techniques used to measure results	Client, support staff
Create desire for stakeholders to be involved	Team leaders
Stimulate interest in the HR department's services	Top executives
Demonstrate accountability for client expenditures	All employees
Market future HR programs	Prospective clients

Table 13-2 shows common target audiences and the rationale for selecting the audience. The potential target audiences to receive information about HR results are varied in terms of job levels and responsibilities. Determining which groups will receive a particular communication piece deserves careful thought, because problems can arise when a particular group receives inappropriate information or when another is omitted altogether. A sound basis for proper audience selection is to analyze the reason for communication.

While this list shows the most common target audiences, others can exist in a particular organization. For instance, management or employees can be subdivided into different departments, divisions, or even subsidiaries of the organization. The number of audiences can be large in a complex organization. At a minimum, four target audiences are always recommended: a senior management group, the

participants' immediate manager or team leader, the project participants, and the HR staff.

Communication Targeted to Specific Audiences

Communication is more effective if it is designed for a particular
group. A single report for all audiences may not be appropriate. The
scope, size, media, and actual information will vary from one group
to another, making the target audience the key to determining the
appropriate communication process. The message should be specifically tailored to the interests, needs, and expectations of the target
audience. The results of a retention solution include the six types of
data developed in this book. Some of the data are developed earlier
in the project and may be communicated during implementation.
Other data are collected after implementation and communicated in
a follow-up study. Thus the results, in the broadest sense, may range
from early feedback in qualitative terms to ROI values in a follow-
up impact study.

To the greatest extent possible, the HR staff should know and
understand the target audience. If possible, the HR staff should try
to understand audience bias as each will have a particular bias or
opinion. Some will quickly support the results, whereas others may
be against them or be neutral. The staff should be empathetic and
try to understand differing views. With this understanding, communications can be tailored to each group. This is especially critical
when the potential exists for the audience to react negatively to the
results.

Careful Selection of Media

Some types of communication may be more effective than others
for a particular audience. Face-to-face meetings with key managers
may be better than special bulletins. A memo distributed exclusively
to top management may be more effective than the company newsletter. A downloadable report on the web may be appropriate for other
audiences. Determining the appropriate method of communication
can improve the effectiveness of the process.

Unbiased and Modest Communication

It is important to separate fact from fiction and accurate statements from opinions. Some audiences may accept communication

from HR staff members with skepticism, anticipating biased opinions. Boastful statements sometimes turn off audiences, and most of the content is lost. Although sensational claims may get audience attention, they often detract from the importance of the results. Observable, believable facts carry far more weight.

Consistency of Communication

The timing and content of the communication should be consistent with past practices. A special communication at an unusual time during the project may provoke suspicion. Also, if a particular group, such as top management, regularly receives communication on HR outcomes, it should continue receiving communication, even if the results are not positive. If some results are omitted, it might leave the impression that only positive results are reported.

Respects Testimonials Are More Effective Coming from Individuals the Audience

The value of opinions is strongly influenced by the source, particularly those who are respected and trusted. Testimonials about HR results, when solicited from respected individuals, can influence the effectiveness of the message. This respect may be related to leadership ability, role, position, special skills, or expert knowledge. A testimonial from an individual who commands little respect or is regarded as a substandard performer can have a negative impact on the message.

Influence of Audience Opinion of the HR Department on Communication Strategy

Opinions are difficult to change, and a negative opinion of HR may not change with the mere presentation of facts. Conversely, the presentation of facts alone may strengthen the opinions held by those who already agree with the HR results. It helps reinforce their position and provides a defense in discussions with others. An HR department with a high level of credibility and respect may have a relatively easy time communicating results. Low credibility can create problems when trying to be persuasive. The reputation of the department is an important consideration in developing the overall strategy.

Critical Nature of Planning the Communication

Any successful activity must be carefully planned to produce the maximum results. This is a critical part of communicating the results of retention solutions. Planning is important to ensure that each audience receives the proper information at the right time and that appropriate actions are taken. The questions presented in Table 13-1 must be addressed when developing the plan.

An important issue is a plan for presenting the results of an impact study. This occurs when a major retention solution is completed and the detailed results are known. This is more specialized than the plan for communicating a progress report because it involves an impact study from a major retention solution. Table 13-3 shows the communication plan for a major retention project with a stress reduction solution. (Excessive stress was causing high burnout and, consequently, high turnover.)

In this example, five different communication pieces were developed for different audiences. The complete report of the ROI impact study, a 75-page document, served as the historical account of the

Table 13-3
Retention Solution Communication Plan

Communication Document	Communication Target(s)	Distribution Method
Complete report with appendices (75 pages)	Client team HR staff Intact team manager	Distribute and discuss in a special meeting
Executive summary (8 pages)	Senior management in the business units Senior corporate management	Distribute and discuss in a routine meeting
General interest overview and summary without the actual ROI calculation (10 pages)	Participants	Mail with letter
General interest article (1 page)	All employees	Publish in company publication
Brochure highlighting program, objectives, and specific results	Team leaders with an interest in the project	Include with other marketing materials

project. It was prepared for the client, the HR staff and the manager of each of the teams involved in the studies. An executive summary, a much smaller document, was designed for a select group of higher-level executives. A general interest overview and summary without the ROI calculation went to the participants. A third document, a general interest article, was developed for company publications, and a brochure was developed to show the success of the retention solution. The brochure was used in marketing the same solution internally to other teams.

These general principles are important to the overall success of the communication effort. They should serve as a checklist for the HR team when disseminating results of retention solutions and strategies.

DEVELOPING THE IMPACT STUDY REPORT

The type of formal evaluation report depends on the extent of detailed information presented to the various target audiences. Brief summaries of project results with appropriate charts may be sufficient for some communication efforts. In other situations, particularly with significant HR interventions requiring extensive funding, the amount of detail in the evaluation report is more crucial. A complete and comprehensive impact study report may be necessary.

Content of the Report

This report can then be used as the basis of information for specific audiences and various groups. The report may contain the following sections:

Management/executive summary

The management summary is a brief overview of the entire report, explaining the basis for the evaluation and the significant conclusions and recommendations. It is designed for individuals who are too busy to read a detailed report. It is usually written last but appears first in the report for easy access.

Background information

The background information provides a general description of the retention solution. If applicable, the analysis and events that led to the implementation of the retention solution are summarized. The solution is fully described. The extent of detailed information depends on the amount of information the audience needs.

Objectives

The objectives for the retention solution are outlined. These objectives provide the framework from which the different types or levels of data will be collected.

Evaluation strategy/methodology

The evaluation strategy identifies all components that make up the total evaluation process. Several components of the ROI methodology, presented in this book, are discussed in this section of the report. The specific purposes of evaluation are outlined, and the evaluation design and methodology are explained. The instruments used in data collection are also described and usually presented as exhibits. Any unusual issues in the evaluation design are discussed. Finally, other useful information related to the design, timing, and execution of the evaluation is included.

Data collection and analysis

This section explains the methods used to collect data, as outlined in earlier chapters. The data collected are usually presented in the report in summary form. Next the methods used to analyze data are presented with interpretations.

Project costs

Costs of the retention solution are presented in this section, by category. For example, analysis, development, implementation, operation, and evaluation costs are recommended categories for cost presentation. The assumptions made in developing and classifying costs are presented here.

Reaction and satisfaction

This section details the data collected from key stakeholders, particularly the participants involved in the retention solution, to measure the reaction and satisfaction with the solution.

Learning

This section shows a brief summary of the improvement in knowledge and skills related to the retention solution. It explains and quantifies how participants have learned new processes, skills, tasks, procedures, and practices needed to make the retention solution successful.

Application and implementation

This section shows how the retention solution was implemented and the success of the application of new skills and knowledge. Key implementation issues are addressed, including any major success or lack of success.

Business impact

This section shows the changes in turnover and retention and other business impact measures that initially influenced the need for the project. This shows the extent to which performance has changed because of the implementation of the retention solution.

Return on investment

This section actually shows the ROI calculation and the benefits/cost ratio. It compares the calculated value with the expected value and provides an interpretation of the actual calculation.

Intangible measures

This section shows the various intangible measures directly linked to the retention solution. Intangibles are those measures not converted to monetary values or included in the actual ROI calculation. They are reported only if there is evidence of linkage to the solution.

Barriers and enablers

The various problems and obstacles affecting the success of the retention solution are detailed and presented as barriers to implementation. Those factors or influences that had a positive effect on the solution also are included as enablers. Together they provide important insight into the factors that can hinder or enhance future projects.

Conclusions and recommendations

This section presents conclusions based on all the results. If appropriate, brief explanations are presented on how each conclusion was reached. A list of recommendations or changes in the solution, if appropriate, is provided with brief explanations for each recommendation. It is important that the conclusions and recommendations are consistent with one another and with the findings described in the previous section.

Developing the Report

Table 13-4 shows the table of contents from a typical evaluation report for an ROI evaluation. This specific study was conducted for a large chemical company and involved an ROI analysis on a retention solution. The typical report provides background information, explains the processes used and, more important, presents the results.

Although this report is an effective, professional way to present ROI data, several cautions must be followed. Because this document reports the success of an HR-initiated retention solution involving a group of employees, complete credit for the success must go to the stakeholders who made the difference and their immediate leaders. Their performance generated the success. Another important caution is to avoid boasting about results. Although the ROI process may be accurate and credible, it may still contain subjective assessment. Huge claims of success can quickly turn off an audience and interfere with the delivery of the desired message.

A final caution concerns the structure of the report. The methodology should be clearly explained in addition to assumptions made in the analysis. The reader should easily realize how the values were developed and how the specific steps were followed to make the process more conservative, credible, and accurate. Detailed statistical analyses should be placed in the appendix.

COMMUNICATING INFORMATION ON RETENTION SOLUTIONS

Perhaps the biggest challenge of communication is the actual delivery of the message. This can be accomplished in a variety of ways

Table 13-4
Format of an ROI Impact Study Report

General Information

Background information on retention solution
Objectives of study

Methodology for Impact Study

Levels of evaluation
The ROI methodology
Collecting data
Isolating the effects of the retention solution
Converting data to monetary values

Data Analysis Issues

Cost of Retention Solution

Results: General Information

Response profile
Success with objectives

Results: Reaction and Satisfaction with Retention Solution

Data sources
Data summary
Key issues

Results: Learning for Solution Success

Data sources
Data summary
Key issues

Results: Application and Implementation of Solution

Data sources
Data summary
Key issues

Results: Turnover Reduction (or Prevention)

General comments
Linkage with other business measures
Key issues

Results: ROI and Its Meaning

Results: Intangible Measures Linked to Solution

Table 13-4
(*Continued*)

Barriers and Enablers

Barriers to solution success
Enablers for solution success

Conclusions and Recommendations

Conclusions
Recommendations

Exhibits

Table 13-5
Areas of Feedback for Retention Solutions

Appropriateness of objectives	Project leadership
Appropriateness of plans	Project coordination
Appropriateness of schedule	Project communication
Progress made with plans	Motivation of project participants
Importance of project	Cooperation of project participants
Support for project	Capability of project participants
Resources for project	Likelihood of project success
Integration of project with other systems	Barriers to project success
	Enablers to project success

and settings, based on the target audience and the media selected for the message. Several approaches deserve additional coverage and are presented here.

Providing Ongoing Feedback

One of the most important reasons for collecting reaction, satisfaction, and learning data is to provide feedback so adjustments or changes can be made throughout the project. In most retention solutions, data are routinely collected and quickly communicated to a variety of groups. Table 13-5 shows the typical areas of feedback provided to several feedback audiences using a variety of media.

Data are collected during the project at four specific time intervals and communicated to at least four audiences—sometimes six. Some of these feedback sessions result in identifying specific actions that need to be taken. This process becomes comprehensive and must be managed in a very proactive way. The following steps are recommended for providing feedback and managing the feedback process (Block, 2001):

Communicate quickly

Whether the results are good or bad, it is important to let individuals involved in the project have the information as soon as possible. The recommended time for providing feedback is usually a matter of days and certainly no longer than a week or two after the results are known.

Simplify the data

Condense data into an understandable, concise presentation. This is not the forum for detailed explanations and analysis.

Examine the role of the solution team and the client in the feedback situation

Sometimes the solution team (or HR executive) is the judge, jury, prosecutor, defendant, or witness. On the other hand, sometimes the client is the judge, jury, prosecutor, defendant, or witness. It is important to examine the respective roles in terms of reactions to the data and the actions that need to be taken.

Use negative data in a constructive way

Some data will show that things are not going so well, and the fault may rest with the HR department or the client. In either case, the story basically changes from "Let's look at the success we've made" to "Now we know which areas to change."

Use positive data cautiously

Positive data can be misleading, and if they are communicated too enthusiastically, they may create expectations beyond what may materialize later.

Choose the language of the meeting and communication carefully

Use language that is descriptive, focused, specific, short, and simple. Avoid language that is too judgmental, broad, stereotypical, lengthy, or complex.

Ask the client for reactions to the data

The client is the No. 1 customer, and the client's reaction is critical since it is most important that the client is pleased with the program.

Ask the client for recommendations

The client may have some good recommendations of changes needed to keep the solution on track or put it back on track if it derails.

Use support and confrontation carefully

These two issues are not mutually exclusive. There may be times when support and confrontation are needed for the same group. The client may need support and yet be confronted for lack of improvement or sponsorship. The solution team may need to be confronted about the problem areas that are developed but may need support as well.

React and act on the data

Weigh the different alternatives and possibilities to arrive at the adjustments and changes that will be necessary.

Secure agreement from all key stakeholders

This step is essential to make sure everyone is willing to make adjustments and changes that seem necessary.

Keep the feedback process short

Do not let it become excessive with long, drawn-out meetings or lengthy documents. If this occurs, stakeholders will avoid the process instead of being willing to participate in the future.

Following these 12 steps will help move the program forward and provide important feedback, often ensuring that adjustments are supported and made.

As briefly described earlier in the chapter, the timing of communication is extremely important. The communication must be routine and continuous to make changes and drive improvement. Figure 13-1 shows an example of communication from a 6-month retention solution project. As the figure illustrates, data are collected prior to the project and at different intervals during the project. Finally, after a 6-month follow-up is completed, the data are presented to a variety of target audiences. The important issue in the planning stage is to address the timing issue along with audiences and information.

Presenting Impact Study Data to Senior Management

Perhaps one of the most challenging and potentially stressful communications is presenting an impact study to the senior management team—the client in a retention solution. The challenge is convincing this highly skeptical and critical group that outstanding results have been achieved (assuming they have), in a reasonable time frame, addressing the salient points, and making sure the managers understand the process used to measure success. Two particular issues can create challenges. If the results are impressive, it may be difficult to make the managers believe the data. On the other extreme, if the data are negative, the challenge is to ensure that managers do not

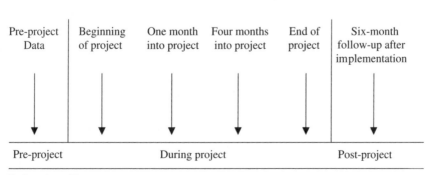

Figure 13-1. Timing of feedback for a 6-month retention project.

overreact to the negative results and seek someone to blame. Several guidelines can help make sure this process is planned and executed properly:

- Plan a face-to-face meeting with senior team members for the first one or two major impact studies. If they are unfamiliar with the complete ROI process, a face-to-face meeting is necessary to make sure they understand the process. The good news is that they will probably attend the meeting because they have not seen ROI data developed for this type of project. The bad news is that it uses some of their precious time, usually 1 to 2 hours for this presentation.
- After the group has experienced a face-to-face meeting with a couple of presentations, an executive summary may suffice. At this point they understand the process, so a shortened version may be appropriate.
- After the group is familiar with the process, a brief version may suffice. A one- to two-page summary with charts and graphs showing all six types of measures usually suffices.
- When making the initial presentation, the results should not be distributed in advance, or even during the session, but saved until the end of the session. This will allow enough time to present the process and react to it before the target audience sees the actual ROI number.
- Present the process step by step, showing how the data were collected, when they were collected, who provided the data, how the data were isolated from other influences, and how they were converted to monetary values. The various assumptions, adjustments, and conservative approaches are presented along with the total cost of the initiative. The costs are fully loaded so that the target audience will begin to accept the process of developing the actual ROI.
- When the data are actually presented, the results are revealed step by step, starting with reaction, moving through to ROI, and ending with the intangibles. This process allows the audience to see the chain of impact with reaction, learning, application, business impact, and ROI. After some discussion about the meaning of the ROI, the intangible measures are presented. Adequate time is allocated to each level of data as needed for the audience. This helps overcome the potentially negative reactions to a very positive or negative ROI.

- Show the costs of additional accuracy, if it is an issue. The trade-off for more accuracy and validity often means more time and direct expense. Address this issue whenever necessary, agreeing to collect more data if required.
- Solicit concerns, reactions, and issues for the process and make adjustments accordingly for the next presentation.

Collectively, these steps will help prepare for and present one of the most critical meetings for the HR staff.

Conduct a Retention Review Meeting

No group is more important than top executives when it comes to building support for managing retention. In many situations, this group is also the client for retention solutions. Improving communications with this group requires developing an overall strategy and building informal and formal relationship with the senior team.

A retention review meeting is an effective way to communicate to top executives about managing retention. While this review can be conducted more frequently, an annual basis is common. The primary purpose is to show top management what has been accomplished in retention management and what is planned for the future. The review also provides an opportunity for input and advice to the HR staff about retention issues, including needs, problems with the present solutions, and evaluation issues. The meeting can last from 2 hours to 2 days, depending on the scope of the meeting and the amount of information. This meeting is best suited for situations where retention is a critical issue, long-term strategies for managing retention are in place, and multiple solutions are being implemented in the same firm. A typical agenda for a half-day version of this review meeting is shown in Table 13-6.

This meeting may be the single most important event on the HR department's calendar during the year. It must be planned carefully, executed in a timely manner, and controlled to accomplish its purpose. This approach has been used in many organizations, and the reaction has been extremely favorable. Executives and managers want to know what the organization is accomplishing with retention, what results have been achieved and, most important, they want to have input on the decisions for retention solutions.

Table 13-6
Annual Review Agenda

Time	Annual Review Meeting Topic
8:00 AM	Review of retention issues and strategies
8:30	Review of turnover data and analysis
9:00	Description of each retention solution and the results achieved
10:30	Significant deviations from the expected results (both positive and negative)
11:00	Basis for determining retention needs for the next year
11:15	Anticipated solutions for the coming year (secure support and approval)
11:30	Proposed evaluation strategy and potential payoffs
Noon	Problem areas for managing retention (lack of support, where management involvement is needed or other potential problems that can be corrected by executive management)
12:30 PM	Concerns of executive management
1:00	Adjourn

The Organization's Publications and Standard Communication Tools

To reach a wide audience, the HR department can use in-house publications to communicate information about retention solutions. Whether a newsletter, magazine, newspaper, e-mail, intranet, or web sites, these types of media usually reach all employees. The information can be quite effective if communicated appropriately. The scope should be limited to general interest articles, announcements, and interviews.

Project results

Results communicated through these types of media must be significant enough to arouse general interest. For example, a story with the headline, "New Flextime Project Reduces Turnover by 10%," will catch the attention of many people because they may have participated in the solution and can appreciate the significance of the results. Reports on the accomplishments of a group of participants may not create interest unless the audience relates to the accomplishments.

For many retention solutions, results are achieved weeks or even months after the project is completed. Participants need reinforcement from many sources. If results are communicated to a general audience, including the participant's subordinates or peers, there is additional pressure to continue the project or similar ones in the future.

Building interest

Stories about managing retention and the results achieved create a favorable image. Employees are made aware that the organization is investing time and money to improve performance and prepare for the future. This type of story provides information about projects that employees otherwise may not have known about and sometimes creates a desire to participate, if given the opportunity.

Stakeholder recognition

General audience communication can bring recognition to participants, particularly those who excel in some aspect of the project. When participants deliver unusual performance, public recognition can enhance their self-esteem.

Human interest stories

Many human interest stories can develop from retention solutions. In one organization, the editor of the company newsletter participated in a comprehensive leadership development project and wrote a stimulating article about what it was like to be a participant. The article gave the reader a view of the entire course and its effectiveness in terms of the results achieved, including a reduction in turnover. It was an interesting and effective way to communicate about a challenging activity.

Case studies

Case studies represent an effective way to communicate the results of a retention solution. A typical case study describes the situation, provides appropriate background information (including the issues that led to the solution), presents the techniques and strategies used to develop the solution, and highlights the key issues in the project. Case studies tell an interesting story of how the solution was developed and the problems and concerns identified along the way. In one fast food company, the new employee orientation was redesigned to reduce turnover in the first 60 days of employment. The success was reported in the company newsletter.

Case studies have many useful applications in an organization. They can offer different perspectives and draw conclusions about approaches or techniques. A case study can serve as a self-teaching guide for individuals trying to understand how retention is managed. Case studies provide appropriate recognition for those involved in the actual case. More importantly, they recognize the stakeholders who achieved the results. The case study format is an effective way to learn about managing retention.

Driving Action from Retention Solutions

The primary reason for collecting and communicating data is to drive improvement. Any type of measurement and evaluation process will yield important data to enable changes or to provide assurance that solutions are working as planned.

Sources of Data for Action

Essentially, all data collection methods have the potential of yielding data that can drive actions for improvement. When stakeholders provide input into the success (or lack of success) of a particular solution, they almost always include information, comments, and suggestions that lead to improvements in the process. This is particularly the case with interviews and questionnaires where specific questions focus on the barriers to success. A series of questions explore reasons for lack of success, uncovering obstacles, inhibitors, and specific barriers that need to change, be minimized, or removed to drive the necessary results.

Conversely, it is helpful to examine the enablers to success. In a series of questions, the issues that have helped make the project successful are uncovered so that this issue can continue to be in place, supported, and perhaps even increased. A comprehensive analysis of barriers and enablers is always recommended on any major project.

Other tactics will uncover data that suggest improvement. Sometimes management support is a critical issue. The degree to which managers are supporting (or not supporting) a retention solution is important. Specific questions about the level of support can uncover dysfunctional situations or, on the positive side, excellent management support practices. Answers to these questions help improve the process when presented to the management team for action. Also, data such as "Recommendations for improvement," "Suggestions for changes," and "Other comments" provide rich information for improvement. Sometimes, unsolicited comments deposited in the organization's feedback system provide valuable data (e.g., labeled "sound off," "feedback," "speak up"). These suggestion/comment systems often provide an avenue for stakeholders to voice opinions about the retention issues and the effectiveness of particular solutions aimed at reducing turnover.

Potential Actions from Retention Solution

Essentially, one of four actions can develop from data collected about the success of the retention program. The first option is to accept the status quo—leave the solution as it is. This is rarely the case, and would only be accepted if all of the data suggest maximum success. Fundamentally, the data are indicating that nothing needs to be changed to improve the program.

A more likely action is to make some adjustments in the retention solution. The results often suggest minor adjustments are needed to fine-tune the process or system so that improvements can be realized.

A third option is to redesign the solution. This action is appropriate when the data show that the solution is not successful and a major redesign or refocus is necessary to make it successful. The solution may have been an appropriate response to the need, however, it was improperly designed or unsuccessfully implemented.

A fourth option is to discontinue the solution. In this case, the data show that the solution is not matching the need and will not reduce turnover or prevent it in the future. The best course of action is to kill it.

These options underscore the importance of having timely data so that actions can be taken quickly, before time and resources are wasted or diverted.

Developing the Action Plan

After it is determined that adjustments or redesign are needed for a major improvement, an action plan should be developed. The action plan details the specific steps that will be taken to adjust, refocus, or redesign the retention solution. Any format will work

Table 13-7
Criteria for Selecting Retention Solutions for ROI Evaluation

- Life cycle of the solution
- Linkage of the solution to operational goals and issues
- Importance of the solution to strategic objectives
- Cost of the solution
- Visibility of the solution
- Size of the target audience
- Investment of time
- Top executives' interest in the solution

provided it follows the SMART requirements (specific, measurable, achievable, realistic, and time-based). The action planning process brings organization, structure, discipline, and follow-through (Phillips, 1998).

Not Every Project Needs an ROI Calculation

As mentioned in earlier chapters, a comprehensive evaluation system that includes ROI is not necessarily appropriate for every retention solution. Minor solutions representing minimal investments and small amounts of time may not be appropriate to evaluate at the ROI level. Table 13-7 lists the issues that must be considered when deciding to take a project to this level of accountability. Solutions that are very expensive, time consuming, highly visible, and very strategic may require a comprehensive evaluation to include all six types of data, with ROI as one of the measures.

Maintaining a Low Turnover Rate

The ultimate goal of the strategic accountability approach to managing retention is to develop a very low turnover rate, which translates into high retention. The starting point in the cycle may vary. This process could be developed in response to a high turnover issue and, as the process develops, causes are identified, solutions are implemented, and results are realized. Ultimately, turnover should reduce. The process could start with the challenge of maintaining a current low turnover rate. The process is the same, but the payoffs are often based on what turnover rate would be realized if the solution is not implemented. Several issues should be examined when attempting to maintain a low turnover rate.

Revisiting the Targets

A low turnover rate is only meaningful relative to what is expected or accepted. In Chapter 3, the concept of setting targets for turnover for a particular group was introduced. Three specific targets were identified: acceptable, employer of choice, and a stretch goal, usually in the top 10 to 25 percent of organizations in the same industry. These targets must be operational to maintain low turnover. As turnover increases to one of these levels, specific actions will be triggered, with some actions more substantial than others. Targets become the trigger points for action.

Special Challenges

Maintaining a low turnover rate presents special challenges. The first is to resist overinvesting in prevention programs. While this may seem like unnecessary advice, some organizations spend large amounts of money developing new programs and projects and solving problems that do not necessarily exist. Consider, for example, a major automobile manufacturer that built an on-site fitness center with the primary objectives to increase the attraction of prospective employees and help retain current employees. These are noble objectives consistent with many attraction and retention goals, but the solution was not needed in this case. The employer enjoyed an excellent reputation in the community with a lucrative benefits package and hourly wage rates almost double that of the state's average. When the company announced a new assembly line opening on the third shift, for example, it was flooded with thousands of applicants, many of them very high-quality candidates. Further investigation revealed an *extremely* low turnover—almost too low. Employees were not leaving because of the excellent work environment and the generous pay and benefits package. The addition of the fitness center could be a positive contribution to the organization, but not for the purpose of attracting and retaining employees.

Another challenge is to consider using leading indicators to spot turnover problems before they become serious issues. As mentioned in Chapter 3, intention to quit is an important leading indicator along with organizational commitment and job satisfaction data.

These leading indicators can be crucial for early analysis and action before turnover develops into a serious problem.

A very important challenge is to take immediate action when a problem is uncovered. Quick action requires rapid analysis of the turnover issue, development of an appropriate solution, and efficient implementation and feedback of the results. The ability to take quick action can prevent a turnover problem from becoming disastrous.

A final special challenge is the notion of complacency. It is sometimes tempting to consider the retention issue as unimportant and move onto other challenges. While it *is* important to move to other critical issues in the organization, turnover should always be monitored, on a leading indicator basis, if possible, to ensure that retention is not becoming an issue. It is counterproductive to wait until turnover becomes an issue to tackle it again. Complacency can cause serious problems, eroding the good things that have been developed previously.

Monitoring Outside the HR Area

Maintaining a peripheral vision provides an awareness of impending trouble on the horizon. For example, the economy and the measures associated with it (described earlier) often become leading indicators of more serious problems to come. If jobs are being created at a faster rate than the local market can handle, a potential turnover issue is developing.

Another issue is monitoring the competition. Very aggressive competitors sometimes feed off the success of others (i.e., employees are recruited within an industry because of the quality, skills, and expertise of the employee in another company). Essentially, competitors are buying capable employees rather than investing in resources to develop them. This can occur unexpectedly as competition becomes more aggressive (or desperate) and searching for quick-fix approaches.

The health of the business must also be monitored—analyzing backorders, revenue, and projections—ensuring that the organization is healthy financially and has adequate back orders and resources to withstand a potential dip in the economy.

OVERCOMING RESISTANCE TO MANAGING RETENTION

Resistance

Logically, it seems obvious that the management team would want to support solutions designed to lower turnover. After all, turnover is the cause of many of the operational issues and most managers would welcome a lower turnover rate. The problem arises in the fact that some managers may not understand the reasoning for a particular solution or do not have time to invest in supporting and reinforcing these solutions.

Most of the solutions described in this book require management involvement. The role of the management team and their influence on the retention issue has frequently been underscored. The manager is the key to this issue. The manager must be involved in the issue and devote serious time to make it work. In exasperation, some managers ask, "Don't we have enough to manage without having to manage retention?" They have many issues that they must organize, coordinate, and facilitate in their work units, and a variety of retention solutions may be an unwelcome addition to their mix of responsibilities. In other cases, some managers have given up on the turnover issue, accepting high turnover as a cost of doing business.

The result of this frustration might be a display of open resistance to managing retention. Table 13-8 shows some typical management

Table 13-8
Open Resistance to ROI

1. It costs too much.
2. It takes too much time.
3. Who is asking for this?
4. It is not in my job description.
5. I did not have input on this.
6. I do not understand this.
7. What happens if the solutions are ineffective?
8. How can we be consistent with this?
9. The process is too subjective.
10. Our managers will not support this.

Table 13-9
Building Blocks for Overcoming Resistance

Finding shortcuts
Monitoring progress
Removing obstacles
Preparing the management team
Initiating projects and solutions
Preparing the staff
Revising policies and procedure
Establishing goals and plans
Developing roles and responsibilities
Assessing the need for managing retention

resistance to the retention solutions. These resistances are sometimes based on myths, whereas others may be realistic. Managers may not have time or see this issue as part of their duties; they may not understand what they should be doing; they have many questions that can create this resistance. Consequently, these items alone can make many of the retention solutions become ineffective.

Actions to Overcome Resistance

It is important to take specific steps to overcome the resistance. The strategic accountability approach, which forms a basis for this book, is client focused. Although retention is a process orchestrated by the HR staff, it is designed for the management team. It requires constant communication with managers to make the team aware of the retention issue, explain their role in the process, and keep them involved in developing solutions. In addition to following the steps in this book, it may require a variety of steps to overcome resistance. Table 13-9 shows the building blocks to overcome resistance for these types of programs. For large organizations with a variety of retention solutions, it may be helpful to focus more time on many of these building blocks to overcome resistance. A special retention function or retention task force may be developed to address these issues. More information on implementation of this kind of process is available in other works (Phillips and Burkett, 2004).

Taking the Long View

It is important to underscore the need for adopting a long-range view for managing retention with this critical challenge. The workforce must be "managed" with a long-term perspective, anticipating downturns in the business so that recruiting can stop. Generally, to have abrupt shifts in employment levels are unnecessary. For example, Cisco Systems had a tremendous recruiting effort halted, followed immediately by massive layoffs. This scenario illustrates that someone was not anticipating or understanding the issue.

To manage the retention issue over the long term, problems should be anticipated to the extent possible, and recruiting channels adjusted to prepare for downturns or major upturns of employment. For example, a major government organization with thousands of research scientists is facing a shortfall of these scientists in the future, as the majority of the workforce in those job categories will retire in the next 5 years. Consequently, the tremendous challenge is to ensure that staffing is appropriate. In another scenario, a company completing a major government contract to assemble weapon systems knew in advance when the assembly line would phase out. With this long-term view, the HR function, in concert with the management team, redirected staff, retrained staff, and even helped in outplacement opportunities. The employees who were destined for layoff were trained in other careers that were desperately needed in their local area. Engineers became building contractors, technicians became heating and air conditioning specialists, and flight line mechanics became diesel mechanics. This required extensive training but served as an orderly outplacement for these employees to direct those careers.

Still another technology organization looked to the future and saw a major shortfall of people available for their jobs. Anticipating that this could lead to high turnover rates, the company embarked on a tremendous internal training program to prepare employees for the shortage of skills, choosing to upgrade their own employees rather than trying to recruit trained professionals. This extensive training, combined with a service commitment in exchange for the training, kept a stable workforce in place during what otherwise might have been an extremely volatile period.

These are only a few examples of organizations that take the long view in terms of their HR staffing issues. While the focus on the book is on retention, it is important to ensure that all the staffing issues are addressed in a consistent, coherent manner.

FINAL THOUGHTS

This chapter presented the final step in the strategic accountability approach for managing retention. Communicating results to drive action and make adjustments is a crucial final step in the model. At the completion of this step, the process continues until turnover is ultimately taken to acceptable levels and maintained at those levels. If this step in the process is not taken seriously, the full impact of results will not be realized. The chapter began with the principles of communicating results, with discussions on communication issues and processes. The various target audiences were detailed and, because of its importance, emphasis was placed on communicating with the executive group. A suggested format for a detailed evaluation report was provided, and much of the remainder of the chapter included ways in which data can be used to drive improvement and maintain a low turnover, particularly taking the long view.

REFERENCES

Block, P. *Flawless Consulting Fieldbook and Companion: A Guide to Understanding Your Expertise*. San Francisco: Jossey-Bass/Pfeiffer, 2001.

Phillips, J.J., series editor. *Implementing Evaluation Systems and Processes*. Alexandria, Va.: American Society for Training and Development, 1998.

Phillips, P.P., and Burkett, H. *The ROI Field Book*. Boston: Butterworth-Heinemann (2004).

FURTHER READING

Block, P. *Flawless Consulting: A Guide to Getting Your Expertise Used*, 2nd ed. San Francisco: Bass/Pfeiffer, 2000.

Carr, D.K., Hard, K.J., and Trahant, W.J. *Managing the Change Process: A Field Book for Change Agents, Consultants, Team Leaders, and Reengineering Managers*. New York: McGraw-Hill, 1996.

Donoghue, K. *Built for Use: Driving Profitability Through the User Experience*. New York: McGraw-Hill, 2002.

Eckes, G. *Making Six Sigma Last: Managing the Balance Between Cultural and Technical Change*. New York: John Wiley & Sons, 2001.

Herman, R.E., and Gioia, J.L. *How to Attract, Optimize, and Hold Your Best Employees*. Winchester, Va.: Oakhill Press, 2000.

Johnson, M. *Winning the People Wars: Talent and the Battle for Human Capital.* London, England: Financial Times/Prentice Hall, 2000.

Larkin, T.J., and Larkin, S. *Communicating Change: How to Win Employee Support for New Business Directions.* New York: McGraw-Hill, 1994.

MacDonald, J. *Calling a Halt to Mindless Change: A Plea for Commonsense Management.* New York: American Management Association International, 1998.

Phillips, J.J., Stone, R.D., and Phillips, P.P. *The Human Resources Scorecard: Measuring the Return on Investment.* Boston: Butterworth-Heinemann, 2001.

Robbins, H., and Finley, M. *Why Change Doesn't Work: Why Initiatives Go Wrong and How to Try Again—and Succeed.* London, England: Orion Business Books, 1997.

Sadler, P. *Managing Change.* London, England: Kogan Page, 1995.

Senge, P.M., Kleiner, A., Roberts, C., Ross, R.B., and Smith, B.J. *The Fifth Discipline Fieldbook: Strategies and Tools for Building a Learning Organization.* New York: Currency Doubleday, 1994.

Slater, R. *The GE Way Fieldbook: Jack Welch's Battle Plan for Corporate Revolution.* New York: McGraw-Hill, 2000.

CHAPTER 14

Case Study Application: Southeast Corridor Bank*

This study demonstrates how a retention improvement program generated extremely high impact, including an impressive return on investment (ROI), using the strategic accountability approach to managing retention described in this book. This case, which analyzes a turnover problem in branch operations, focuses on how the specific causes of turnover were determined, how the solutions were matched to the special causes, and how the actual calculation of the impact of the turnover reduction is developed. The strength of the case lies in the techniques utilized to ensure that the solutions are appropriate and that the turnover reduction represented a high payoff solution.

BACKGROUND

Southeast Corridor Bank (SCB), a regional bank operating in four states with 60 branches, had grown from a single-state operation to a multistate network through a progressive and strategic campaign of acquisitions. As with many organizations, SCB faced merger and integration problems, including excessive employee turnover. SCB's annual turnover rate was 57 percent, compared to an industry average of 26 percent. The new senior vice president for human resources (HR) faced several important challenges when he joined SCB; among them was the need to reduce turnover. Although man-

---

*A slightly modified version of this case was published in a companion book of case studies, *Retaining Your Best Employees*, Patricia P. Phillips (Editor), American Society for Training and Development, Alexandria, Va., 2002.

agement was not aware of the full impact of turnover, they knew it was causing operational problems, taking up much staff and supervisor time, and creating disruptive situations with customers.

STRATEGIC ACCOUNTABILITY APPROACH

The strategic accountability approach, outlined in Figure 14-1 and described in detail in Chapter 2, is the basic model for this case study. The process brings accountability to the retention issue in eight steps.

The approach is strategic since it considers the retention issue to be an important part of strategy. The executive team is very involved in this issue. With many firms, retention has become a strategic issue because it often means the difference between mediocre and excellent profits. Accountability is incorporated throughout the process

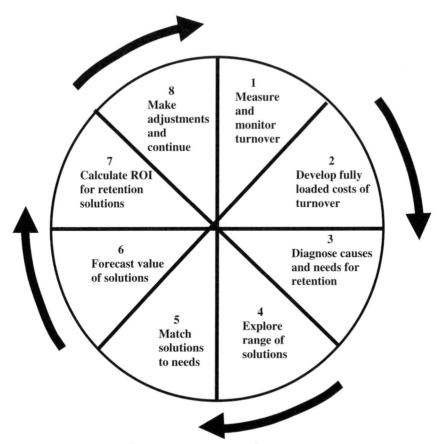

Figure 14-1. The strategic approach to managing retention.

to fully understand the cost of the problem, cost of the solutions, potential impact of the solutions, and actual impact of the solutions—all in monetary terms. The approach moves logically from one issue to another through a series of steps necessary to manage the process. Stay on track is easy because each of the different issues must be addressed before moving onto another issue. This approach brings structure and organization to the retention, rather than or implementing solutions without analysis.

Step 1: Measuring and Monitoring Turnover

To properly monitor and measure turnover, several issues must be considered, as follows:

- Define turnover consistently
- Report turnover rates by various demographics
- Report rates by critical job groups
- Include costs with turnover
- Compare data with benchmarking targets
- Develop trigger points for action

Step 2: Developing a Fully Loaded Cost of Turnover

The impact cost of turnover is one of the most underestimated and undervalued costs in the organization. It is often misunderstood because turnover statistics often do not reflect the fully loaded costs of turnover. These fully loaded costs are not regularly reported to the management team, and they therefore do not know the actual cost. It can be extremely frightening for the management team when fully loaded costs are calculated for the organization for an entire year.

Only the costs for recruiting, selection, and training are usually considered when exploring turnover. These costs are often easily calculated and sometimes inappropriately reported as the cost of turnover. In reality, other costs should be included. A more comprehensive listing includes 12 categories as listed in Table 14-1.

Step 3: Diagnose Causes and Needs for Retention Improvement

Determining the cause of turnover is a critical and ellusive issue. Some causes may be obvious, while others can be extremely elusive.

Table 14-1
Recommended Categories for Accumulating Turnover Costs

Exit costs	Lost productivity
Recruiting costs	Quality problems
Employment cost	Customer dissatisfaction
Orientation cost	Loss of expertise/knowledge
Training cost	Management time for turnover
Wages and salaries while training	Temporary replacement costs

Collecting appropriate data is often a challenge because of the potential for bias and inaccuracies that surface during the data collection process. Several diagnostic processes are available.

Step 4: Explore a Range of Solutions

Organizations are very creative in their approach to the turnover problem. This results in hundreds of excellent solutions. The critical issue is to ensure that the solution is feasible for the organization. Most solutions can be categorized as follows:

- **Joining the organization,** which includes image and market performance, recruitment, selection, job fit, orientation, and initial training.
- **Establishing an appropriate work environment,** which includes job satisfaction, work place design, safety, supportive culture, job security, life balance, diversity, and quality of leadership.
- **Creating equitable pay and performance processes,** which includes pay, benefits, rewards, recognitions, and job performance.
- **Building motivation and commitment,** which includes empowerment, teamwork, ethics, trust, organizational commitment, professional growth, and career advancement.

Step 5: Matching Solutions to Needs

This step goes hand in hand with the issue of forecasting the value of solutions presented next. The development of the two issues should be parallel since the solutions selected for implementation are assumed to meet specific needs, making the forecast of the anticipated value imperative. When attempting to match solutions to need, the following five key issues are considered:

- Avoid mismatches
- Implement only a minimum number of solutions
- Select a solution for a maximum return
- Verify the match early
- Check the progress of each solution

Step 6: Forecast Value of Solutions

Developing a forecast for the value of a solution allows the team to establish priorities, work with a minimum number of solutions, and focus on solutions with the greatest return on investment. A difficult, challenging, and, sometimes risky, issue, forecasting is an expert estimation of what a solution should contribute. It is imperative to accumulate as much data as possible to back up the estimate and build credibility around the process. The payoff value can be developed if the percentage of expected turnover reduction can be estimated with credibility. For example, if the No. 1 cause of turnover is addressed and removed with a solution, what percentage of the turnover would actually be eliminated? Sometimes employees can provide input for this issue as data are collected to identify the causes of turnover. This step may require several "what if" decisions with employees while making various assumptions about the data. This step may also involve building on previous experiences to the extent possible. In some cases, the experience of other organizations can be helpful.

Step 7: Measure ROI for Retention Solutions

Another often neglected step is the actual calculation of the impact of a turnover reduction strategy. This step is often omitted because it appears to be an add-on process that may be unnecessary. If accumulating solutions is the measure of success of turnover reduction or prevention, the impact to those solutions may seem to have no value. From a senior executive's point of view, accountability is not complete until impact and ROI data have been collected, at least for major solutions. The ROI methodology generates six types of data about the success of a turnover reduction strategy:

1. Reaction to and satisfaction with the solution
2. Skill and knowledge acquisition

3. Application and implementation progress
4. Business impact improvement
5. Return on investment, expressed as an ROI formula
6. Intangible measures not converted to monetary values.

This definition also includes a technique to isolate the effects of a turnover solution. The ROI process has achieved widespread applications for the evaluation of all types of programs and solutions (Phillips, 2002).

Step 8: Make Adjustment and Continue

The extensive set of data collected from the ROI process will provide information to make adjustments and changes in turnover reduction strategies. The information reveals success of the retention solution at all levels from reaction to ROI. It also examines barriers to success and identifies specifically what kept the solution from being effective or prevented it from becoming more effective. It also identifies the processes in place that enable or support a turnover reduction solution. All of the information allows for adjusting and/or repositioning the solution so that it can be revised, discontinued, or amplified. The next step in the process goes back to the beginning, monitoring the data to ensure that turnover continues to meet our expectations . . . and the cycle continues.

Measuring and Monitoring Turnover at SCB

SCB monitored turnover by various categories and defined them as either voluntary separations or terminations for performance. Departures due to retirement and/or disability were not included in the definition. A turnover for performance was an important issue that could be rectified if the performance deficiency could have been recognized or prevented early.

The turnover rate was monitored by job group, region, and branch. Branches had the highest turnover rate, averaging some 71 percent in the previous year—far exceeding any expectations and industry averages (e.g., turnover compared with other financial institutions and data from the American Bankers Association). In addition to branches, turnover was considered excessive in a few entry-level, clerical job classifications in regional and corporate offices.

Impact of Turnover at SCB

The impact of turnover was developed at the beginning of the study. External turnover studies in the banking industry had revealed that the cost of turnover for bank employees was 110 percent to 125 percent of annual pay. Using the categories listed in Table 14-1, this fully loaded cost was published in several trade publications. When reviewing the proposed program and the proposed method for calculating the payoff, the senior executive team suggested a lower value. In essence, the senior team thought that turnover was not quite that expensive and suggested only 90 percent (0.9 times an annual pay).

DETERMINING THE CAUSE OF TURNOVER

Three basic techniques were used to pinpoint the actual cause of turnover. First, as described briefly above, the analysis of individual job groups and tenure within job groups provided insight into where turnover was occurring, the magnitude of the problem, and some indication of the cause. Much of the turnover occurred in the early stages of employment (e.g., in the 6- 18-month category).

Second, exit interviews from departing employees were examined to determine whether specific reasons for departure could be pinpointed. As with most exit data, accuracy was a concern as the departing employees may have been biased when reporting the reason for leaving. The stigma of individuals not wanting to burn bridges left the data incomplete and inaccurate.

Third, recognizing this problem, the HR team used the nominal group technique to determine more precisely the actual causes of turnover. A highly structured and unbiased focus group, this process is described next.

Nominal Group Technique

The nominal group technique was selected because it allowed unbiased input to be collected efficiently and accurately across the organization. A focus group was planned with 12 employees in each region for a total of six groups representing all six regions. In addition, two focus groups were planned for the clerical staff in corporate headquarters. This approach provided approximately a 10 percent sample and was considered a sufficient number to pinpoint the problem.

Participants for focus groups represented areas of highest turnover. They described why their colleagues were leaving—not why *they* would leave. Input was solicited from participants in a carefully structured format, using third-party facilitators. The data were integrated and weighted so that the most important reasons were clearly identified. This process has the advantages of low cost, high reliability, and being unbiased. Data were captured in a 2-hour meeting in each regional location. Only 2 days of external facilitator time was necessary to collect and summarize data for review.

The nominal group technique unfolds quickly in 10 easy steps as follows.

1. The process is briefly described along with a statement of confidentiality. The importance of participant input is underscored and participants understand what they must do and what it means to SCB.
2. On a piece of paper, participants are asked to make a list of specific reasons why they feel their colleagues have left SCB or why others may leave in the future. It is very important for the question to reflect the actions or potential actions of others, although their comments will probably reflect their own views (and that is what is actually needed).
3. In a round-robin format, each person reveals one reason at a time and it is recorded on a flip chart. At this point, no attempts are made to integrate the issues, but just to record the data on paper. It is important to understand the issue and fully describe it on paper. The lists are placed on the walls so that when this step is complete, as many as 50 or 60 items are listed and visible.
4. The next step is to consolidate and integrate the lists. Some of the integration is easy because the items may contain the same words and meaning. For others, it is important to ensure that the meanings for the cause of the turnover are the same before they are consolidated. When integrated, the remaining list may contain 30 or 40 different reasons for turnover.
5. Participants are asked to review all of the items and carefully select the 10 items they consider to be the most important causes and list them individually on index cards. At first, participants are not concerned about which cause is No. 1 but are instructed to simply list the 10 most important ones on the cards. Participants usually realize that their original list

was not complete or accurate, and they will pick up other issues for this list.

6. Participants sort the 10 items by order of importance, the No. 1 item being the most important, and No. 10 the least important.

7. In a round-robin format, each participant reveals a cause of turnover, starting from the top. Each participant reveals his or her No. 1 item, and 10 points are recorded on the flip chart next to the item. The next participant reveals the No. 1 issue and so on until the entire group offers the top cause for turnover. Next, the No. 2 reason is identified, and 9 points are recorded on the flip chart next to the item. This process continued until all cards have been revealed and points recorded.

8. The numbers next to each item are totaled. The item with the most points becomes the No. 1 cause of turnover. The one with the second most points becomes the second cause of turnover and so on. The top 15 causes are then captured from the group and are reported as the weighted average cause of turnover from *that* group.

9. This process was completed for all six regional groups and the clerical staff groups. Trends began to emerge quickly from one group to the other. The actual raw scores from each group were combined for the integration of the six regional focus groups.

10. The top 15 scores are the top 15 reasons for turnover in the branches and clerical groups.

Specific Needs

Table 14-2 shows the top 10 reasons for employees leaving only the bank branches. A similar list was developed for the clerical staff, but the remainder of this case study will focus directly on the efforts to reduce turnover in the branch network. Branch turnover is the most critical issue with the highest turnover rates and representing the largest number of employees. The results of the focus groups developed a clear pattern of specific needs. Recognizing that not all of the causes of turnover could be addressed immediately, the bank set out to work on the top five while a variety of options for solutions were considered. Eventually, a skill-based pay system was implemented.

Table 14-2
Top Ten Reasons Why Branch Employees Leave the Bank

Reasons for Turnover in the Branch Network

1. Lack of opportunity for advancement
2. Lack of opportunity to learn new skills and new product knowledge
3. Inadequate pay level
4. Not enough responsibility and empowerment
5. Lack of recognition and appreciation of work
6. Lack of teamwork in the branch
7. Lack of preparation for customer service problems
8. Unfair and unsupportive supervisor
9. Too much stress at peak times
10. Not enough flexibility in work schedules

Table 14-3
Proposed Job Levels

Banking Representative Level	Job Duties	Hourly Wage Rate ($)
I	Basic teller transactions (deposits, check cashing, etc.)	6.00
II	Same as above, plus opening and closing accounts, CDs, savings bonds, special transactions, etc.	7.50
III	Same as above, plus limited liability consumer loans, applications for all consumer loans, home equity loans, referrals for mortgage loans, etc.	9.00

SOLUTION: SKILL-BASED PAY

The skill-based pay system addressed the top five issues. The program was designed to expand the scope of the jobs with increases in pay for the acquisition of skills and provide a clear path for advancement and job growth. Jobs were redesigned from narrowly focused teller duties to an expanded job, labeled Banking Representative. The teller job title was eliminated, and the tellers became Banking Representative I, II, or III. Table 14-3 shows the basic descriptions of the jobs with new initial wage rates. A branch employee would be considered a Banking Representative I if he or she could perform one or two simple tasks, such as processing deposits and cashing checks.

As Banking Representatives I took on additional responsibilities and performed different functions, they would be eligible for a promotion to Banking Representatives II. If they performed all the basic functions of the bank branch, including consumer loan applications, promotions to Banking Representatives III was appropriate. Branch employees could progress as they developed job-related skills. Centralized training opportunities were available to develop the needed skills while structured on-the-job training was provided through the branch manager, assistant manager, and teller supervisor. Self-study, videos, and distance learning were also available to help learn new skills. The concept of multiple tasks was aimed at broadening responsibilities and empowering employees to perform a variety of tasks needed to provide excellent customer service. Pay increased following skill acquisition and demonstrated accomplishment, recognized accomplishments, and increased responsibility.

Although the skill-based system had some definite benefits from the employee perspective, there were also some benefits for the bank. Not only was turnover expected to be lower, but actual staffing levels could be reduced in larger branches. In theory, if all employees in a branch could perform all the duties, fewer employees would be needed. Previously, minimum staffing levels were required in certain critical jobs and those employees were not always available for other job duties.

In addition, improved customer service was anticipated. This new approach would prevent customers from waiting in long lines for specialized services. For example, in the typical branch bank, it is not unusual to see long lines for special functions (i.e., opening a checking account, closing out a CD, or taking a consumer loan application) while teller functions (paying and receiving) often have little or no waiting. With each employee performing all the tasks, shorter waiting lines would not only be feasible, but expected.

To support this new arrangement, the marketing department referenced the concept in promotion of the branch staff and products and services. Included with the checking account statements was a promotional piece labeled, "In Our Branches There Are No Tellers." This document described the process and explained that all the branch employees could perform all branch functions and consequently provide faster, efficient service.

MEASURING SUCCESS

Measuring the success of the new solution required collecting data at four levels. At the first level, reaction and satisfaction is measured during meetings with the employees and during regularly scheduled training sessions. This measurement provided input on employee acceptance of the new arrangement and different elements of the program. Using brief surveys, data were collected on a 5-point scale. As expected, the results were positive, averaging a 4.2 composite rating, with 5 representing exceptional.

At the second level, learning is measured in two different ways. For each training and learning opportunity, skill acquisition and knowledge increase is measured. Informal self-assessments are taken for many of the programs. A few critical skills required actual demonstration to show that employees could perform the skill (e.g., documentation, compliance, and customer services). When learning measurements revealed unacceptable performance, participants were provided an opportunity to repeat training sessions or take more time to practice. In limited cases, a third opportunity was provided. After 1 year of operation, only two employees were denied a promotional opportunity due to their performance in training programs.

At the third level, application and implementation was measured by collecting four types of data as shown in Table 14-4. Actual participation in the program reflected the willingness for individuals to pursue skill acquisition through a variety of efforts. The results were impressive.

In all, 95 percent of the branch employees wanted to participate in the program. The remaining 5 percent were content with the Banking Representative I classification and were not interested in learning new skills. Requests for training and learning opportunities

Table 14-4
Selected Application and Implementation Data

Application and Implementation Progress		
	1 Year Prior	1 Year Post
Participation in program	NA	95%
Requests for training	45 per month	86 per month
Review situations	NA	138
Actual promotions	139	257

were a critical part of the formal processes. Employees had to map their own developmental efforts, which were approved by the branch manager. Some 86 requests per month were logged, almost taxing the system for providing training and learning opportunities. Reviews of the status and progress—to be considered for the promotion for the next level—were significant, with a total of 138. This review was the formal way of demonstrating skills for promotion. Promotions increased quickly, as much as double that of previous promotions in the branch network. As the table shows, actual promotions 1 year prior to the program was 139, increasing to 257 one year after the program was initiated.

Nine categories of business impact measures were monitored and are shown in Table 14-5 with the definitions. In all, nine categories of data were expected influenced to some degree by this project, although the first four were considered the primary measures.

The most important expected benefit was turnover reduction. The major goal of the project was that the total avoidable turnover

Table 14-5
Business Measures Influenced by the Project

Business Impact Measures

1. Branch employee turnover (monthly)	Avoidable turnover. Total number of employees leaving voluntarily and for performance reasons divided by the average number of employees in the branch for the month. This number is multiplied by 12 to develop the annual turnover rate.
2. Staffing level	The total number of employees in the branch, reported monthly.
3. Customer satisfaction	Customer reaction to the job changes (faster service, fewer lines) measured on a 1 to 5 scale.
4. Job satisfaction	Employee feedback on selected measures on the annual feedback survey process.
5. Deposits	Savings, checking, and securities deposits by type and product.
6. Loan volume	Consumer loan volume by loan type.
7. New accounts	New accounts opened for new customers.
8. Transaction volume	Number of face-to-face transactions, paying and receiving, by major category.
9. Cross selling	New products sold to existing customers.

should be reduced. The second measure was staffing levels. With more highly skilled employees, fewer staff should be necessary, at least for the larger branches. The third measure was customer service. With fewer customers waiting in line and less need to move from one line to another, customers should be more satisfied. The fourth measure is job satisfaction; employees should be more satisfied with their work, their job, and career possibilities. Finally, there was an expected increase in volume attributed to the project because fewer customers were waiting in line. Consequently, customers would visit more often or would not leave in frustration because of delays. This should result in increases in deposits, consumer loan volume, new accounts, transaction volume, and cross-selling measures. Additionally, these last five categories were operational measures of each branch and were expected to change very little because of this project.

Isolating the Effects of the Skill-Based Pay Project

An important issue was to isolate the actual impact of the skill-based pay project from other influences. In almost any type of situation, multiple influences drive specific business measures. To add credibility and validity to the analysis, a specific method was used to isolate the effects of the project for each data item used in the ROI calculation. As shown in Table 14-6, the method used for isolating

Table 14-6
Business Measures and Planned Analysis

Data Item	Method of Isolating the Effects	Method of Converting Data
Employee turnover	Branch manager estimation Staff estimation	External studies
Staffing levels	Branch manager estimation	Company payroll records
Customer service	Customer input	NA
Job satisfaction	Staff input	NA
Deposits, loan volume, new accounts	Branch manager estimation	Standard value (% margin)
Transaction volume Cross selling	Branch manager estimation Staff estimation	Standard (average % margin)

the effect of the project on turnover reduction was to obtain estimates directly from branch managers and the branch staff. In brief group meetings, the branch staffs were provided the results of the turnover reduction and were asked to allocate the percentage linked directly to the skill-based pay effort. Each branch provided this information.

As a first step in the process, branch team members would discuss the other factors that could have contributed to turnover reduction (only two were identified). They were asked to discuss the linkage between each factor and the actual turnover reduction. This discussion, in a focus group format, improved the accuracy of this estimation. However, since it is estimation, an error adjustment was made. Individuals were asked to indicate the level of confidence in their allocation of turnover improvement to the skill-based pay project using a scale of 0 to 100 percent. With this scale, 0 percent means no confidence and 100 percent means absolute certainty. The confidence percentage was used as a discount for the allocation. For example, if an individual allocated 60 percent of the turnover reduction to this specific project and was 80 percent confident in that allocation, the adjusted value would be 48 percent (60 percent times 80 percent). When collected properly, this method of isolation provides a conservative estimate for the effect of skill-based pay on turnover reduction. In this example, the branch manager input was combined with the staff employees on equal weighting. Essentially, the results were averaged.

For staffing levels, actual improvements were adjusted with the branch manager estimation. In essence, using the process described above, branch managers indicated the degree to which the new project resulted in actual staff reduction. Staff reductions only occurred in 30 percent of the branches (i.e., the larger ones), and this estimate only involved those branch managers. Since no other factors contributed to this staff reduction, branch managers gave the entire reduction amount to the skill-based project.

Table 14-6 shows the planned method for isolation for each measure that is a part of the planning for the study. Increases in deposits, loan volume, new accounts, transactions, and cross selling were minimal and were influenced by many other variables. Consequently, no attempt was made to isolate the effect on them or use the monetary improvements in the ROI analysis. However, they are listed as intangibles, providing evidence that they have been driven with the turnover reduction program.

Survey cards completed at the end of a transaction and deposited at the entrance to the branch provided a sample of customer service reactions. The customers appreciated the new approach, liked the service delivered, and indicated that they would continue to use the branch. The annual employee job satisfaction survey showed improvements in advancement opportunities, a chance to use skills, pay for performance, and other related issues. Customer service and job satisfaction measures were not isolated or converted to monetary volume and consequently not used in the ROI calculation. However, these measures are very important and influential in the final evaluation and listed as intangible benefits.

Converting Data

Table 14-6 also shows the method used (or planned) to convert data to monetary value. Turnover was converted to monetary value using a value from external studies. The specific amount was calculated using 0.9 times the annual salary as the cost of one turnover. This value was considered a conservative amount since several studies had values ranging from 1.1 to 1.25 times annual earnings. More importantly, the value was developed and agreed to in a meeting with the senior management prior to the actual calculation of values. The average annual salary of the branch staff below the branch manager level was $18,500. Collectively, the staffing reductions translated into significant savings far exceeding expectations. For each turnover reduction, a $16,650 (18,500 × 0.9) savings was realized. Table 14-7 shows the turnover reduction of 174. The contribution factor (the percentage of the reduction linked to the solution) and confidence estimate error adjustment is multiplied by the 174 to yield 120 prevented turnovers. The contribution factor and confidence estimates were obtained in branch meetings, described earlier. The cost of a turnover ($16,650) is multiplied by 120 to yield an annual value of almost $2 million. That amount is doubled for a 2-year savings. At this point in data collection, the second-year value is not known and a second-year forecast is needed.

The method for converting staffing levels to monetary value was to use the actual salaries for those job levels eliminated. Only a few branches were affected. The actual number was multiplied by the average salary of the branch staff. The value was captured for 1 year and projected for another year assuming the same level. A 2-year time frame was used because it was considered a conservative way to evaluate (i.e., 1 year of actual data and the forecast of 1 year). Although the program should provide extended value, additional

Table 14-7
Calculation of Business Results

	Prior Year	One-Year After	Actual Difference	Actual Business Results Contribution Factor	Confidence Estimate	Adjusted Amount	Unit Amount	Annual Benefits	Two-Year Benefits
Turnover	71% (336)	35% (182)	174	84%	82%	120	$16,650	$1,998,000	$3,996,000
Staffing levels	480 (average)	463 (end of year)	17	100%	100%	17	$18,500	$314,500	$629,000

benefits beyond the two years were excluded. This is the conservative basis of the ROI methodology.

Analysis

The turnover reduction at the branches was significant, moving from 71 percent to 35 percent in 1 year. Although some smaller branches had no staffing changes, the larger branches had fewer staff members; 30 percent of the branches were able to employ at least one less staff member either part-time or full-time. Also, 10 percent of the branches were able to reduce the staff by two individuals.

Table 14-7 shows the calculations of the annual and projected values for the total benefits for the two-year period. Different scenarios could have been considered, such as capturing the first-year value only. Benefits had to be captured or projected for the same 2-year period as the costs. The total 2-year benefit was $4,625,000.

Project Cost

Table 14-8 shows the fully loaded project cost of the skill-based project. The initial analysis costs were included and included time, direct costs, and travel expenses for focus groups. The development of the program included the time and materials. The next two categories were the branch staff time and represented an estimate of all the time away from normal work to understand the program and

Table 14-8
Fully Loaded Project Costs

Project Costs	Year 1	Year 2
Initial analysis	$14,000	—
Program development	2,500	—
Participant time	345,600	195,000
Branch manager time	40,800	30,200
Salary increases	446,696	203,900
Administration/operation	4,600	4,100
Evaluation	3,000	—
TOTAL	$857,196	$433,200

learn new skills. The next category is the actual salary increases, that is, the additional salary in the branch as a result of a potential early promotion. The total amount of first-year promotions ($977,600) was reduced by the rate of promotions in the year before the solution was implemented.

Administration and operation was ongoing and involved the time required from the HR staff to administer the program. Finally, the evaluation costs were included and represented the costs related to developing the impact study project. The total cost presented in this table contains several of the items in a 1-year actual and 1-year forecast while the other items are the total cost of the project. The total 2-year cost was $1,290,396.

ROI and Its Meaning

The 2-year monetary benefits are combined with costs to develop the benefit/cost ratio (BCR) and the ROI using the following formulae.

$$BCR = \frac{\text{Solution benefits}}{\text{Solution cost}} = \frac{\$4,625,000}{\$1,290,396} = 3.58$$

$$ROI = \frac{\text{Net solution benefits}}{\text{Solution cost}}$$

$$= \frac{\$4,625,000 - \$1,290,396}{\$1,290,396} \times 100 = 258\%$$

This BCR value indicates that for every $1 invested in the project, $3.58 is returned. In terms of ROI, for every $1 invested, $2.58 is returned after the costs are captured. These results are excellent, since most of the ROI studies have target (expected) values in the 25 percent range. The ROI is only one measure and should be considered in conjunction with the other measures. It is an estimate that is developed utilizing a conservative approach. It probably underestimates the actual return from this project.

Communication Results

The results were communicated to the senior management team in an executive staff meeting where approximately 30 minutes were allocated to the project. The communications were very critical, and three points were made:

- The project was quickly reviewed, including the description of the solution.
- The methodology used for evaluating the project was described.
- The results were revealed one level at a time presenting the following six types of data:
  1. Reaction to, and satisfaction with, the skill-based pay system
  2. Learning the system and how to use it
  3. Application/implementation of the system
  4. Business impact of skill-based pay
  5. Return on the investment in skill-based pay
  6. Intangible measures linked to skill-based pay

This presentation provided a balanced profile of the project and was convincing to the senior management team. The intangibles were important, particularly the customer service improvement. Overall, the senior team was very pleased with the success of the project and impressed with the analysis. This was the first time that an HR solution had been evaluated using a balanced measurement approach, including ROI.

LESSONS LEARNED

Although this study was on track with the right solution, a few lessons were learned. Perhaps it would have been safer to forecast the ROI at the time the solution was implemented. Forecasting is an important step in the strategic accountability approach to managing retention. It was considered, but not pursued. However, increasing the branch salaries to the extent planned for this solution is a risky scheme. It would be difficult to retract this program if it did not show enough value to make it worthwhile. A forecasted ROI could provide more confidence at the time of implementation.

Also, branch managers and regional managers were not entirely convinced that skill-based pay would add value. Additional effort was needed to capture their buy-in and help them understand the full cost of turnover. They needed to see how this system could alleviate many of their problems and add monetary value to the branches.

Finally, branch manager time was underestimated, as these managers had to deal with numerous requests for training and juggle schedules to ensure the staff maintained the training they needed. Managers also had to provide additional training and spend the time necessary to confirm that bank representatives had obtained the skills necessary for promotion.

DISCUSSION QUESTIONS

1. This case study illustrates how the actual causes of turnover are developed. What is your reaction to this process?
2. Why do many organizations spend so little time determining the causes of turnover?
3. Calculating the ROI of a turnover reduction program is rarely accomplished yet can have tremendous benefits. Why is this step often omitted?
4. How can the data from this project be used in the future?
5. Critique the overall approach to this retention project, highlighting weaknesses and strengths.

REFERENCE

Phillips, P.P. *The Bottomline on ROI*. Atlanta, Ga.: CEP Press, 2002.

Index

About the Authors

JACK J. PHILLIPS, Ph.D.

Jack J. Phillips is a world-renowned expert on measurement and evaluation and developer of return on investment (ROI), a revolutionary process that provides bottom-line figures and accountability for all types of training, performance improvement, human resources, and technology programs. He is the author or editor of more than 30 books—12 focused on measurement and evaluation— and more than 100 articles.

His expertise in measurement and evaluation is based on more than 27 years of corporate experience in five industries (aerospace, textiles, metals, construction materials, and banking). Phillips has served as training and development manager at two *Fortune 500* firms, senior HR officer at two firms, president of a regional federal savings bank, and management professor at a major state university.

In 1992, Phillips founded Performance Resources Organization (PRO), an international consulting firm that provides comprehensive assessment, measurement, and evaluation services for organizations. In 1999, PRO was acquired by the Franklin Covey Company and is now known as The Jack Phillips Center for Research. Today the center is an independent, leading provider of measurement and evaluation services to the global business community. Phillips consults with clients in manufacturing, service, and government organizations in the United States, Canada, Sweden, England, Belgium, Germany, Italy, Holland, South Africa, Mexico, Venezuela, Malaysia, Indonesia, Hong Kong, Australia, New Zealand, and Singapore. He leads the Phillips Center in research and publishing efforts that support the knowledge and development of assessment, measurement, and evaluation.

Phillips's most recent books include *The Human Resources Scorecard: Measuring the Return on Investment* (Boston: Butterworth-Heinemann, 2001); *The Consultant's Scorecard* (New York: McGraw-Hill, 2000); *HRD Trends Worldwide: Shared Solutions to Compete in a Global Economy* (Boston: Butterworth-Heinemann, 1999); *Return on Investment in Training and Performance Improvement Programs* (Boston: Butterworth-Heinemann, 1997); *Handbook of Training Evaluation and Measurement Methods*, 3rd edition (Boston: Butterworth-Heinemann, 1997); and *Accountability in Human Resource Management* (Boston: Butterworth-Heinemann, 1996).

Phillips has undergraduate degrees in electrical engineering, physics, and mathematics from Southern Polytechnic State University and Oglethorpe University, a master's degree in decision sciences from Georgia State University, and a Ph.D. in human resource management from the University of Alabama. In 1987 he won the Yoder-Heneman Personnel Creative Application Award from the Society for Human Resource Management.

Phillips can be reached at The Jack Phillips Center for Research, P.O. Box 380637, Birmingham, AL 35238-0637; 205-678-8038; fax: 205-678-0177; email: serieseditor@aol.com

ADELE O. CONNELL, Ph.D.

Adele Connell received her Ph.D. degree from the University of Utah where she specialized in organizational, interpersonal, and small group communication, business, and behavioral statistics. While completing her doctorate degree, she was a full-time adjunct professor for Weber State University's School of Business and consulted for a variety of organizations including General Motors, General Dynamics, NASA, Soil Conservation Service, AIMs Research Center (Department of the Navy), The City of Los Angeles, IRS, Boeing, and Ford.

Following her work in academia, Connell spent over a decade working in the financial services and call center industries for companies such as Allstate, American Express Traveller's Cheque,

Discover Card, and Advanta MasterCard BusinessCard. In these organizations, she has worked in the areas of operation, sales, training, leadership, and quality. She has written several training manuals on quality, problem solving, business writing, leadership, and has one internet-based course entitled "Negotiation for the Sales Professional."

Connell has over 20 years of military service and is a Colonel in the U.S. Army Reserves. She is assigned to the 96th Regional Readiness Command located at Ft. Douglas in Salt Lake City, Utah. She is the mother of four children.

Contact with the author is encouraged and welcomed. She can be reached at Post Office Box 705, Tooele, Utah 84074; office: 435-843-4306; cell: 435-850-6300; e-mail: adele.Connell@franklincovey.com or adeleconnell@hotmail.com

Do You Know How to Retain Your Best, Most Valuable, and Productive Employees?

Retaining high-performing employees is tough for most organizations, despite well-conceived efforts to reduce turnover. *Retaining Your Best Employees* is a resource designed especially to help you keep your most valuable employees satisfied and at their jobs. This book takes you on a case study tour of the best retention strategies from organizations just like yours and lets you to apply these valuable lessons to your own situation. How do other organizations manage retention, and what effect do retention policies have on employees? How well do reward and recognition programs work? Does an internal degree program reduce turnover? You'll find answers to these and many other questions in this important book.

ASTD Press

800.628.2783 ext.250

1888-6222